THE VULNERABILITY OF PUBLIC HIGHER EDUCATION

THE VULNERABILITY OF PUBLIC HIGHER EDUCATION

Michael Bernard-Donals

THE OHIO STATE UNIVERSITY PRESS
COLUMBUS

Copyright © 2023 by The Ohio State University.
All rights reserved.

Library of Congress Cataloging-in-Publication Data
Names: Bernard-Donals, Michael F., author.
Title: The vulnerability of public higher education / Michael Bernard-Donals.
Description: Columbus : The Ohio State University Press, [2023] | Includes bibliographical references and index. | Summary: "In the last forty years, public higher education in the United States has become vulnerable due to changes in funding and public opinion of higher education. Through case studies, mostly involving education policy changes, this vulnerability is reframed as a tool that university faculty can use to adapt their future work"—Provided by publisher.
Identifiers: LCCN 2023025357 | ISBN 9780814215555 (hardback) | ISBN 0814215556 (hardback) | ISBN 9780814283158 (ebook) | ISBN 0814283152 (ebook)
Subjects: LCSH: Universities and colleges—United States—Faculty. | Education, Higher—Aims and objectives—United States. | Academic freedom—United States.
Classification: LCC LB2331.72 .B46 2023 | DDC 378.1/20973 —dc23/eng/20230814
LC record available at https://lccn.loc.gov/2023025357

Other identifiers: ISBN 9780814258897 (paperback) | ISBN 0814258891 (paperback)

Cover design by Brad Norr
Text design by Juliet Williams
Type set in Adobe Minion Pro

CONTENTS

Acknowledgments		vii
INTRODUCTION	The Vulnerability of Public Higher Education	1
CHAPTER 1	Commonplaces of Governance	22
CHAPTER 2	Faculty Rights and Responsibilities and the Urgency of Justice	44
CHAPTER 3	Academic Freedom, Democracy, and Professional Rights	68
CHAPTER 4	Expertise, Discipline, and Faculty Autonomy	93
CHAPTER 5	The Vulnerabilities of Institutional Diversity	121
CHAPTER 6	Becoming Rhetorical	149
Works Cited		173
Index		185

ACKNOWLEDGMENTS

I didn't intend to write this book. Nine years ago, I was enjoying my term as director of the Mosse/Weinstein Center for Jewish Studies at the University of Wisconsin–Madison and finishing up two projects that were consistent with a line of thinking I'd been pursuing for a number of years on Jewish rhetoric and the commonplaces of memory that were associated with it. In 2014 I was encouraged to apply for a position in the provost's office, and after being tapped to serve as the vice provost for faculty and staff, I began my work in university administration, and everything changed. It's not that I didn't know how universities worked: I'd been a department chair and a center director, had run a first- and second-year writing program, and had been involved in shared governance at a number of levels—departmental, college, and university. But what I began to understand, during my years in the provost's office, was that universities are, as David Labarree tells us in the title of his book, a perfect mess: a mess in that they have become intellectual and economic engines in an unplanned, ad hoc fashion and perfect in that they have managed, in that unplanned way, to mostly fulfill their role in creating educated, engaged, and critically aware citizens who will become, if they are not already, members of a dynamic public.

I also learned, however, that the social, political, and financial dynamics of the university were not well understood by the vast majority of my faculty and staff colleagues. The policies and procedures in place to grease the machinery of the public university were sometimes not particularly well suited to the lived lives of those faculty and staff members, who have been largely steeped in a tradition (and the commonplaces) of publicity, deliberation, and democracy, of academic freedom and the ideal of unencumbered intellectual work, as well as a sense of meritocracy, in which the best work in the classroom, the archive, the laboratory, and the public would secure for them greater autonomy from the hue and cry of a highly fractured public sphere. But those commonplaces didn't satisfactorily describe the landscape of public higher education, either in Wisconsin or in the US. I served in the provost's office during a time, in Wisconsin, when a Republican governor took pains to erode faculty members' tenure protections and governance rights and to eviscerate public funding for their work; when the governor's appointees on the Board of Regents seemed to think faculty members needed to be protected from themselves and turned to the very worst forms of bean-counting accountability measures; a time when, in universities in the Big Ten Academic Alliance and elsewhere, presidents were being plucked from the worlds of business and politics without much faculty input and faculty members were being dismissed from their jobs without due process. Toward the end of my term, the country was roiled by a racial reckoning sparked (this time) by the murder of George Floyd by police officers in Minneapolis, and by a worldwide pandemic that saw university administrators make drastic changes to the way universities were run, often with little or no deliberation with those who run them, the faculty and staff. The public university in my state, and in states around the country, was in crisis, and vulnerable. And the learning curve for dealing with these changes, and that vulnerability, was difficult.

As it happens, I wasn't alone on that learning curve, and I couldn't have had better teachers, mentors, and colleagues, among them the other vice provosts in faculty affairs in the Big Ten Academic Alliance. Terry Curry at Michigan State University, Blannie Bowen at Penn State University, Steve Abel at Purdue, and Abbas Benmamoun at Illinois were among the first people I met as liaisons to the BTAA's Academic Leadership Program, and they were welcoming to me as a newcomer to the group and extremely generous with their time in helping me understand the relation of governance to policy, of faculty work on the ground to the perceptions of faculty work in university administration, governing boards, and the public. They'd been in academic leadership long enough to see their universities shift under their feet and were at universities where those changes led to crises of significant proportion. Those in the BTAA liaison group whose wisdom, practical advice, sage counsel, and exceptional work ethic were so exemplary include Karen Stubaus at Rutgers, Kathy Bieschke at Penn State, Rebecca Ropers at Minnesota, Judy Walker at

Nebraska, Helen Malone at Ohio State, Eliza Pavalko at Indiana, Peter Hollenbeck at Purdue, and Bill Bernhard at Illinois. At later stages of the project, some were also generous enough to talk me through how diversity initiatives at their universities worked and how much distance there was between their universities' policies and the lived lives of the faculty those policies were meant to protect and support. Charity Farber, at the BTAA office in Urbana-Champaign, is a dynamic leader whose broad view of public higher education is second to none, and she is a very good friend to boot.

I was also lucky to have teachers and experienced university leaders closer to home at UW-Madison. While I only worked briefly with him in the provost's office, Paul DeLuca demonstrated a forthrightness and candor that were a welcome introduction to what a provost could be. I was very fortunate to have worked closely with Sarah Mangelsdorf, whose intelligence and sensitivity as provost over five years were simply outstanding examples to follow; she helped me recognize that being a leader was not incompatible with being an empathetic and decent human being. I also worked with some extremely talented vice provosts. Steve Cramer, vice provost for teaching and learning, helped me recognize that sometimes just getting people on the same page was exhausting work, but well worth it, and Patrick Sims, vice provost for the Division of Diversity, Equity, and Educational Achievement, shared with me a healthy impatience for transforming the culture at public universities in a way that matched the lofty language of diversity initiatives with a change in the way we saw ourselves and our colleagues and for sometimes making ourselves and those in leadership uncomfortable in doing so. Maureen Noonan Bischof—Mo—has been not only an exceptional role model, whose patience, tolerance for dissent, and empathy for those with whom she worked are extremely tough acts to follow; she was also a good friend, confidante, and partner in getting into "good trouble."

My education in the politics of higher education, and in understanding the limitations of even extremely sound policy and strong shared governance, was enhanced by my work with a number of colleagues whose dedication to change in the political arena was as urgent as their recognition of the vulnerability of higher education in the institutional one. My time working actively in PROFS, the Public Representation Organization of the Faculty Senate, gave me an intimate understanding of how state and federal policy—and politics—were often warped by polarization that was not reflected in the sentiments of the state's and nation's citizens, its publics. Jack O'Meara, PROFS's legislative liaison, taught me that realism and cynicism aren't the same thing and that even extremely uncomfortable conversations with state and local politicians are crucial to helping change the minds of intransigent lawmakers, even if it means saying things that people don't want to hear; Michelle Felber, who essentially runs the operation without getting nearly enough credit for it, is a gifted political thinker whose insistence on listening to the faculty was always in my ear. PROFS members and past presidents Bill Tracy, Judith Burstyn, and Mark Cook (with whom I also served on the executive committee of the faculty senate) showed me that persistent advocacy and steel backbones are keys to making change. As a member, and later president, of the senate's executive committee—the University Committee, which serves as something like a constitutional court and leadership council—and then later in the provost's office, I worked closely with three gifted governance coordinators (secretaries of the faculty): David Musolf, who managed to keep in his head the complex and sometimes troubled decades-long history of shared governance at UW-Madison and wielded that memory as a tool for faculty rights; Steve Smith, whose time in the office brought decency, a fierce dedication to fair play, and a drive for equity that transformed the role; and Heather Daniels, whose time as governance coordinator for academic staff makes her an advocate for parity and solidarity among employment "classes." Jake Smith, as the senate's parliamentarian, and as a mensch, taught me that Robert's Rules, far from an encumbrance, can be wielded to ensure inclusion, robust deliberation, and justice and Heather McFadden, who served for a time as the chair of academic staff governance, helped me understand how to use my privilege as a wedge to include the voices of those who are so often left unheard.

After leaving the provost's office, where I had the distinct advantage of seeing firsthand both how vulnerable the faculty's rights and responsibilities can be in a neoliberal public and how the work of talented people can turn those vulnerabilities into a foundation for change, I set to work. I'm extremely grateful to the university and to its related organizations for the funding and the time required to do so. In addition to the provosts for whom I worked insisting that scholarly work is part and parcel of administrative work, I have been fortunate to work in a department—from which I was largely absent for seven years—that insists that my experience in administration is valuable to my scholarly work. Anja Wanner in particular, who was department chair during much of my time in the provost's office, was incredibly supportive of my work. I'm grateful, too, to the Wisconsin Alumni Research Foundation, whose award of a named chair also came with research funding generous enough to free me to engage in research, as well as to collaborate with talented colleagues and graduate students, in ways that I hadn't imagined before. The funding made possible by the university allowed me to attend a workshop sponsored by the Rhetoric Society of America, led by Nathan Stormer, that started my education in the relation of rhetoric to vulnerability. I'm also particularly grateful to very talented doctoral students from programs at our university in English and communication arts. James Ryan, now an assistant professor at one of the campuses of the University of Alaska system, worked closely with me for a year, helping me piece together databases, publicly available documents, and research on the development of higher education in the US. James also helped sort through the enormous archive he assembled to identify the patterns that emerged in cases of faculty dismissal without cause, of reach-in by governing boards and university presidents, of initiatives designed to bolster the diversity and equity at the faculty and staff level, and of interdisciplinary efforts to break through the institution's methodological silos (and all while writing a book of his own). Gabe Carter not only added to and helped fine-tune the archive but also read early drafts of some of the book's chapters, identifying where the arguments held together and where they didn't and making excellent suggestions for revision. Brooke Hubsch provided sharp, incisive readings of the chapters, putting her finger on methodological blind spots and theoretical imprecisions and making strong counterarguments that helped strengthen the project's trajectory, while Nick Avery read through the entire project at its near-final stages, giving it a polish it wouldn't otherwise have. I'm grateful for faculty colleagues who were also instrumental in this project's genesis: Adam Nelson saw a draft of the book proposal, asked tough questions about the directions in which the project was going and about its theoretical underpinnings, and provided a comprehensive bibliography so that I could understand how universities in the US came to be what they are today. Venkat Mani read parts of the book as they were underway and provided friendship and support all along the way. And Sonia Baku, an incredibly talented writer, gave me an aesthetic and moral standard to which to aspire.

While the general contours of the notions of vulnerability that I am working with in this project had been worked out by the beginning of fall 2021, a doctoral seminar I taught during the four months of that semester, titled Rhetoric, Violence, Vulnerability, helped me hone it and connect it with the idea of commonplaces that serves as one of the book's generative engines. In addition to Gabe Carter, Nick Avery, and Brooke Hubsch, the members of that seminar were Theo Boluwatife Okunlola, Diego Alegria Corona, Nathan Wood, Tom Chang, Ali Rushevics, Gina Atkins, Nora Harris, and Erin Miller. The concepts, questions, and theoretical positions staked out, deliberated, and tested by the students in that seminar are all visible in this book, and I am grateful to all the seminar participants for their willingness to stick their necks out and try on new ideas.

Among the reasons this book exists is that I couldn't get an idea out of my head, an idea put there by Taralee Cyphers at The Ohio State University Press.

While wandering around the book exhibit at the MLA conference in 2017, we began talking, and she asked me if I was working on anything. I laughed under my breath: I was in the provost's office, and I had plenty to work on, just not much that would show up in print. Looking for a way to respond, I mentioned a piece on higher education and mobility that I'd published in *Philosophy and Rhetoric* that year and told her that if I had another book in me, it'd follow some of the ideas staked in that essay. Cyphers said that it sounded interesting and to contact her when I was ready to put together a proposal. So as my term in the provost's office was winding down, and as I began to cast around for ideas, that conversation stuck with me, and I began to outline what would eventually become this book. I did not know at the time I spoke with her at MLA that Cyphers is an outstanding editor, with a remarkable eye for an idea's, and a project's, potential strengths and weaknesses, and her suggestions early on in the writing helped give the book its current shape and trajectory. Her guidance throughout the process, from the proposal stage to editing the finished product, has been simply outstanding, and I'm incredibly grateful for her work and for the question she lodged in my head more than six years ago.

Finally, I'm grateful to my family for their endless love and support.

An earlier, shorter version of chapter 1 appeared in *Rhetoric Society Quarterly* in its fall/winter issue in 2022 (52.5) as "Commonplaces of Governance and the Vulnerability of Faculty Work." Some of the ideas in chapters 4 and 6 originated in essays published in *Philosophy and Rhetoric* in 2019—"Rhetorical Movement, Vulnerability, and Higher Education" (52.1)—and 2022—"Academic Freedom's Rhetorical 'Grey Zone'" (55.1).

Support for this research was provided by the University of Wisconsin–Madison Office of the Vice Chancellor for Research and Graduate Education with funding from the Wisconsin Alumni Research Foundation.

INTRODUCTION

The Vulnerability of Public Higher Education

For anyone who's been paying attention, public higher education in the US has been in a precarious position for at least the past forty years. When I began this project in earnest during the summer of 2020, during a worldwide pandemic that forced most universities to shut down in-person teaching and, in the case of research universities, all but their most crucial research operations, a number of trends were already underway. State funding for public universities had been falling for decades, and the financial crisis of 2008 and the short-lived recession brought on by COVID made things worse. According to a report issued by the State Higher Education Officers Association (SHEEO) in 2021, states' financial support of their public universities over the last twenty years (since 2001) has decreased by nearly 15 percent.[1] The decreases in funding have meant that these states—which in some cases provided over half their universities' total overall funding forty years ago—have

---

1. The changes in funding vary significantly by state: while Illinois has increased its per-student funding by nearly 86 percent and Connecticut has increased its funding by over 50 percent (the two largest increases), states like Pennsylvania, Iowa, and Indiana have seen decreases of between 30 and 40 percent since 1980; thirty-seven states have seen their FTE allocations to their public universities decrease since 2001.

forced their public universities to look elsewhere for the funding to support their missions.²

This financial shift is important not just because of what it tells us about who now shoulders the cost of public higher education but also because it signals a larger cultural shift in the commonplaces we have traditionally used to describe the relationship between public universities and the communities they serve. For a long time, the largest share of the cost of educating students was borne by the states because their citizens and legislators recognized their obligation to provide a college education to their citizens' children. Higher education has been seen, particularly since the Morrill Acts of 1862 and 1890, as a public good, an instrument through which the children of the laboring, agricultural, and other emerging middle and professional classes would have access to training in the liberal arts and sciences, training that in previous generations had only been available to children of the elite, those who could afford the tuition and other costs associated with a university education. More recently, with students and their families now paying more tuition, per student, than state legislatures, higher education has, de facto, become not a public good but a private one, available to those who can afford it.

The *ways* we measure the "goods" associated with higher education have also shifted in the last forty years. The most recent example is a survey from the Pew Research Center released in the summer of 2019. The top-line result from the survey is that since 2012, perceptions of higher education have changed significantly, with only half of survey respondents believing that colleges and universities have a positive effect "on the way things are going in the country these days" (Parker).³ But when a reader gets into the data, some of the reasons for the opinions become clearer; one of the most significant

---

2. In my home state of Wisconsin, the latest "Budget in Brief," the glossy publication produced with data from the office of the Academic Planning and Institutional Research, shows that while in 1976 the University of Wisconsin–Madison was provided around 43 percent of its overall funding from the state, in the 2020–21 fiscal year, only 17 percent of its funding was provided by the state. By contrast, 11 percent of the university's funding came from its students and their families in the form of tuition in 1976, while by the most recently completed fiscal year, students' contributions to their education nearly doubled, to 21 percent. In addition, "auxiliary" operations—which include parking lots and structures, dormitory fees, and meal plans paid for by students and their families—also doubled, from 11 percent to 22 percent of the university's overall funding.

3. Most of the reporting on the survey focused on the stark divide in the results depending on whether respondents affiliated with the Democratic or Republican party, with only one-third of Republican-leaning respondents noting universities' positive effects on the country and nearly two-thirds noting their negative effects (in a 2012 Pew survey, the numbers had been reversed), whereas Democratic-leaning respondents by more than a two-to-one margin saw universities' positive effects, a result that has not changed since the 2012 survey.

causes of the shift has to do with just what "good" public higher education does. Among the top three reasons for attending college cited by college students surveyed by Pew, two were job related: that college "opened doors to job opportunities" (53 percent agreed) and that it "help[ed] develop specific skills and knowledge for the workplace" (49 percent agreed). The other reason for attending college: helping students grow personally and intellectually (62 percent agreed). While people see value in higher education that *includes* intellectual growth, more emphasis is placed on the individual graduate's earning power, their place in the workforce, and the leverage that a four-year college degree can get them in the marketplace.

The Pew survey also tells us about perceptions of the faculty who teach at these public universities, those who shoulder the burden of the shifts in the material realities of their colleges' public missions, and hence the commonplaces associated with that publicity (the idea of "public-ness"). One survey question asked whether respondents have confidence that college professors act in the public interest. Much of the attention in the wake of the survey focused on the difference in responses by political affiliation.[4] But the fact that the Pew survey would ask respondents to answer this question at all suggests that one of the fundamental assumptions about a university education, and especially a public university education—that a college education is good for the nation because it educates the nation's citizens and enriches the public discourse—is up for grabs, and it's the faculty who are the reason it's up for grabs.

The public—and their representatives in state legislatures around the country or on college and university governing boards—have responded to the concerns not by providing adequate funding for their state colleges and universities but by submitting bills and policies that address faculty rights and responsibilities. Some of those bills are focused on campus speech, what students and especially professors can and can't say, or can and can't prevent others from saying, at their universities (both in the classroom and outside of it). For a while these bills focused on whether universities had the ability to block certain controversial speakers (provocateurs, really) from campus— people like Milo Yiannopoulos—or how to penalize students who used the heckler's veto to silence such speakers. But in the last couple of years, other such bills have focused on faculty members. In Wisconsin, a bill proposed in the state assembly would have prevented faculty members from calling out, for example, hate speech or microaggressions in their classrooms and from disagreeing with students for their positions or opinions in the classroom, even

---

4. Pew reports that while 86 percent of Democratic-leaning respondents had a fair or great amount of confidence that university faculty were working in the interests of the public, only 38 percent of Republican-leaning respondents believed so.

regarding material associated with the course being taught, and would have penalized the university with monetary damages in cases where faculty did so (Wisconsin Assembly). Other states have proposed similar legislation. In a number of instances, the problems with public higher education are addressed by governing boards extending their reach into faculty affairs—attempting to rectify the problem that students aren't being properly prepared for the workforce—by creating accountability measures that purport to ensure that faculty members are doing their jobs. As I describe in one of the book's chapters, one such measure is the post-tenure review process, by which tenured faculty members are evaluated periodically, usually every five years, to ensure that they are continuing to teach, do research, and support their universities through service. What happens, often enough, is that the review process is changed, not by faculty members themselves (or even their deans or provosts) but by members of their governing boards or state legislatures, and the criteria used for the evaluations make it far more likely that faculty members will be disciplined or dismissed, not because they haven't done their jobs but because they *have*. Their work is seen as controversial, or their views as not congenial to their students', or their programs—often associated with the study of race, or gender, or social justice—as unpopular or outside the "political mainstream." And in the year leading up to the writing of this book, state legislatures have been busy banning the teaching of certain subjects, usually those associated with race and gender, that might cause "discomfort, guilt, anguish, or any other form of psychological distress" in students learning about, for example, structural racism (see, e.g., South Dakota Legislature).

VULNERABILITY

My point in rehearsing these instances of the erosion of public higher education is that, as I describe in the chapters that follow, the material conditions for those who live, study, and work at public universities in the last couple of decades are very different from those that existed when the familiar commonplaces of public higher education were established in the years between the first Morrill Act and the Second World War. Those commonplaces—that public universities are designed to provide an education in the arts and sciences to the children of the laboring and emerging executive classes, to give them the opportunity to learn methods of analysis and engagement that will inform their ability to deliberate about the direction of the nation and to participate robustly and in an informed way in those deliberations—are no longer suitable in a (neo)liberal society in which, in its late capitalist stages, individual relations are characterized by separation and by their apparent "random motion," a "profoundly unsettled" state (Walzer 148). The public, whatever it is—that the term has been in dispute since its coinage two and a half millennia ago is significant—shifts over time. For Michael Walzer—and I agree with him—the public is in constant shift, oscillation, and movement, so much so that the way we have come to understand the work that gets done at public universities by its faculty sometimes bears little relation to the dynamics of those universities or the publics where they reside. Think about faculty members' own arguments about public higher education's value: about its contributions to democracy and the formation of an informed public; about scholarly work's relative autonomy, as expertise grants faculty members a concomitant autonomy in the governance of their institutions; about the protections of free speech that grant university faculty a related protection, in academic freedom, to engage in arguments that are considered marginal by members of the public; about how the lived lives of faculty members and the policies devised to protect their work are in alignment due to the ability of critical, thoughtful experts to deliberate rationally. These arguments don't align with the material realities of their universities, which are characterized by a deep skepticism of expertise, the splintering of the public, an erosion of deliberation in the face of that skepticism, and a devaluation of free speech. As I argue throughout this book, faculty members' understandings of and arguments about their work and the work of public higher education are in fact *encumbered* by commonplaces whose vectors have changed significantly over the last forty years.

I argue further that faculty work in public higher education is *vulnerable*, in two senses of the term. As I've described above, and as will become evident in the case studies that form the centers of the chapters that follow, public higher education and the faculty members who promulgate the education provided at their universities are vulnerable to the changes at those universities over the last four decades. The number of faculty members has declined relative to non-tenure-track instructors, support staff, scientists and laboratory workers, and administrative staff and executives since the 1970s, and the decline has drastically affected the nature of their rights and responsibilities to their institutions and to the publics they purportedly serve. The decline has made them more susceptible to the accountability measures established by boards and state legislatures and created instances of precarity—particularly among those who have not earned tenure, women, and faculty of color—that make their circumstances more like those who can be disciplined and dismissed for reasons other than cause and without due process. In this definition of vulnerability, faculty members are susceptible to harm, to deteriorating conditions at universities brought on by a lack of public funding and the related demands of funded research and, at the same time, staying in their lanes—their designated roles in governance over the limited portfolio of the teaching and research enterprises—while avoiding issues that might raise the hackles of a public that increasingly demands that their children receive an education that gives them entry into the workforce, a credential that can be "cashed" in the marketplace, and that doesn't involve changing those students' political, cultural, or religious beliefs. These faculty susceptibilities—such as discipline or dismissal for engaging in controversial research or creating areas of research that challenge the orthodoxies of departmental, disciplinary, or methodological consensus; limitations on participation in shared governance that prevent them from engaging in changing the conditions of their workplaces; or being hired into departments that promise to be congenial places to work that instead turn out to be riven by structures of racism, homo- or transphobia, or sexism—align with what Danielle Petherbridge calls "situational vulnerabilities," "forms of relationality, social practices or institutions in which [a person] is unable to prevent abuses of vulnerability or that undermine what [the person] takes to be important for [their] well-being" (599). These abuses include not only physical injury but also "underprivilege, or degradation, [instances of] social injury that subjects are motivated to contest because they strike at the core of their personhood" (597). While these forms of vulnerability are inevitable in relations of power that one finds in institutions such as states or their apparatuses (including universities)—consistent with the Foucauldian idea that subjects are always already constituted by disciplinary forms of subjection—they are exacerbated when the approaches to ameliorating them are encumbered by modes of thought and language that are not critically aligned with the material conditions that create those forms.

But vulnerability has a more general, and in my (and Petherbridge's) understanding, productive meaning, one that I also explore in this book. It provides the basis for a set of commonplaces that more adequately represents the conditions of the contemporary public and, as a result, the contemporary conditions of faculty at public universities. In this definition, derived from the work of Judith Butler, Petherbridge, Sara Ahmed, Erinn Gilson, and others, vulnerability is best described as a constitutive openness to the other, as a condition in which we are thrown into a world with subjects that are unknown to us, that—in Walzer's terms—form collectivities, split off from those collectivities, and re-form into other, distinct collectivities (154). In this condition, subjects are constantly in motion and consistently engaging in forms of relation that "indicat[e] the richness of [material and bodily] encounters with the other and with the world," the "psychological openness that affirms the individual and provides [them] with the capacity for a positive relation-to-self." It leads to an "interdependence that attends to the subject in [their] needfulness and that requires forms of social action and cooperation" notwithstanding that those forms of action and cooperation take place in networks of power and potential—some would say inevitable—abuses of power (Petherbridge 598). In this sense, vulnerability carries with it a critical capacity that allows subjects to form relations of solidarity based on their mutual recognition of one another and the situational vulnerabilities in which they find themselves mired, one that requires forms of justice that are related to the law, what Burke called the constitutions that provide the frameworks within which disagreements can be aired and deliberated, which include university bylaws, shared governance documents, laws passed by state legislatures, and even unwritten codes of decorum, disciplinarity, and collegiality. But such relations must sometimes operate *in spite of* the law, particularly where the law stands in the way of doing justice and where it contributes to or exacerbates instances of situational vulnerability. This project involves identifying the ways in which the rhetorical misalignment between the material conditions at public universities and faculty (and institutional) approaches to and pursuit of their work creates vulnerabilities that are best described as situational, while also recognizing how those approaches reflect a more general sense of (constitutive) vulnerability that opens up novel ways for faculty members to engage with one another, with their work, with their legislatures, and ultimately with their publics. My aim is to advance a theory of vulnerability in public higher education whose ramifications, in practical terms, bear further exploration.

COMMONPLACES

In this project, *commonplace* refers to a term or set of terms whose meaning is understood to be more or less stable and whose significance is recognized mutually by those who use those commonplaces, generally as substitutes for a more complex set of meanings. The significance of a given commonplace changes over time, though commonplaces frequently carry with them vestiges of their former meanings. My argument in this book is that the commonplaces used by faculty members to describe the work of higher education have become misaligned with the conditions that have historically given them meaning. There are two principal commonplaces on whose terrain the misalignment is most plain in discussions of public higher education. They run consistently not only through discussions of the purposes for college and university education but also through the description of the work of the faculty in a public higher education context. These commonplaces, while often used distinctly in discussions of higher education, are conceptually related. The first is *responsibility*, the idea that subjects or agents have a more or less univocal will through which they take action and create effects in or on the material world. Chad Lavin, in his book on responsibility and politics, describes responsibility in the liberal context as the idea that actors and events in historical contexts enable events; that there are more or less well-defined boundaries between subjects and objects, structures and agents, the public and the private; and that in light of the contours of this liberal public sphere, agents can be assigned responsibility, and collectivities of agents may bear responsibility for the aims and consequence of their actions. This idea of responsibility can be traced back to Aristotle, in the *Nichomachean Ethics,* where he distinguishes between voluntary and involuntary actions (Lavin 6). What's important about the Aristotelian distinction, for Lavin, is that it begins a line of reasoning that suggests that there are two types of responsibility: individual responsibility, where individual subjects are responsible for their actions—and where, in more contemporary liberal theorizations, those individuals' responsibilities are coupled with rights which emanate from freedom and will that allow the subject to act in and on the material world—and collective responsibility, where individuals' rights and responsibilities are consolidated in order to maintain the peace and act consensually in the furtherance of the collective (public) good. As Lavin puts it, "The institutions of liberal democracy—especially representative government and a free press—are primarily mechanisms for consolidating aggregates of individuals into autonomous and coherent collective agents with the same characteristics [that John] Locke ascribes to individuals. . . . Liberal governance enables distributing responsibility for state action to its constituents" (9).

The work of the faculty in public higher education has, since the last third of the nineteenth century, been considered such a distributive institution, one in which the responsibilities of the collective are consolidated in order to achieve the public good. The historian of education Christopher Loss has traced this relationship closely in his book *Between Citizens and the State.* There he argues that since the creation of the truly public university system after the Morrill Acts, a close relation between higher education and national aims has existed, but this relationship grew more explicit in the years leading up to the Second World War and accelerated in the years afterward. Higher education was at times rather unabashedly used as a tool of state policy, from creating better citizen-soldiers during the wars (research showed that better-educated soldiers were more apt to follow orders and to understand the significance of their army's campaigns) to better reintegrating veterans after the war through the GI Bill, from providing a global education to Americans and providing an American education to noncitizens during the Cold War to supporting the rights of women and people of color during the late stages of the civil rights movement. The relationship wasn't always direct—that is, it wasn't necessarily that the government provided funding for faculty positions or research initiatives—but shifts in national ideology were mirrored and supported by leaders and faculty at public universities. Toward the end of his book, Loss traces the shift, beginning in the 1970s, that occurred as a result of the downturn in state funding for public higher education due to the structural slowdown of the nation's manufacturing economy. This shift resulted in an erosion of "responsibilities-based" theories of education—such as during the world wars, when higher education was seen as a right for those who had fulfilled their responsibilities as citizen-soldiers—in favor of "rights-based" theories—such as, in the 1960s and 1970s, when Black and women's power movements galvanized young people to see themselves as citizens due to their identities rather than their participation in national service. That these shifts occurred at the same time as the rise of conservatism meant that there would be an inevitable backlash against higher education, and particularly public higher education, which by the late 1970s and early 1980s began to appear as a breeding ground of identity politics and "arcane subject matter" (Black studies, gender studies) that no longer deserved government largesse or political "protection."

The idea of paired responsibilities and rights is very much woven into the principles of public higher education and its accountability to the state through its production of well-educated citizens who are able to participate, *as* citizens, in the deliberative process of self-governance and public engagement. The American Association of University Professors (AAUP) was created during the second wave of public higher education—the second Morrill Act, passed in 1890, expanded the reach of the land grant colleges to the former Confederate states, making the public university a national rather than simply a sectional achievement—and the rise of the Progressive movement at the beginning of the twentieth century, and it was designed primarily as an effort by university faculty members to curtail what they saw as the unchecked power of presidents and governing boards over the academic mission of the university. In the 1890s the presidents or trustees of a number of institutions dismissed members of the faculty for their politics or because they were teaching subjects deemed controversial or contrary to prevailing economic or other theories, and the AAUP, organized in 1915, formalized the idea that university faculty members bore a responsibility to the public. Specifically, the organization argued that faculty members' years of study, and the expertise granted by their credential and their continued scholarly exploration of their subjects, gave them special rights—namely, the autonomy to oversee and deliver on the academic mission of the university, to establish the university's curriculum, to teach and do research on their subjects of study—and also special responsibilities. The first right—the right to academic freedom—was dependent on the second—their responsibilities to their students, to the institution, and to the broader public—and taken together they reflected "two communities to which professors belonged: that of their discipline and that of their institution. In turn, as a member of an institutional faculty, . . . the professor was also a member of a larger professional body: the professoriate," a body that, despite its autonomy, worked in the service of the public good and that public's "progress" (Tiede 76, 71). In the words of the AAUP's 1940 "Statement of Principles," which I take up in detail later on, the goal of the association is "to promote public understanding and support of academic freedom and tenure and agreement upon procedures to ensure them in college and universities. Institutions of higher education are conducted for the common good" and carry with that responsibility "duties correlative with rights" (AAUP 3). The difficulty, of course, is that notions of publicity and the accompanying responsibility have shifted dramatically over the last forty years: while, as the "protector of the cognitive structure of the modern national state," the university represented a paradigm of responsibility "whose chief characteristic was its autonomy," there is today a "greater questioning of the [status of] knowledge" and faculty expertise, whereby "consensus on what constitutes knowledge has been replaced by dissensus, and culture, once preserved and reproduced in the university, is more contested than ever" (Delanty 2, 4).

Closely associated with the commonplace of responsibility is that of *democracy*. According to James Cattell, president of Columbia University from 1891 to 1902, "True democracy does not consist of government by the uninformed, but of government by those most competent, selected and responsible to the people" (qtd. in Tiede 27), and academic freedom and the responsibilities incumbent on university faculty were designed to create a citizenry of the informed: expertise, with the autonomy it granted by way of academic freedom, was in a direct relationship to the promulgation of a democratic state, where faculty members' roles in academic governance were correlative to informed citizens' roles in governance of that state. In terms defined by historian of higher education William Tierney, the "public good rests on a shared commitment between higher education and society," whereby education, "specifically public universities, exists because of the obligation to serve public needs and to provide a place for the growth of knowledge" (Holley 201). Public education derives "from a fealty to the public good—not simply to educate the citizenry for jobs, skills, and citizenship but also to be a public place where thoughtful debate and examination about the polis might occur" (Tierney 2). The university is an instrument of democracy insofar as it creates a public good in two senses: as a site of knowledge production and as a "site for the production of critical perspectives and for the development of autonomous citizens and leaders" (Pusser 17). This is a decidedly *rhetorical* notion, one that extends as far back as the pre-Socratic philosophers; whereas Aristotle understood democracy as a political system in which all governed all with no distinction between the skills and capacity for deliberation of citizens (a notion that was exclusive of women, slaves, and noncitizens), Isocrates saw that democracy *required* citizens to be educated, and he saw himself as both a citizen *and* an educator whose skills as a rhetorician—to deliberate on matters of public concern—were instrumental to proper governance. To be a citizen in a democracy required that the citizen bear responsibility for the direction of the polis and so was responsible for one's own action and for the will of the collective. For someone like Isocrates, that acting-together required of a polis—of a true demos—the capacity to educate the soul, the psyche (*psuche*) through governance, which is "literally a *self-governance*, . . . a *deliberate* act of coming together. Reflective self-governance does not come about through sheer repetition of good habits . . . [but rather through] a deliberate and daily pursuit" through education (Haskins 92–94).

The democratic ideal is very much the cornerstone of the idea, for faculty members at public institutions, of academic freedom. In order for citizens to deliberate—in Isocrates's terms, for them to educate their souls—they need to have what the constitutional scholar Robert Post calls democratic competence, which is the requirement that speech not only be free but also be cognitively empowered to distinguish the elements of deliberation. While everyone's speech and the opinions made public through that speech should be treated with toleration and equality, democratic competence requires "that speech be subject to a disciplinary authority that distinguishes good ideas from bad ones" (Post, *Democracy* 34). University professors, each with disciplinary expertise earned through years of training and the evaluation of that expertise by their colleagues, must be "shield[ed] from unchecked political control" by legislatures, governing boards, and administrators to create "authoritative disciplinary practices that produce expert knowledge" (35), and the disciplinary control over the dissemination of that expert knowledge must be granted to the faculty, so long as—per AAUP guidelines—those faculty members are deemed to also have maintained their responsibility to their professions and to the public good. Expertise needs to be protected because it's "crucial to conveying factual knowledge that cognitively empowers public opinion . . . because it serves the value of democratic competence" (40). But this idea of faculty work, hewing to the rights-and-responsibilities model of faculty autonomy and governance as fulfilling a democratic purpose, is problematized in a neoliberal era. As Gerard Delanty notes,

> the modern university has been the expression of the Enlightenment idea of the "republic of science:" the autonomy of [expert] knowledge that has an emancipatory role to play. This model of knowledge—as coherent, autonomous, transcendent, self-referential—confers upon the university and its priestly caste of intellectuals the role of the guardian of knowledge that must be transmitted to society.... [However, under the] dual process of globalization and fragmentation [cited by people like Walzer,] knowledge ... is being detached from its traditional reliance on the nation state and its custodians [and is being] fragmented, that is, knowledge is losing its ability to provide a sense of direction for society and is breaking up into specialist discourses that arise in the context of globalization. (105-6)

This means that we may need new commonplaces—or to reformulate the ones we have, of responsibility and democracy—in order to achieve the aims of public higher education and that faculty will need to find new orientations to their publics in order to do so.

FACULTY WORK

Before providing an outline of what those other commonplaces might look like, I want to describe the aspects of faculty work in which the current commonplaces of responsibility and democracy are in play and that will serve as the focus for the chapters that follow. They include faculty members' role in the shared governance of public universities and in particular the rationales used by faculty members for the protection of that role in an increasingly managerial institution; the relation of faculty rights and responsibilities to their institutionalization in university policy and how those policies, understood as a written constitution or set of laws, at times work against the mobility of the public and academic freedom of faculty to pursue their work without encumbrances of politics or bureaucratic reach-in; and the institution of tenure meant to protect that freedom. They also include the argument for faculty autonomy based on the idea of disciplinary expertise—autonomy both from meddling by deans and provosts, by legislators or governing boards, and from the public's sometimes partial understanding of faculty work and expertise more generally—and the problems posed for that argument by intellectual work that spans and breaches disciplines and the administrative structures designed to support it. And they include the drive by faculty to diversify the perspectives taken by those in labs and classrooms in order to democratize higher education as well as the legal and administrative framework meant to support those efforts while also being responsive to a public whose notion of democracy differs sometimes radically from that of the faculty and their institutional representatives. The centerpiece of this project is a set of case studies that address significant aspects of faculty work in public higher education: (1) the idea of public goods and the "compact" between a university's faculty and the citizens of the state, (2) the expectation that faculty have an obligation to engage in the governance of the university, (3) the idea that faculty members' rights depend on their adherence to a code of ethics for their responsible conduct as teachers, researchers, and institutional citizens, (4) the notion that tenure is a right conferred on the faculty to provide them freedom to pursue potentially controversial lines of research, (5) the sense that disciplinary expertise provides faculty autonomy in the governance of academic matters and maintains certain conventions, and (6) the notion that a culture in universities that honors the diverse experiences and contributions of their faculty members provides a publicly valuable educational milieu. The chapters set the case studies into historical and theoretical context, particularly in relation to the traditional paradigm of liberal democratic rights and responsibilities, and they examine ways of understanding those case studies, and the principles they illustrate, through an alternative to the neoliberal paradigm of public higher education, one built on an ethics of vulnerability and destituent power.

The shared governance of universities, the focus of chapter 1, is a relatively new practice. Until the late nineteenth century, American universities were governed by a president and a lay governing board to which the president reported; faculty were seen more or less as hired hands and deemed responsible for student conduct in the classroom and in the dormitories more than for their expertise in the subjects they were teaching. This began to change in the decades prior to the First World War, when many Americans sought their doctorates at European (mainly German) research universities, where faculty members had more room to pursue their scholarly research, were trained more professionally in established academic disciplines, and had more freedom from the nation-states that funded them. With this experience in mind, university faculty members in the US began to bristle at the late nineteenth- and early twentieth-century backlash against intellectuals specifically and against "progressives" more generally, and they agitated for a greater role in governance, particularly over their role in the setting of the university's academic mission. That public universities were growing larger, and educating a greater number of more diverse students, also meant that their presidents and boards were willing to delegate some of the leadership of their institutions to department heads and deans. By the middle of the twentieth century, while faculty had begun to secure a governance role in their universities, the democratic principles on which that role had been founded were already shifting, in large measure because the autonomy on which the role was founded began to be seen by state legislators and governing boards as *delimiting* rather than expansive. If governance was founded on faculty members' disciplinary autonomy—they were, after all, the experts in their fields and so should be granted authority over how their subjects were taught and how credentials were given—then that autonomy should be limited in matters beyond faculty expertise (such as university budgets and finance, or contracts, or working conditions, and so on). In other words, the argument used to establish a faculty role in governance—democracy and expertise—was being used to limit that role.

As I noted earlier, the idea that faculty work is undergirded by a series of rights and responsibilities is at the foundation of the AAUP's principles of academic freedom. As I show in chapter 2, what often goes unexplored in this loose relationship is the extent to which those rights and responsibilities are distributed, and often interwoven, in ways that complicate the relationship. Just about every public university in the country has a statement on faculty rights and responsibilities in a format that looks very much like an institutional constitution, Burke's written and sometimes tacit agreements on what is and isn't negotiable, and how those negotiations take place, in a public or community. Those statements assume that rights and responsibilities, based on a notion of freedom (and with it, the constraints that may be placed on freedom), can be more or less clearly identified and, through the application of policy, regulated. Two issues need to be accounted for, though. The first is that any glance at a university's statement on rights and responsibilities reveals any number of publics and institutions to which a faculty member is responsible: their students, their departments, their deans, their universities, and their publics (in the form of the students' parents individually and in the aggregate and in the form of that broader public represented by the respondents in the Pew survey). And the responsibilities to any one of these groups or entities often pull against the faculty member's responsibilities to some other group or entity. The second issue is that while public universities have devised (sometimes elegant) policies and procedures to guard against the abrogation or violation of faculty members' rights and responsibilities, often those policies *permit* violations that appear to fly in the face of the public good. And this is because rights and responsibilities are understood to reside within a set of policies that are akin to what the philosopher Emmanuel Levinas would call a "politics," a set of behaviors on which, through deliberation, we agree. They reside instead, I will argue, in an "ethics," an urgent call to respond that isn't bound by consensus, constitution, policy, or the law. Justifying rights and responsibilities of faculty on the basis of consensus, policy, or law often ignores the urgency of the response that is called for.

Academic freedom, and the tenure protections that come with it, is also a relatively new feature of higher education in the US. Tenure itself wasn't truly formalized until the 1940s, and academic freedom, as defined by the AAUP, is a version of the freedoms witnessed firsthand by American academics training in Germany, where universities were understood to be a state apparatus and yet granted autonomy to run their own affairs. But in that short period, academic freedom and tenure have come to be seen as cornerstones of a public university education: without the freedom to pursue their work to whatever ends it might lead, faculty will always be at the mercy of the public's changing understanding of expertise, of science, and of how the world works. So academic freedom is recognized by faculty members as an advantage for the public. It provides what Post calls democratic competence, the ability to sort good ideas from bad ones in service of genuine and informed public discourse. But as I explore in chapter 3, it's that very autonomy—the expertise of the faculty member—protected by academic freedom that also distinguishes the faculty member from their neighbor and from the demos, so while it secures their membership in the community of experts, it puts them outside the community of their democratic peers. It's this commonplace—that tenure protects academic freedom, and in so doing functions as a public good and a means of enhancing democracy—that becomes problematic. According to Walzer, one's identity and membership in the neoliberal community is defined by a constant shifting, a movement between and across voluntary and involuntary affiliations. The sense of the public good—and of the demos's willingness to abide the understandings of it provided by those in the demos most capable of defining it, experts—is also constantly in flux. So any understanding of academic freedom that does not also recognize the radical mobility of the demos, let alone of the nature of freedom itself, will fail to convince members of the demos who see expertise to be at odds with the common good. That understanding fails to grasp the inseparability of the demos and the institution, even despite the latter's relative autonomy from the former.

Disciplinary autonomy of the faculty is also related to commonplaces of the public good and of the democratizing power of public higher education. As Christopher Loss and others have argued, that disciplinary autonomy led universities to serve as the research engines of the nation-state in the First and Second World Wars and the Cold War, and while the economic model has shifted, as I noted in the opening pages of this introduction, the ideological one has not. And yet toward the end of the Cold War and after it, American universities began to pursue much more vigorously truly interdisciplinary work to address "wicked problems"—depletion of fossil fuel reserves, urban and suburban infrastructure needs, the intransigence of poverty despite robust social safety-net programs—that couldn't be "solved" in any single disciplinary home. The turn toward interdisciplinarity, the focus of chapter 4, was intended not only to catalyze new areas of research, and to capitalize on the growth of federal research as a funding opportunity to replace lost state dollars, but also to address the deteriorating ethos of the expert, the university faculty member who is traditionally seen as someone who "prizes individuality over teamwork and the discovery of specialized knowledge over problem based collaboration" (Crow and Dabars 18), and whose disciplinary expertise is closely tied, both institutionally and culturally, to an academic department. The drive—and institutionalization—of interdisciplinary faculty work is intended to work against the tyranny of the academic discipline (and department) by bringing together experts in multiple fields to deploy that expertise on problems relevant to the broader public, thereby bolstering the ethos of the expert and restoring some of the cachet lost through political efforts to undermine the university and its disciplinary relevance. It is also meant to create a sense of accountability by the university to its publics by directing the expertise among its faculty members to focus more clearly on neoliberal economic needs, such as the creation of biomedical or pharmaceutical interventions to sustain life or the advancement of nanotechnology to support the nation's information technology networks, rather than allow the disciplines and their centripetal internal dynamics to determine the direction of primary research, which may or may not have a direct, translational effect on the public good. As I describe, the shift into interdisciplinary work to solve thorny public and policy problems may well improve the appearance of the university, in the sense that the institution has greater accountability to the public that pays its bills, but it also has the capacity to undermine the autonomy and independence of the individual faculty member by directing their research programs toward projects that are more readily fundable by the federal agencies that set the policy agenda and by weakening their institutional (that is, governance) autonomy in the university itself. So while the ethos of the university, as an institution, may well shift in the eyes of the public due to its transdisciplinary turn, the ethos of the expert faculty member, and of their work in the disciplines, may also be undermined at their own institution.

Finally, the drive for faculty diversity is also premised on notions of the public good. As I note later, universities underwent a number of shifts in the 1970s and 1980s; in one of these shifts, the idea that public universities were in service to the public good through the creation of new knowledge was challenged by critics who saw universities' purpose not as creating proprietary knowledge but as providing access to understanding one's self, one's identity, and one's place in the world. This shift represents a move away from a responsibility-based education to a rights-based one, one embraced particularly by people who were historically underrepresented in higher education. A second shift, related to and in response to the first, was toward the increased regulation of the public university. If universities were about providing access not to the economy but to one's identity, then this sort of "social engineering" needed to be reined in and managed by the state, and part of this management took the form of initiatives around inclusion and race—through "affirmative action"—that regulated the ways in which the democratization of the faculty, through diversity programs, takes place. As I describe in much greater detail in chapter 5, in navigating the often complicated political and legal landscape of diversity, universities are so focused on policy fixes that they often ignore just how fraught the lived lives of their faculty really are. Programs, such as the "targets of opportunity" initiatives that I explore in the chapter, are often so focused on the numbers of faculty from underrepresented groups that they don't take account of the quality of life—and the vulnerabilities—experienced once the faculty members arrive and begin working on campus.

COMMONPLACES OF VULNERABILITY

Vulnerability is a more useful way to describe the conditions of public higher education than terms that more aptly reflect conditions over a century old. In adopting commonplaces associated with vulnerability, we aren't necessarily *becoming* vulnerable so much as we're recognizing the conditions in which we already find ourselves. Vulnerability need not only be seen as a susceptibility to harm, though heaven knows that public universities and their faculty members are susceptible to institutional harm. Rather, vulnerability, understood as a radical openness to others, has the capacity to reorient faculty work and to provide ways for faculty, in pursuing that work, to shift the relations of materiality and power that have proved so intransigent in the last few decades. The chapters that follow describe how these commonplaces can, in faculty work in the public university, change the conditions of that work. The first of these commonplaces is the idea of vulnerability itself, specifically in its definition as a general *openness to others*. As Danielle Petherbridge has shown, that openness is constitutive—we are who we are by means of the demand for openness and relationality—and it is accompanied by a *critical* dimension, which provides human subjects the ability to recognize and assess different forms of vulnerability and particularly those forms that have the potential to injure, to exclude, to damage, or to demean those others with whom we engage. To be open to others means that we are responsible for our capacity for engagement—we are *response-able*—and that responsibility, that capacity for response (what Diane Davis has called a *rhetoricity*), often exceeds the disciplinary, methodological, constitutional, and political terms that encumber models of governance, of academic freedom, of diversity, and, frankly, the democratic project itself.

To be vulnerable is also to be *mobile*, a second commonplace of public higher education in its current condition. To refer to Walzer once again, contemporary neoliberal society is defined—unlike traditional liberal ones—by constant shifts in one's affiliation, in one's identity, and in the social structures and networks within which institutions exist. While civil society relies on institutions and the state to organize and bring some coherence to those affiliations, their more rapid movement means that the institutional energy required to manage that coherence becomes greater and greater, leading to a continuum with top-down managerial strategies on the one end and what looks like chaos on the other. To be constitutively open to others—to be defined by those constantly shifting relations of openness—means that we're perpetually in motion, and the means by which academics find their mooring in public universities, such as departmental units, the protections and the gravity of tenure, and disciplinary methodologies, are also constantly shifting. But being mobile doesn't mean having no moorings whatsoever; it doesn't mean that it's necessary to give up governance, or tenure, or departmental homes. It means, though, that whatever structures we build to recast faculty work in a context of vulnerability (both constitutive and situational), we need to be cognizant of what Alessandra Von Burg calls the *stochastic* quality of that work, a quality that destabilizes distinctions between insides and outsides of institutions, communities, and the demos and that, in that destabilization, also forces us to recognize the *potential* in that mobility, what Nathan Stormer has called the potential to be otherwise, what the Greeks called *physis*, a changeableness and an inconstancy. Later in this book I describe the connection between the stochastic nature of vulnerability and what Deleuze and Guattari called "nomadism," in which subjects are constantly on the move, in organizational structures—if they can be called that—"whose irreducible parts (atoms) occupy or fill a smooth space in the manner of a vortex, with the possibility of springing up at any point" (381). This kind of movement renders subjects—and members of university faculties—vulnerable, but also laden with the power of mobility.

One of the difficulties of faculty work that I describe later, and particularly in the chapters on discipline and interdisciplinarity and on academic freedom, is its reliance on the concept of autonomy, an autonomy founded on expertise. Faculty members are in some sense defined by their work, what Aristotle called one's proper *ergon*, where membership in disciplinary and intellectual communities is more or less fixed. But as I've suggested here, and as I demonstrate later, faculty members find themselves between and among a number of different communities, more specifically between their *oikos*, their institutional responsibilities, and the polis, their responsibilities to the broader public. It's in that space, the threshold, that Deleuze and Guattari, Giorgio Agamben, and Jean Luc Nancy, each in their own way, see a power that they call inoperative or destituent. Its power, derived from mobilities associated with constitutive vulnerability, is an inoperative one: in this model, there is no proper ergon, no proper work, for the inoperative or destituent subject. Agamben writes that such a subject is "devoid of any specific vocation" and is "a being of pure potentiality (*potenza*), that no identity and no work could exhaust" ("Elements" 8). As such, its power is "liberated and suspended from its 'economy,' from the reasons and aims that define it" in ordinary circumstances (9). What this means is that a faculty member's work resides between two spaces, public and institutional, and that it is potentially liberated from the democratic commonplaces that undergird traditional notions of governance, diversity, academic freedom, and faculty rights and responsibilities. It provides a different kind of freedom, one that is fraught with danger at the same time that it provides a kind of breathless potential.

These two commonplaces—vulnerability and mobility—and the power inherent in them can lead to new forms of solidarity. The forms of governance and faculty members' notions of rights and responsibilities are typically understood in terms of responsibilities defined by policy: faculty members—defined by the academic freedom they have by dint of tenure—are quite proprietary about their roles (in teaching, research, and service), as they should be. But as I described earlier, the protections of tenure and a role in governance have become far less common in the contemporary public university than they were even forty years ago: non-tenure-track and part-time faculty members outnumber their tenured colleagues at some public universities by more than two to one, and the conditions of those tenured and tenure-track faculty have come to look more and more like those of their untenured colleagues, not to mention those members of public university communities who have been relegated to what are typically called "supporting" roles. But the existence of vulnerable, precarious bodies in the public university creates the possibility for both resistance and solidarity among those bodies, whose critical capacity to recognize and assess the conditions of precarity and vulnerability are crucial to ensuring the mobility, and the potential, of those individuals. As I describe in the chapter on diversity initiatives, the vulnerability and precarity experienced by all those who work at public universities, and particularly those who experience heightened conditions of precarity, create what Stefano Harney and Fred Moten call an "undercommons," a ruptural space amid the institution that gives refuge to those who are at the institution's margins—not just faculty but also the staff who go unrecognized by the faculty, or the students whose social conditions render them less mobile in institutional spaces such as bursars' offices and private dormitories—and that also presents a potential threat to the (invulnerable) logic of that institution. Those who reside in this space—who are, by dint of the conditions of structural or situational vulnerability, unrecognized—are also on the move. They are "bodies that cause[ ] discomfort (by not fulfilling an expectation of whiteness)" (Ahmed 41) and are forced to "work[ ] out the mechanisms of distribution through which [the institution] reproduces the conditions of existence" (32). The person who is actively engaged in these spaces is *mobile* but also a person who "creates trouble" and, in the spaces at the margins of the institution, causes trouble together with others who occupy that same space.

The commonplaces I've outlined, and their potential to exert the power of a certain kind of solidarity, can be located in a notion of rhetorical education founded on the vulnerabilities inherent in intellectual labor and the critical perspective such labor entails. Rhetorical education's critical perspective, as a practice that retheorizes structures of (intellectual and institutional) power in relation to constitutive (rather than situational) vulnerability in ways that mutually and continually condition one another, is necessary to ensure that vulnerability is not abused. Such a rhetoric is underwritten by the sense of vulnerability and the potential force of destituency, which better position us to engage with legislative and economic threats without having to resort to the (heretofore unsuccessful) language of public goods and civic duty and to critically examine and open up the norms of faculty work. In the case studies that form the core of the book, my focus is on the work of the *faculty* at public universities and on examining the *public*—and hence *rhetorical*—character of that work in the context of the institutional aims of those universities. It is intended to diagnose the problems inherent in understanding the work of the universities as *public* and to provide alternative models of the work's public dimensions, using rhetorical principles—consensus, timeliness, the nature of the polis, and figural displacement—as key terms in those models. I draw out the implication of this neoliberal subjectivity for the work of public higher education, considering what it would mean for faculty members to be constantly on the move and for the intellectual and governance work they do to be only the temporary stabilization of a disciplinary or institutional community. A rhetorical engagement in which subjects are in constant flux, where institutions are continually evolving, and where faculty work involves potentiality more than stability (in Giorgio Agamben's terms, *destituency*) is *vulnerable*: it puts us at risk while providing the critical capacity to ameliorate that risk. Rhetoric—and *rhetorical education*—provides the means by which both student and scholar understand the potential that resides in destituency, vulnerability, and risk. While there are *situational* vulnerabilities that place higher education at risk—the adjunctification of faculty, the marginalization of interdisciplinary faculty and of faculty of color, annual reductions in funding, and administrative reach-in by activist boards, to name only a few—there are significant positive implications for *constitutive* vulnerability, the vulnerability that makes us capable of mobility, engagement, and openness to others and that can be marshaled to rethink the idea of publicity, the commonplaces of higher education, and the idea of public higher education itself.

CHAPTER 1

Commonplaces of Governance

In the fall of 2019, the University of Alaska was at the turning point of a budget crisis. The state's Republican governor, Mike Dunleavy, announced that in the face of declining state revenues, the university system's funding would be reduced by $134 million, or 41 percent. The university's president, Jim Johnsen, scrambled in the months between June and October to propose a number of options that would lessen or forestall the cuts, options that would have involved the dismissal of faculty and that were proposed quickly with virtually no faculty input. By late fall, the governor partially backtracked on the budget, and the worst of the crisis was averted. But the financial crisis at the University of Alaska was, at its heart, a crisis of shared governance, the principle that the operations of a university are to be distributed between its governing board, its president, and its faculty and staff, each according to their particular area of expertise. Principles of shared governance recognize that all these entities have a role to play in developing policy, responding to material and financial exigencies, and determining the direction of the university and that shared governance is achieved through the formation of consensus to maintain financial, educational, and institutional stability. The crisis in Alaska precipitated votes of no confidence against President Johnsen in two of its campuses' faculty senates, on the grounds that Johnsen and the board of regents had failed to engage with members of the faculty in responding to the governor's budget proposals, proposals that would have redirected or eliminated programs at each of the university's three research-oriented campuses. Johnsen, according to the faculty, had failed to share governance to achieve a consensus on the academic mission of the university with those whose job was to create and sustain its academic programs.

What happened in Alaska is playing out across the landscape of American public higher education. With decreased funding from their states, smaller numbers of students in the enrollment pool, and significant pressures to reconfigure how faculty conduct research and engage the technologies of teaching, universities are facing the question of whether faculty, with all the other demands on their time and labor, "can work effectively on [this] scale" and specifically whether shared governance's aims of providing order and stability by means of consensus are reasonable in the current circumstances (Bowen and Tobin 183, quoting Kerr). Do the principles that underlie shared governance—that faculty have a significant role in operating their institutions, that faculty and administrators share aims if not the means to achieve them (that is, consensus), and that the sharing, if not the distribution, of governance, has a tendency to maintain the stability of an institution in the face of significant change—retain their efficacy in the face of these changes? In this chapter, I examine the commonplaces that serve to bolster our contemporary understanding of university shared governance and the practices of governance that are animated by them. Perhaps the most central commonplace used to develop arguments for faculty and shared governance is the idea of *the university as a public good*: that as a community of scholars dedicated to the preservation and creation of knowledge, the university works best if it invests those responsible for the dissemination and creation of knowledge, the faculty, with a stake in its governance, since they know best the landscape of their disciplines, of the classroom, and of their local units and how they fit together. Of course the expertise of the faculty does not (necessarily) include every aspect of the university, and principles of governance reflect this through the idea of *faculty members' proper sphere,* that faculty members' roles in governance will reflect their expertise, mainly academic affairs, including criteria for professional advancement; the curricula and programs of their departments, schools, and colleges; and the teaching and research conducted with their students. All of this, in the words of Clark Kerr, is intended to provide the institution a sense of *stability, security, and continuity* (see *The Uses of the University* 71–72) that preserves not only the work of the institution but the institution itself.

Examining the commonplace of the university as a public good, and the attendant ideas of faculty members' spheres of responsibility and of the stability required for faculty members to do their work, yields a clearer understanding of their efficacy as rhetorical, that is, as a means of establishing the discursive ground on which conflicts can be resolved and disorder and potential violence averted. The principles of shared governance are a peculiarly American invention, developed in the last hundred years or so as a means of ordering the increasingly complex organization of public higher education while maintaining its civic responsibilities to educate the children of the country's working and professional classes. After examining the development of shared governance as a (rhetorical) means of providing order through consensus, I closely analyze recent instances of governance crises in American higher education. My goal is threefold: to determine the efficacy of governance commonplaces—publicity and consensus, faculty responsibility and autonomy, and institutional stability—for public higher education at its current conjuncture; to understand the consequences of their rhetorical failure; and to propose an alternative set of commonplaces with which to address a period in American public higher education characterized not by stability but by movement, unsettlement, and vulnerability.

GOVERNANCE: STASIS AND MOBILITY

The characteristics of shared governance—to achieve consensus, to admit faculty to governance in their role as experts, and to reach consensus by means of deliberation—emerged alongside the development of public higher education and the professoriate in the US. Before 1890 faculty had virtually no role in university governance; the college president governed the university as a sovereign. The historian Laurence Veysey characterizes the years beginning with 1890 as a period of the "rise of administration" because in these years the number of administrators—deans, business and support staff, and senior faculty who served as de facto department chairs—grew significantly in order to manage increasingly complex institutions, with larger campuses, greater numbers of students, and an ever-expanding curriculum that reflected the new fields that were emerging and along with them the professionally trained faculty who taught them. As noted earlier, the demand for governance that wasn't autocratic—where presidents ruled like sovereigns—came from faculty, many of whom had advanced degrees from Germany, where faculty had a modicum of autonomy that was unheard of in the US. Administrators, from the president on down, came to understand that to share governance was simply to avoid the pushback that would inevitably come from these newly empowered faculty members (Veysey 308).

In fact, governance *had* to be shared because of the conditions at the universities. Committees were formed to help create order in the chaos, and then deans gained power as they took over from the badly organized committees; assembly-line methods of student registration and course-numbering systems became commonplace. But while the pressure to share governance appeared to come about in response to practical problems, it also suggested something else about the apparent heterogeneity of the new public university landscape. It helped make universities look more similar to one another than different as the practices adopted by one university—Harvard, or Johns Hopkins—were copied by others. Through the growth of governance, universities were becoming not only stable but uniform in their missions and distributive, if not democratic, in their sharing of authority. "Bureaucratic modes served as a low but tolerable common denominator, linking individuals, cliques, and factions who did not think in the same terms" (Veysey 315). This kind of governance allowed faculty the (academic) freedom to pursue their intellectual interests, to pursue their research along robust methodological lines, and to work inside their own more or less self-governed departmental units.

This brief history highlights two tendencies in governance noted by Clark Kerr: one toward the avoidance of strife and conflict, with the aim of achieving stability, and one toward self-deliberation and an openness to mobility and change. At the time, the former tendency had more gravity and force than the latter. Kerr, in his book on the "multiversity," writes that at a time when the "university [was] being called upon to educate previously unimagined numbers of students; to respond to the expanding claims of national service; to merge its activity with industry as never before; to adapt to and rechannel new intellectual currents" (65), it needed to create an environment that gave its faculty members a sense of stability, security, continuity, and equity (71–72). But "there is a kind of 'guild mentality,'" Kerr goes on, "in the academic profession, as in many others," and the result was not so much an openness to change but the development of spheres of relative autonomy and expertise. This relative autonomy is reflected in the American Association of University Professors' (AAUP's) statement on shared governance, originally written in 1966 jointly by the AAUP, the American Council on Education, and the Association of Governing Boards of Universities and Colleges (AGB). In its first major section, its authors write: "Although a variety of such approaches [to joint efforts at governance] may be wide, at least two general conclusions regarding joint effort seem clearly warranted: (1) important areas of action involve at one time or another the initiating capacity and decision-making participation of all the institutional components, and (2) differences in the weight of each voice, from one point to the next, should be determined by reference to the responsibility of each component for the particular matter at hand" (AAUP, "Statement on Government" 136). For the faculty, this means that their primary area of governance should be education and student affairs; in addition, "scholars in a particular field or activity have the chief competence for judging the work of their colleagues" (136, 139).

But this distribution and sharing of governance is nonetheless contextualized more broadly with this line from the statement's introduction: "Regard for the welfare of the institution remains important *despite the mobility and interchange of scholars*" (AAUP 135–36, emphasis added). Kerr's qualities of stability and security give faculty the capacity for an intellectual and deliberative openness and mobility that is implicit in the idea of faculty autonomy but latent in the commonplaces of publicity and consensus as a public good, a capacity that is most often suppressed in governance crises like the ones I examine shortly. Inherent in the commonplaces of stability is a tendency toward mobility, unsettlement, and openness.

Speaking of the rules of shared governance, Rob Deemer and his colleagues write that "bylaws are much like a constitution. . . . Consider that a constitution's primary function is to provide a framework within which disagreements can be aired, examined, debated, and eventually resolved" (10). The constitution is a means by which experienced faculty members' institutional memory is solidified and by which new members of a faculty can be oriented "to the meaning, practice, and significance" of the institution's ideologies (11). An argument could be made, however, that simply designating which individual or group *owns* the authority and responsibility does not go far enough to be effective. In an essay on the relation of governance to responsibility, Steven C. Bahls puts his finger on the problem with the consensual models of governance: they depend on a "view of shared governance focused on rights and territories and move toward a view that ensures joint accountability for the institution as a whole" (87). If everyone is in their lane, their understanding of the deliberation, let alone the self-deliberation, necessary for engagement that achieves justice is limited to the ways in which they have been interpellated as faculty, or deans, or board members. It's as if the stability of governance becomes important for its own sake; in pursuing it, the intellectual mobility—the "interchange of scholars," or what Gerard Delanty calls reflexive knowledge production—of self-deliberation that it's meant to allow for often becomes de-emphasized. The model also ignores what happens when one of those lanes belongs to non-tenure-track faculty, with marginal rights and territories, who are more mobile in the sense that they are—by dint of their precarious employment status—unmoored from their units and institutions, and so also from frameworks of deliberation (see Kezar and Maxey 29–34).

This model of governance founders in the current context of public higher education, notes Michael DeCesare. For one thing, more and more board members (increasing numbers of whom come from the corporate world), focused on maximizing profit and increasing organizational efficiency, are uninterested in sharing responsibility with faculty who, in staying in the classroom and the laboratory, might just as well cede governance of the institution to those who know how to run businesses. Interdependence between and among faculty, staff, and administrators, let alone boards, seems hugely inefficient. Second, there are structural changes that threaten the notion of shared governance, including a growing belief by members of the public that higher education is less about the creation and dissemination of knowledge than about preparing individuals for the workforce. "If faculty are to impart the habits of mind necessary for citizens to participate in democracy, [they] need a central role in the governance of [their] institutions. But if [they] are to simply train obedient workers to participate in a ruthless labor market, [they] do not" (DeCesare 151). Politicians, too, have become more demanding of accountability from colleges and universities, on the same principle that they should create well-trained workers, and as a result they have line-item funded institutions not with general purpose revenue but with job training and professional centers on the campuses. DeCesare notes that at the time of the writing of his essay, legislatures in various states had proposed "political litmus tests for hiring faculty," legislatures in two states had introduced "bills . . . to eliminate tenure, and, in Kentucky, the [governor unilaterally abolished and reconstituted] a state university's board of trustees" (152). Finally, he cites the AGB's white paper "Shared Governance: Changing with the Times," which suggests that changing conditions in higher education, including the increasing pace of emergencies fiscal and cultural, the growth in faculty unionization efforts, and the threat posed by open meetings laws to lay bare the deliberations of governance bodies, mark the need to reassess whether governance as practiced really works as it should.

Bahls cites Richard Morrill, the former president of the University of Richmond, who "observes that faculty define themselves as autonomous professionals who have the right, and in the eyes of many, the obligation to work independently. He observes the natural tension between faculty who value autonomy and boards and presidents who value order and dependability. Administrators seek to make order out of chaos, while faculty members see administrative efforts to increase order as efforts to corporatize higher education" (110). It could also be that faculty see administrators trying to impose order on a kind of scholarship and work that is, at its best, all about chaos, disorder, and complexity (the kind of self-deliberation Isocrates describes as sensitive to contingency); requires dexterity and mobility; and may run afoul of the law, or policy, or practice. It's a different kind of dynamis, or power, altogether.

CASE STUDIES: GOVERNANCE, RHETORIC, AND REASON

In the remainder of this chapter, I complicate the idea of governance as consensus used by so many scholars of higher education by putting some pressure on its commonplaces: how does governance's *rhetoric* of publicity, autonomy, and consensus bear up under current material conditions? What shared governance practices discussed in the last section omit is the extent to which governance functions rhetorically as an instrument of mobility and change, one that opens the door to the very unsettlement that its advocates hope to avoid. While it might be too much to say that shared governance in higher education has its roots in rhetorical principles, governance itself has historically been associated with the formation of right reason, the creation of stable publics that are not regularly disrupted by the vagaries of material and potential violent change and that are put into practice through deliberation. Shared governance is so mundane an aspect of faculty responsibilities—listed on one's curriculum vitae as "service," traditionally the least visible and least respected of the three principal pillars of faculty work (along with teaching and research)—that it often becomes most heavily felt when threatened by administrative overreach, or by legislative fiat, or sometimes just by ineptitude or failure of communication. As Steven Bahls puts it, governance is about aligning and pursuing priorities, sharing accountability in doing so, and "developing a system of checks and balances for addressing more routine, nondirectional decisions" (100), in which "nondirectional" means the routine, day-to-day decisions that take place in departments, schools, and colleges. What follow are case studies where governance becomes particularly visible because it is under assault, either by members of the institution itself (faculty, deans, chancellors) or by forces and stakeholders outside the institution but crucial to its functioning (legislators, governors, members of governing boards). They demonstrate the extent to which the commonplaces we typically use to describe the faculty's relationship to an institution through governance—that faculty have a special relationship to the workplace in higher education, one where they have a specific sphere of work; that institutions function best when they are more or less stable; that the outcome of governance, intimately tied to deliberation, is consensus; that the aim of faculty work, and of universities, is to inculcate critical engagement with and to create knowledge and in so doing to create an well-educated and engaged citizenry—come to a point of crisis, forcing us to rethink not only what governance is and does but what faculties at universities are and do.

Failures of Consensus and Deliberation

The case of the University of Alaska with which I began this chapter was a crisis brought on to some extent by forces well beyond the control of the board of regents there, including a drastic fall-off in the price of petroleum, which is responsible for a significant portion of the funding available to the state to run its government, agencies, and K–12 and higher education. In 2015, not long after taking on the presidency of the University of Alaska System, Jim Johnsen worked with chancellors of the campuses and the board of regents to create what was called the "Strategic Pathways" (SP) to "meet Alaska's needs for higher education with fewer resources from the state" by "maximiz[ing] value to Alaska through excellent, accessible and cost-effective higher education" ("Strategic Pathways"). Among other aims, SP was to reduce program duplication by creating specific educational initiatives at each of the three main University of Alaska campuses and reducing funding to programs that were not crucial to those initiatives. After the 2015–16 academic year, when faculty at the university's campuses were presented with the plan for SP, they began to ask, through their faculty senates, for opportunities to participate in the planning and to better understand the efficiencies that were touted in the plan. But the senates were not given the information they requested about the "efficiencies" in the Strategic Pathways, and as a result, the senates of UA Fairbanks and UA Anchorage drafted resolutions of no confidence in President Johnsen (see "University of Alaska Anchorage Resolution"). The board of regents went ahead with Strategic Pathways anyway.

In the spring of 2019, largely as a result of a decrease in oil revenues, the governor warned that there would be budget cuts, and the legislature asked the board of regents to create a committee to study whether the three main campuses could merge their operations and, for the purposes of accreditation, be considered a single university with three campuses. The state legislature then passed a budget that included $320 million for the university system over the objections of the governor, and on the day before the deadline for passage, Governor Dunleavy vetoed $134 million in support for the university, a 41 percent decrease in funding. The legislature attempted to override the veto but didn't reach the required threshold. Now the university had to figure out how it was going to keep its doors open, with President Johnsen warning of layoffs of as many as two thousand people; he told a reporter that "there's nothing that escapes a cut of this magnitude" (Bohrer).

Within three weeks, the board of regents declared financial exigency, a technical term that typically means the university faces a situation so dire that it must act in unusual and expedient ways to manage a budget crisis, often including the termination of tenured and untenured faculty members and eliminating programs. The University of Alaska policy on exigency doesn't follow the AAUP's guidelines on the process, which requires that a faculty body participate in the decision that a condition of financial exigency exists or is imminent and that there be a process in place through which faculty who are identified for termination can appeal before a faculty committee (see AAUP, "On Institutional Problems Resulting from Financial Exigency" 148). At UA the board can unilaterally declare that the conditions for exigency exist, and the grievance process does not make clear whether a faculty body will hear grievances, only that a hearing officer has jurisdiction (see University of Alaska Board of Regents Policy on Financial Exigency).

By August, the board of regents and President Johnsen had negotiated with the governor to reduce the cuts to the university's budget to $70 million over three years and rescinded the declaration of exigency. But the board also took up Johnsen's earlier plan, into which faculty claimed to have had no input, to consolidate the three campuses into a single university for accreditation purposes. Because the governance bodies at the three main university campuses had not been consulted—about the Strategic Pathways two years earlier and now on financial exigency and the merger plan—the faculty senates of all three campuses voted no confidence in the president; the UA Anchorage Senate resolution reads in part that "President Johnsen has repeatedly ignored the accreditation concerns raised by faculty and other shared governance groups" and "has repeatedly and willfully ignored the need for inclusive dialogue and decision making input from the chancellors, shared governance, and community stakeholders" and called on the board of regents to suspend Johnsen's actions on consolidation ("University of Alaska Anchorage Resolution").

The UA case represents an instance of what happens when the deliberations that constitute governance—founded on rhetorics of publicity, autonomy, and consensus—are bypassed, in part because those commonplaces ignore the extent to which governance also involves mobility and change, opening the door to the very unsettlement its advocates hope to forestall. James Crosswhite, in his exploration of the formation of the Western rhetorical enterprise, describes rhetoric as "a capability for deliberation and judgment in conditions of uncertainty where there are conflicting conceptions of what is good" (2) and as a way to put "an end to violence and [serve as] the beginnings of politics, as well as the birth of a new kind of human being" (11). It makes possible "dynamic resolutions of conflict in discourse and in processes of justice" and learning "what it means to do justice to each other's lives and experiences" (12, 13). Consistent with this view, governance is seen as a means of avoiding strife and violence and of reaching sympathetic accord with one's fellow humans. Yet, in "A Critique of Violence," Walter Benjamin makes a useful distinction between practices that bring individuals into accord with *the law*—in the context of higher education, the policies, rules, documents, and principles that govern academic and administrative actions—and those that move individuals into accord with *justice,* the ultimate ends toward which those policies are meant to lead. There's an intimate connection between violence and the law: violence functions as the means by which law is created and preserved. True violence—a force that diverts movement toward an end and in doing so causes harm—takes place when the implicit (coercive) violence of the law can't guarantee the state's outcome. In the UA case, the financial crisis caused such a circumstance, the solution to which its administration believed was available not by means of deliberation but by means of what Benjamin calls law-preserving violence. Benjamin notes that it is by means of language, "the sphere of human agreement . . . the proper sphere of 'understanding,'" that the rights of the person may be vouchsafed against law-preserving or law-making violence and might instead be accorded justice (286). But in the UA crisis, faculty were bypassed in governance not only because the law—policy—permitted it but also because UA's president and board saw governance only as a means to stability: the means became the ends because the mobility inherent in governance—and self-deliberation—was seen as a threat commensurate with the threat of a financial meltdown.

Moreover, the case suggests—as Benjamin notes—that even the sort of deliberation that did take place involves its own sort of violence. In Plato's *Protagoras,* as Crosswhite puts it, the "mutual advent of human political society and rhetoric lie in a sense of justice and a sense of shame and in their use to resolve conflicts discursively" (137). Governance provides us, in this view, the means, through rhetorical practice, to achieve a peace that comes of the ability to form sociality or community, where conflict is unavoidable but doesn't lead to strife or violence but rather a "generative and productive ideal" (164). But while this view of governance, as made possible by means of rhetoric, is aimed at the idea of justice, it often leads to stability's opposite. As any rhetorician recognizes, the discursive attempt to find a route to a reasoned conclusion in Plato's dialogues often ends in the frustration of the interlocutors: they throw in the towel, they stop arguing altogether, they make their excuses and leave the site of the argument, or they get so angry that they threaten violence. This is because we *expose ourselves to one another* through the deliberative process, and in so doing we are susceptible to becoming other than what we are. *This is the potential mobility inherent in governance that works against stability and continuity*—and that Johnsen and the Alaska regents wished, apparently, to avoid.

Deliberation in the context of governance requires, in Ekaterina Haskins's view, a self-understanding, so "citizenly discourse, *logos politikos*, is constituted precisely by a series of pleas in which unification is urged and common identity affirmed in response to division and strife" (90). Through her reading of Isocrates, Haskins argues that reflective self-governance "does not come about through sheer repetition of good habits that someone else had laid down. It is a result of a deliberate and daily pursuit," one that opens the rhetor and the interlocutor up to possibilities that lie beyond the social codes and virtues of the polis and that requires a continual reassessment of the shape of the polis, and its constitution, over time (94). Haskins points out that Isocrates's *Areopagiticus*, when read together with the *Nicoles*, suggests as much: "The soul of the city is nothing other than its constitution, since it has as much power as the intellect does in the body. For it is this that deliberates in all matters, preserves what is good, and avoids misfortune" (*Areopagiticus* 14). But like Benjamin's distinction of law and justice, such (self)deliberation requires discursive maneuvers that go beyond the adherence to the law, beyond the politeia, beyond constitution and "overflows the parameters of written laws" (Haskins 93). Governance is not commensurate with the formation of consensus; rather, in this latter (Isocratean) view, it is highly sensitive to the contingencies of power and may hit on a principle located quite outside the law or policy. It's a practice that requires a certain dexterity and mobility, and while it may avoid violence and strife between and among interlocutors in the process of deliberation itself, it may well also work against the law or policy or practice. Governance, in this view, *is* mobility, since rhetoric, governance's medium, is not so much a praxis as it is a dynamis, a capacity, a power.

In the Alaska case, the intimate connection that Benjamin saw between violence and the law played out in its financial crisis. The permissive policies for exigency, the material conditions of scarcity, and the severe limitations on the authority of the faculty through its deliberations in the senate made possible a set of circumstances where budget cuts signed into law by Governor Dunleavy were met by the unilateral declaration of exigency that easily would have led to the elimination of faculty positions and the consolidation of, and elimination of programs in, the UA system's campuses. The "Critique of Violence" suggests that deliberation provides the possibility that the rights of the person may be protected from violence and instead be accorded justice. But one of the conditions of achieving such consensus or accord is requiring the formation of sympathy, which guards against the demonization of one's interlocutors and which, in the words of James Crosswhite, "keeps one in the argumentative situation, persevering in the hope and practice of nonviolence and refusing the temptations of force" (154). In the summer and fall of 2019, no deliberations with the faculty—or with any stakeholders beyond the board of regents—took place, and no sympathy was formed. In fact, the opposite happened: one sort of violence, in this case the threat of layoffs and program elimination, was met with another sort of violence, a vote of no confidence by the faculty at the three UA campuses. As Barrett and Quarless note in their essay on shared governance, "Representative engagement is the 'public common' of the faculty in both governance and representation" (64). But the public common at the University of Alaska was entirely bypassed, and any deliberations occurred out of sight of the public. Students who were asked about the fiasco as it was occurring in real time fully understood the consequences of what was happening. "This is a huge budget cut," said Audrey Kirby, a student at UA Fairbanks who was interviewed for an *LA Times* story on the financial woes of the university. "If they were to [go through with the budget cuts and the ensuing merger proposal], it would have devastating impacts on Alaska" (Bloomberg). Even when the university is seen not as a creative engine for the formation of critically engaged citizens but as an engine for the economy, the failure of deliberative governance has the same effect: it marginalizes the well-being of those "customers" it was created to serve. The financial events in the state of Alaska in the summer and fall of 2019 were textbook examples of circumstances that needed to be addressed expediently; by ignoring the deliberative process, the university's board of regents created a circumstance of greater crisis and violence than they had when the events began.

President Johnsen resigned from the UA presidency in the late spring of 2020.

Public Goods and Faculty Responsibilities

In the years between 2015 and 2017, a proposal to change the University of Wisconsin's institutional mission led to its own crisis of governance. The institution's mission is codified in chapter 36 of Wisconsin state statute, which also outlines the faculty's responsibilities in governance. Relying heavily on the trope of public goods, the relevant section of chapter 36 reads:

> The mission of the system is to develop human resources, to discover and disseminate knowledge, to extend knowledge and its application beyond the boundaries of its campus and to serve and stimulate society by developing in students heightened intellectual, cultural and humane sensitivities, scientific, professional and technological expertise and a sense of purpose. Inherent in this broad mission are methods of instruction, research, extended training and public service designed to educate people and improve the human condition. Basic to every purpose of the system is the search for truth. (Wisconsin State Legislature)

In 2015 Republican governor Scott Walker introduced a biennial budget bill, Act 55, which would have made changes to chapter 36, including the language on the university's mission. That section, had it been passed, would have read:

> The mission of the system is to develop human resources to meet the state's workforce needs, to discover and disseminate knowledge, and to develop in students heightened intellectual, cultural and humane sensitivities, scientific, professional and technical expertise, and a sense of purpose. (Hamer)

What's missing in the proposed revision is the extension of knowledge beyond the boundaries of the campus (what's often called the "Wisconsin Idea"), the improvement of the human condition through teaching and research, and the search for truth that underwrites the university's activities.

The reaction against this revision was swift. Faculty were as angry about the fact that the change was introduced quietly as they were about the substance of the change itself; the change was discovered by the Center for Media and Democracy (CMD), and UW-Madison journalism and mass communication professor Robert Dreschel worried about the justification the governor's office used to hide the process of drafting the bill (Hamer). The governor initially suggested that the introduction of the change was a drafting error, though records requested by the CMD showed that the changes were directed by Walker himself. They were ultimately withdrawn, and this section of state law reads as it did in 2014 (Strauss). But the larger point is that the proposed change makes clear the economic and cultural context the university confronted in 2015 and still confronts today, one in which the public good no longer drives the mission of public higher education and deliberation, whether in the classroom or in the faculty senate, is secondary to the neoliberal demand for a well-trained workforce.

This is the crux of the other changes introduced by the budget bill (Act 55) into chapter 36, specifically those that amended the section on the role of the faculty in governance. Wisconsin statute gave them exceptionally broad authority "for the immediate governance of [the] institution and [to] actively participate in institutional policy development" (Wisconsin State Legislature). In this governance model, faculty have a special relationship to the institution that employs them, as—per the AAUP—"appointees, but not in any proper sense the employees," of the university's president or trustees, because the faculty member's responsibility "is primarily to the public itself," and faculty are, by dint of their expertise in their subject matter, "no more subject to the control of the trustees, than are judges subject to the control of the president" that appointed them (AAUP, "1915" 295). Their proper sphere is over the university, not only the domain of their area of expertise or of the teaching and learning enterprise. The change to 36.01(2) was a declaration that the university was not a place where professionally trained experts sought after truth and disseminated it to students and the public "exempt from any pecuniary motive" (294) but rather was precisely pecuniary; it was also a declaration that faculty were employees, not appointees, because their job wasn't about the creation of knowledge but about creating other employees. This is borne out in the language of Act 55. In the section of chapter 36 defining the roles of the faculty, the lines about faculty being "vested with responsibility for the immediate governance of [the] institution and [to] actively participate in institutional policy development" were struck, and their role was limited to "advising the chancellor" on educational activities and personnel matters. And just in case the relationship between the chancellors of the institutions and their faculties wasn't clear, the bill added a section, "Meaning of 'subject to' in certain provisions." It reads, "'Subject to the responsibilities and powers' means subordinate to the responsibilities and powers'" (Wisconsin State Legislature).

These changes, one of which was forestalled and one of which was passed into law, reflect two significant problems with the public-goods commonplace. First, in the state of Wisconsin—and since the midterm elections of 2010, in a great number of states whose legislatures and governors' offices became more conservative and more pro-business—the idea of the university as public good has given way to the notion that it's a private good and that by receiving taxpayer funds to support them, the universities and their faculties were responsible for the number of jobs they produced. Though Governor Walker's proposed change in the language of the university's mission never made it into the 2015 budget bill, the language of human resources and workforce needs is common in many legislators' accounts of the value of higher education, in Wisconsin and elsewhere. That language reflects the idea that faculty members are employees, not appointees, and have no special status that distinguishes them, or their rights and responsibilities, from those of other employees whose responsibilities are to their stakeholders (and shareholders) and to their boards. Second, faculty members, however they are defined, have not only a proper sphere of responsibility but a sphere that is significantly delimited. While deliberation may be all well and good, it needs to take place in the library, the laboratory, and the classroom; it has no place in other aspects of the governance of the university. And even there, deliberation is subordinate to the powers of the chancellors and to the board of regents. In this case, justice has been subordinated to the law, in the sense that the faculty's responsibility for governance of the institution as a whole has been undermined by policy. Whatever power (dynamis) that governance might catalyze that could overturn disciplinary, intellectual, methodological, or institutional orthodoxies has been delimited, subordinated not only to the power of the chancellor and the board of regents but also to the ideologies of efficiency and order that Kerr warned about in his lectures on the challenges faced by the contemporary "multiversity."

The Wisconsin case also places in stark relief the idea that shared governance's aim is to avoid strife and conflict and to achieve institutional stability, a tendency that often enough leads, in rhetorical terms, to a language of preservation. But as I suggested earlier, there is a second and opposite tendency inherent in the first, one that derives from the principle of autonomy of the faculty, autonomy granted by their expertise and their capacity for creating new knowledge even in relatively conservative institutions. Describing the modern "multiversity," Kerr writes that at a time of great transformation, institutions need to create an environment that gives faculty members a sense of stability, security, and continuity (71–72). But as I noted, Kerr goes on to describe "a kind of 'guild mentality' in the academic profession," the result of which is a relative independence of mind and autonomy (73; see also Geiger 201–3). It's a relative autonomy codified in the AAUP's statement on shared governance, which reflects the aspirations, if not the reality, of governance in US universities. But as I've also noted, the distribution and sharing of governance, with the faculty maintaining governance in their own (educational) lane, is contextualized more broadly with this line from the statement's introduction: "Regard for the welfare of the institution remains important *despite the mobility and interchange of scholars*" (135–36, emphasis added). Kerr's qualities of stability and security are vouchsafed *in order that* faculty may maintain a physical and—I would add and emphasize—an intellectual and deliberative mobility implicit in the idea of faculty autonomy but latent in the commonplaces of publicity and consensus as a public good. It's this idea of mobility that is most often suppressed in crises of governance.

During the same year that the University of Wisconsin's mission and shared governance were thrown into crisis, the trope of faculty autonomy was trumped by the realities of "accountability" in a proposal by the board of regents for a new system of post-tenure review. In a newspaper article describing the exigence for the policy, the chair of the task force assigned to write the policy, board of regents member John Behling, is quoted as saying, "The Legislature beat us up and consistently used the term accountability. . . . If we don't add post-tenure review into the [tenure] policy, I fear we will get forced into a tenure policy that is unlivable. . . . If we address this 'phantom' of accountability, we as a system will be much better served" (Schneider, "Regent"). The UW system task force included some faculty members, though it was small and did not include representatives from most of the campuses (the UW-Madison representative was its provost), and many on the task force seemed to agree with Behling that the need for the policy was spectral. The task force produced a system-wide policy that required the inclusion of administrative review of tenured faculty along with peer review, and the board gave campuses one year to develop their own campus policies and to submit them for approval. The UW-Madison faculty senate executive committee chair charged a committee to write its campus policy that included nine members of the faculty. By the fall of 2016, the UW-Madison committee had come up with a policy, but board committee chair Behling refused to approve the policy unless it had even stronger provisions for administrative review of faculty in addition to the peer review, pressing the campus on "accountability," which by this point was less spectral, apparently, to Behling than it had been a year earlier.

As each UW system campus had to contend with accountability policies that were created by a board that refused to recognize the appropriate sphere of authority that faculty members' distinct status as professionals gave them, the wielding of a different kind of power (or violence) emerged to displace notions of public goods and of faculty autonomy. Language—in the form of policies presented to the faculty and in the form of a repeated refusal to give ground on the matter of administrative review during post-tenure review—functioned *as* violence, as a form of "law preserving" action that doesn't require deliberation at all. For Benjamin, the "sphere of human agreement" that is "wholly inaccessible" to violence or force is language. But the post-tenure review negotiations, between faculty members who seemed to experience great consternation over the misunderstanding of their proper sphere of influence and board members who saw demands for accountability trumping any urgency to remain within their policymaking sphere, show how hewing to the letter of a policy in the face of cries of unfairness or overreach is incompatible with justice, which requires a different kind of deliberation, one that eschews notions of consensus and responsibility in the face of the law. The board did not seem to be interested in creating the "sympathy" that deliberative engagement requires, nor did the faculty seem to recognize that the language of reason would fail in the face of the violence of a policy that insisted on keeping faculty in their (narrow) lane.

CONCLUSION

In his book on faculty governance, Larry Gerber points to a US Supreme Court case that serves as a watershed moment in how universities understand shared governance and faculty autonomy. The case was brought in the 1970s by the administration of Yeshiva University against its faculty, who wanted to organize as a bargaining unit. The court decided in 1980, by a 5–4 majority, in favor of the administration, allowing it to block its faculty from organizing. In his dissent, Justice William Brennan wrote:

> Education has become "big business," and the task of operating the university enterprise has been transferred from the faculty to an autonomous administration, which faces the same pressures to cut costs and increase efficiencies that confront any large industrial organization. The past decade of budgetary cutbacks, declining enrollments, reductions in faculty appointments, curtailments of academic programs, and increasing calls for accountability to alumni and other special interest groups has only added to the erosion of the faculty's role in the institution's decision-making process. (qtd. in Gerber 133)

Faculty decisions, Brennan went on to add, are made to serve the faculty's "independent interests" to create effective learning, teaching, and research environments (132), using the argument that faculty, by dint of their expertise, have a right to governance. But Brennan's argument is dependent on both the trope of faculty autonomy and the trope of public goods—even if they have eroded to some degree—and shows that the "special status" or "proper sphere" of faculty results not so much in stability as in stasis. Faculty expertise grants faculty a right to participate in deliberation about policy, but in doing so it also delimits their authority, confining it to the disciplinary and methodological structures designed to contain their expertise rather than serving as an engine for broader deliberative power.

Interestingly, it's Bowen and Tobin, in their book about the difficulties of making good on the promise of shared governance, who propose a way out of the problem, one that—given that both authors were presidents of relatively conservative private institutions (Princeton University and Hamilton College, respectively)—is fairly radical. They begin by wondering, with Kerr, whether the size and scale of the modern university, particularly those institutions that have an explicitly public mission founded in the Morrill and Smith-Lever acts, makes it impossible for faculty to work at that scale while maintaining their own expertise, worrying that the centripetal forces of expertise will serve an equally centripetal force on their ability to govern beyond preserving the status quo (Bowen and Tobin 183). For this reason, they go on, "we do not think that the most urgent need today is for a 'greater sense of order and stability.' It is rather for organizational machinery that can facilitate an all-encompassing set of strategic decisions that allocate human and capital resources effectively and provide a compelling set of incentives for faculty to pursue system-wide goals. Such machinery cannot be simply consensus-driven" (183–84). They instead recommend "horizontal thinking," a more "networked" approach to issues "without expecting to control outcomes" (184). Rather than simply cite, as Gerber and Kerr do, the growing pressures for accountability and efficiency demanded by legislators and others in a neoliberal economy, Bowen and Tobin also cite the significant changes that information technology is bringing to higher education, not least in the promulgation of information and communication in governance, including a "compression of time and space," suggesting that "vertical models of decision-making in the academy, focused on departmental [and other 'proper spheres' of] authority, have to give way to more horizontal ways of organizing discussion" with "mutual openness" (206, 207, 211).

For such models to work, we need to consider both looking beyond the tropes of goods and adopting commonplaces that better suit the material circumstances facing public higher education. If liberal notions of publicity and autonomy can no longer be comfortably overlaid on a neoliberal and managerial institution, one characterized by movement, vulnerability, and a shifting of identities, then it makes sense to consider governance as a mode of self-questioning, along the lines of Haskins's rendering of Isocrates. Here, governance is the opening up of the deliberative space to perspectives that are not only not one's own but also incommensurable to the self, and as a result the opening of the subject to potentialities that are altogether alien and perhaps not recognizable at the point of deliberation at all. Deliberation opens the rhetor and the interlocutor up to possibilities that lie beyond the social codes and virtues of the polis, requiring a continual reassessment of the shape of the polis, and its constitution, over time. But there are matters beyond the law, because the polity "overflows the parameters of the written laws," and so governance, as it is made manifest through internal and external deliberation, doesn't conform to law or policy. In instances where the goal is to achieve something like justice, governance has to reach beyond consensus, consent, or received ideologies and orthodoxies and must instead work as a coming-together that is sensitive to power and may find a course of action outside the bounds of law, policy, or custom, at least as defined by the institutions themselves. It's practice that requires a certain dexterity and mobility, and while it may avoid strife between and among interlocutors in the process of deliberation itself, it may at times also represent—to the institutions whose activities called for the deliberation in the first place—a kind of mobility, exogamy, or violence. The principle of governance, in this view, highlights its mobility rather than its tendency toward stability.

What does this mobility look like, and how does it function as a means to achieve a course of action outside the bounds of policy or the law? First, consider Bowen and Tobin's concern about scale, and about the "lanes" granted by expertise to which faculty seem to have been relegated in the case studies I've presented. Governance characterized by its willingness to exceed policy, law, discipline, and proper spheres (suggested by Haskins's reading of Isocrates) understands deliberation as requiring human activity unconfined to institution, polity, or discipline but instead exceeding them. In Giorgio Agamben's work on stasis, particularly his 2013 essay "Elements for a Theory of Destituent Power," he describes a notion of human activity that serves as an engine for ethical action in a world characterized by flux and change. Proper human activity—mobility—is "a threshold of articulation" between stability and interminable flux. How, he asks, can we think about human activity that is also clearly related to brute materiality without reducing the latter to something altogether exogamous or exceptional; how can we act in a way that retains the capacity for doing something that goes beyond the expected, the deliberative, the law? Such action doesn't reside in the faculty member's special status as expert, if we mean the disciplinary knowledge that authorizes their autonomy in overseeing the academic matters of a university, their identities as appointees but not employees, and—in terms found in Wisconsin statute prior to 2015—"the immediate governance of [the institution]." These definitions of power can have debilitating effects in the face of crisis.

Instead, consider the deliberative power of faculty residing in their having no proper work—no "lane" to stay in—at all. Agamben calls this kind of power destituent, of "pure potentiality (*potenza*)" ("Elements" 8); it is a power in which human activity is more properly said to be mobile, neither entirely a reaction to one's circumstances nor the result of a deliberative engagement with the cultural and discursive context in which one is immersed, potentially outside the law or constitutions. Thinking of faculty as having this kind of destituent power would suggest that maintaining tropes of governance that hew toward proper spheres, of stability, and to consensus as a means of achieving public good may do more harm than good. It suggests that exploring the means of exerting that power in their work to transform their places of labor and the university more broadly may well appear to be potentially violent, disorienting, and perpetual. If we think of the AAUP's statements on governance as delimiting a "proper work" (*ergon*) for faculty (and for deans, administrators, and boards), on this alternate view, faculty *have no proper work* and are instead *argos,* inoperative, and as a result, a pure potentiality. Argos requires a kind of destituent stance in faculty toward their institutions, one that has significant implications for shared governance.

There are models for this kind of power already in practice, though—perhaps ironically—they are visible more on the international stage than in the US context. In his assessment of the way the internationalization of higher education has changed the nature of faculty work, William Plater writes that as the economy becomes hyperglobalized, other countries are moving away from seeing higher education as a public good and closer to seeing it as an engine of economic growth and hence an instrument of the market and market power. These changes, Plater argues, inevitably shift the nature of faculty work, the curriculum, how faculty members are recruited, the nature of tenure and long-term contracts, and the notion of faculty mobility and autonomy. Plater writes that "in the face of the massification of education worldwide and the attention to the cost of higher education in the United States, the fundamental model of educational organization is fair game, and—as the increased adjunctification of the faculty has documented—the faculty model is especially vulnerable" (Kezar and Maxey 165). To address this vulnerability, Plater suggests a "flatter" higher education model that upends or levels hierarchies such as faculty ranks, administrative levels, and the tenure system. Individuals at work in higher education would be much less closely affiliated—or unaffiliated altogether—with institutions, or states, or nations and could "market themselves as educational providers via technology and global communication" (163). "Why shouldn't underemployed doctoral students at US institutions (and others) accept concurrent virtual part-time employment at colleges in emerging economies?" he asks (164). Why shouldn't underemployed PhDs do the same? The point is that in the hyperglobalized economy, there will inevitably be a mismatch between the realities of the higher education market and the commonplaces on which higher education was founded, and when this mismatch occurs, and particularly as the professionals working in higher education continue to stratify (tenured, tenure-track, long-term instructional staff, short-term and contingent staff), there will be more, not less, mobility in the work of higher education. Such mobility calls for more urgency—more sensitivity to complexes of power in the face of vulnerabilities and injustice—and more solidarity. I say more about what these alternative models look like—the disciplinary organization of universities, faculty conduct, academic freedom, and diversity and inclusion—in subsequent chapters.

The cases in Alaska and Wisconsin show that governance on the deliberative model fails because the contingencies and vulnerabilities caused by the neoliberal shift in higher education—with its attendant mobilities—render it inoperative. The university president (in Alaska) and the state legislature and the board of regents (in Wisconsin) simply overrode the policies of their universities, in part because of a failure to develop what Crosswhite calls sympathy: there was nothing, presumably, that bound the two constituencies together. But there are models of governance *founded* on the recognition of mutual vulnerability—the recognition that the conditions of tenured faculty look more and more like the conditions of their nontenured colleagues (as diagnosed by Kezar and Maxey, esp. 23–42; Schuster and Finkelstein; and others), conditions that also further marginalize their influence in governance founded on public-goods and formation-of-consensus commonplaces. Such models make possible new forms of solidarity that unite those who share vulnerabilities. Such models make use of the potential violence inherent in mobility and produce action at the margins of policy and the law. In fact, as I've tried to emphasize, deliberation might be better seen as the creation of openness and vulnerability—characterized as a general openness to the other (Petherbridge 591)—rather than the cultivation of sympathy. Vulnerability simply *is* the constant state of mobility in which humans are bound to live, and rhetoric, insofar as it is a form of exertion of the will through deliberation, is a mobility that by definition also contains a potential violence within it, insofar as it is a destituent force.

Rhetoric also carries with it ethical and political responsibilities, the first of which involves recognition: recognition of the other with whom one is implicated and the (vulnerable) circumstances in which that recognition is made possible. For Petherbridge, vulnerability and the interdependence that results from a recognition of others as fundamental to who we are (as becoming other) requires forms of relationality and care as well as "forms of enculturation, socialization, and cooperation" (595). These forms of relationality are not the building of consensus or the forging of public goods but rather the recognition of "our reciprocal vulnerability . . . [and the] open-ended nature of the human condition" in which "forms of relationality, social practices or institutions [make a person] unable to prevent abuses of vulnerability or that undermine what she takes to be important for her well-being" (598, 599). Recognizing and ameliorating those conditions—unilateral abrogations of policy, undermining of faculty members' conditions of employment, de facto disenfranchisement of non-tenure-track faculty (and more and more frequently, of those on tenure-track and tenured lines)—and the commonplaces of governance to which we've become accustomed require that we call out the situational vulnerabilities in concert with those with whom we share conditions of precarity (600–601).

Michael Walzer has diagnosed the contemporary moment as characterized by "a society where individuals are relatively dissociated and separated from one another, or better, where they are continually separating from one another" (148). If he's right, then the deliberation involved in shared governance isn't so much a "sympathy" as it is a relationality in which those who engage in it are also constitutively vulnerable. To protect shared governance against the predations of a penurious legislature provides no guarantee that the will of the faculty will prevail; faculty members, as *inoperative,* are potentially "liberated and suspended from its 'economy,'" rendering it "open" (Agamben, "Elements" 9, 17). It also means that if solidarities render academics open to mutual vulnerability, strife and potential violence in the governance process isn't avoidable but is in fact *un*avoidable. This kind of solidarity isn't required prior to the formation of new critical and material relations that depend on mobility; the solidarity *of* vulnerability engages the conditions of mobility, precarious as they are, as novel forms of destituent power. Such forms could well include a rejection of governance as consensus-forming and deliberation and the adoption of collective action—temporary engagements of resistance and refusal, of forming coalitions that look different, are mobile and potential, and are formed differentially depending on the issue. It would require the formation of common cause between newly vulnerable tenure-track and tenured faculty with their perpetually vulnerable non-tenure-track instructional staff, graduate student colleagues, and other members of the "precariat." Partly, such a governance strategy involves the forcing of recognition by institutional and legislative actors that "the faculty," whose participation in governance is dependent on their autonomy, are differently configured—and exert their autonomy differently (and differentially)—than the commonplaces of public goods and deliberation may suggest. *This* alternative form of deliberation has as its aim—as potential and destituent—to unsettle us and the disciplinary and institutional conventions that tend toward fixity, in a way that recognizes both our mutuality and the extent to which that mutuality is threatened by *situational,* as opposed to constitutive, vulnerability. The aim of governance, then, is not only to force institutions to recognize these risks but also to reconfigure them.

CHAPTER 2

Faculty Rights and Responsibilities and the Urgency of Justice

By the early twentieth century, members of university faculties had become experts, with disciplinary specializations and a degree of autonomy in their spheres of influence, mainly having to do with academic affairs. With the establishment of the American Association of University Professors in 1915, faculty work became explicitly linked to service to the public. The AAUP's 1915 statement establishes the claim that faculty "are the appointees, but not in any proper sense the employees, of the university" and that "the responsibility of the university teacher is primarily to the public itself, and to the judgment of his own profession," while he also "accepts a responsibility" to the authorities—such as the president and the board of trustees—of the university. To put things simply, by the early twentieth century, faculty had special rights, but they also had certain responsibilities closely related to those rights.

It's this pairing, faculty rights and faculty responsibilities, that I explore in this chapter, in particular the tensions that this pairing raises for the work of public higher education. Much could be said about the extent to which the faculty's "special rights" at public universities have been threatened by legislatures and boards of trustees; however, my goal here is to examine the dynamics of the rights-responsibilities dyad in the work of the faculty itself and specifically to understand the extent to which the pairing, and its establishment in policy as a "constitution," at times forestalls or blocks the moral and ethical urgency required by faculty to ensure that their intellectual work is matched by their observance of their responsibilities to the various stakeholders, not least to members of the public. The rights-responsibility pairing is consistent with what Chad Lavin calls liberal social theory, which in part understands responsibility as a causal relationship: as relatively autonomous subjects, we produce action, we make things happen, and it is the results of those actions for which we are responsible. Systems of punishment and reward are grounded in this kind of causality, and while they admit to certain special cases, typically we understand that because we are owners of our own subjectivity, "we *have* responsibility"; we "(tacitly or explicitly) enter into reciprocal relations that lead us to adopt an obligation toward particular (types of) behaviors" (Lavin 13).

But this model of faculty responsibility understates the extent to which freedom is intimately tied to constraint, that we are born into relationships and socialized into forms of action that lead us to define "freedom" in ways that other members of our community might not agree to. Faculty members are responsible to the profession, their students, the administrative apparatus of the institution, citizens, taxpayers, and so on; the list of possibilities is long. One's responsibility to the institution—to observe, for example, your obligation to teach courses when you say you will teach them—may well be in direct conflict with one's obligation to provide an education to those for whom temporal and spatial specificity is a hindrance (remote learners or students with certain disabilities, to name only two obvious possibilities). Finally, even if the rights-responsibility pairing is intended to ensure that faculty members retain the ability to engage with one another and their students in intellectually full and dynamic ways, their engagement with the broader public context in which that work takes place may require different action and a different sense of responsibility. As I describe shortly, the policies—constitutions—universities create to ensure that faculty meet their responsibilities often fail to acknowledge the radically distributed nature of those responsibilities, especially when—in offering due process to those involved in a dispute over those responsibilities—determining who's responsible gets in the way of the urgency of *justice*. And it's justice that ameliorates the vulnerability and harm caused by an imbalance in and the complexity of the relations of power and precarity that reside in the "academically free" spaces of the classroom, the laboratory, the office, or the community.

In what follows, I analyze the way that responsibility is defined in policy in public higher education, paying particular attention to the way that policy functions, in Kenneth Burke's terms, as a constitution, expressing the ethical aspirations for how members of a community engage with one another. I am interested in how policy configures those ethical obligations through an embodiment whose aspirations are often at odds with how decisions get made in actual cases. The cases I explore—instances of faculty misconduct in which the matter of faculty responsibilities is in dispute—demonstrate the consequences of hewing to policy that clearly delineates faculty rights and responsibilities but, in so doing, loses sight of the ethical urgencies and the structural and ideological vulnerabilities that policy is supposed to mitigate. In the chapter's conclusion, I suggest an alternative to the politics of responsibility on which faculty work is so often based, one that foregrounds *justice* over responsibility, and *freedom* over rights.

The rhetorical justification for the creation of a rights-responsibilities model for faculty work was derived from universities' roles in creating a deliberative public. Faculty members took up their public responsibility in the key of professional duty, "began to see themselves as part of a professional class[,] and observed how their actual status differed from those of other professions" (Tiede 21). Larry Gerber, author of *The Rise and Fall of Faculty Governance*, noted the problem with the rhetoric of democratization serving as the basis for asserting rights, and accepting responsibilities, for faculty members. He writes that "a college or university may be a community," a public, "but it is not a polity in which all are entitled to an equal voice in determining the way the institution ought to be run" ("Professionalization" 23). There is a conflict between the notion of responsibilities to a public, as the argument ran in some quarters as influenced by the rise of the Progressive moment, and responsibilities to the norms and standards of a profession or discipline, not only because the profession's standards and paradigms, not to mention ethics, were far narrower than those of the broader public but also because the public's sense of what was acceptable for faculty was often vastly different from the faculty's own sense of it. Tiede notes that the historian Richard Hofstadter, in his book on anti-intellectualism in the US, saw the Progressive Era as a moment of "rapprochement" between the principles of democracy and those of expertise and that "the use of democratic rhetoric to advance the reform of university governance was as much a reflection of [a view] of democracy as it was a reflection of [the view] on basing democratic governance on expertise" (Tiede 27). Hofstadter's thesis was that the anti-intellectual strand of American public opinion has waxed and waned over time, so the calibration of rights and responsibilities, and their translation into constitutions or policies, is a constantly shifting series of adjustments between and among one's professional obligations to conduct teaching and research according to the standards set by disciplinary expectations, one's institutional obligations to teach and conduct research for the good of the members of the academic community, one's responsibility to the demos (the education of engaged citizens), and one's own sense of right and wrong conduct as a liberal (and relatively autonomous) subject. In other words, it's never clear, as Lavin notes in his assessment of liberal notions of responsibility, where one's responsibility as a faculty member lies, which also means that one's rights could well be considered similarly foggy. Matthew Finkin and Robert Post note that in the AAUP declaration of principles, faculty are "appointees, but not in any proper sense the employees" of the university (AAUP, "1915" 295). The rights of a faculty member to hew closely to their professional standards of conduct are relatively autonomous from their responsibilities to the broader public's right to the education that founds responsible citizenship. So, while "universities can advance the sum of human knowledge only if they employ persons who are experts in their disciplines and only if universities liberate these experts to apply freely the disciplinary methods established by their training" (Finkin and Post 37), those disciplines would seem, in the AAUP's formulation, to be relatively homogenous and entirely self-policing.

A quick look at one of the more comprehensive statements provided by the AAUP—a statement that forms the basis for many of the institutional statements on faculty rights and responsibilities found on the websites of and in legal offices at public universities—shows the paradoxes, or at least the confusion, of those public and institutional responsibilities. The AAUP "Statement on Professional Ethics," created by the Association's Committee on Professional Ethics and adopted in 1987, begins with the premise that "membership in the academic profession carries with it special responsibilities." The statement lists twenty-six responsibilities for faculty divided into five areas, with the first four responsibilities being to the profession, the second nine to students, the next six to institutional and professional colleagues, the next three to their institutions, and the final three to the broader public community.[1] Rather

---

1. The lists include the following: Seek and state the truth where [faculty] see it; Develop and improve their scholarly competence; Exercise critical self-discipline and judgment in using, extending, and transmitting knowledge; Practice intellectual honesty; Encourage free pursuit of learning in their students; Hold the best scholarly and ethical standards of the discipline; Respect students; Foster honest academic conduct; Ensure that their evaluations of students reflect each student's true merit; Respect the confidential nature of the relationship between professor and student; Avoid exploitation, harassment, or discriminatory treatment of students; Acknowledge significant academic or scholarly assistance from students; Protect students' academic freedom; Do not discriminate against or harass colleagues; Respect and defend the free inquiry of associates; Show due respect for the opinions of others; Acknowledge academic debt; Strive to be objective in their professional judgment of colleagues; Accept their share of faculty responsibilities for the governance of their institutions; Seek above all to be effective teachers and scholars; Maintain their right to criticize and seek revision; Give due regard to their responsibilities to the institution in determining the amount and character of the work done outside it; Recognize the effect of their decision to terminate or interrupt their service upon the institution; Have the rights and obligations of other citizens; When speaking

than an overlapping set of nested responsibilities, it's equally possible to see a conflict between and among responsibilities to local communities and to the broader public or polis. Patricia Owens argues, by way of Arendt, that there is a clear relation between the narrower realms of institutions and the public, between a hierarchized and self-policing realm and the more democratized and deliberative realm of the demos; the spheres cannot be separated (see esp. 300–301). In the case of universities, I would hypothesize that the range of narrower, institutional responsibilities correspond with what Arendt calls the oikos, the institutional responsibilities of faculty members, the discipline-specific, professional norms of conduct prescribed by professional organizations; the broader public norms of ethical conduct correspond to the polis. This distinction roughly lines up with Finkin and Post's formulation of the distinction between "professional norms" and "public opinion" (154). But whereas Finkin and Post and Tiede (and others who've written about academic freedom's rights-and-responsibilities model of faculty work; see also Bowen and Tobin, chapter 4; Gerber, *Rise and Fall*) see a clear relation between responsibility to institutional and to broader public criteria for faculty work, despite the tensions between them, I argue that there's a hiatus, an aporia, between and among the institutional, professional, and public responsibilities. If one is able to associate institutional and public responsibilities with, respectively, the self-policing and more circumscribed realm of the oikos and the broader public and civic responsibilities of the polis, there is not only a tension between them but also, per the formulation about oikos and polis provided by Giorgio Agamben, a "threshold," a process of "decentering" of both the individual poised as a resident of both realms and the structures of responsibility themselves ("Elements" 5–6). There's a "displacement" that "confuses what pertains to the oikos with what is particular to the polis," in which the bonds created in the one are integrated into the bonds of the other, estranging both realms (Agamben, *Stasis* 15). As I show, this aporetic moment, the hiatus, between public and professional responsibilities often serves as a hindrance to the promulgation of faculty work because it's understood to be an imprecision, a slippage between two kinds of responsibilities. I'd also argue that if one sees this hiatus as Agamben does, as a displacement that has productive rather than destructive value, then it may lead to a quite different understanding of the relation between faculty rights and responsibilities on the one hand and the urgency of their application on the other.

---

or acting as private citizens, avoid creating the impression that they are speaking or acting for their college or university; Have a particular obligation to promote conditions of free inquiry and to further public understanding of academic freedom.

CONSTITUTIONS, POLICIES, FREEDOM, AND JUSTICE

What makes theorizing responsibility so difficult in a neoliberal paradigm is that the complexity of intersubjectivity is difficult to disentangle. The rights that faculty members claim are an ever-moving array of individual, institutional, and citizens' rights, and there will be conflicts between and among them, conflicts that can serve as impediments to work, and frankly to achieving the just outcomes to which the work aims. Among the responses to this conundrum, Chad Lavin points out, is a materialist approach, one "predicated upon the idea that subjects . . . are consolidations of historical forces that are afforded capacities to act by virtue of a complex interchange of historical institutions" (22). Michael Walzer, in his book on liberalism and egalitarianism, puts it this way: "Most of us are born into or find ourselves in what may well be the most important groups to which we belong—the cultural and religious, the national and linguistic communities within which we cultivate not only identity but character and whose values we pass on to our children (without asking them)" (x). Faculty members find that they have absorbed the values of the institutions to which they belong, the intellectual communities in which they practice their academic work, and the publics to which they and their students belong (in addition to the cultural, religious, national, linguistic, and other communities with which they are engaged). Those values, too, are in turn passed along to colleagues, to students, and to the public (sometimes by asking them, and at other times not). I would be hard-pressed to determine which of these associations—institutional, cultural, linguistic, professional, and so on—would rightly fall into the oikos or the polis because, while broadly "public," they seem also to have a familial dimension, a hierarchized and enforced sociality that seems more arbitrary and less deliberative than what the classical terms suggest of the associations they require. But that's just the point: those associations are complex ones, and we are multiply responsible for actions that we take and for relationships in which we are implicated.

Not only are these relationships complex; they're also constantly shifting. Per Walzer, the neoliberal context is a condition of unsettlement, and it's just this unsettlement that rights and responsibilities, codified by universities in policies and procedures and in statements of professional ethics, are supposed to adjudicate, if not entirely settle. But what Lavin asks—and this is at the heart of my argument as well—is whether it might not be better to worry less about adjudication and more about amelioration: "For postliberals, . . . the project is . . . to recognize the unavoidability of rifts and vulnerabilities so as to render us less anxious over our failed endeavors to autonomy and more generous toward our interdependent Other" (128). Both Walzer and Lavin wonder whether we should make "radical mobility a regulative idea" (Walzer 76).

The matter of regulation is where policies—or constitutions—come in. We tend to think of policy (or statements of professional ethics or lists of rights and responsibilities) as the codification of modes of conduct or as expressions of a community's rules of engagement, not unlike how some university administrators or members of boards of trustees understand shared governance. But constitutions and policies aren't so much a user's manual as they are arguments, justifications, or wishes. "Constitutions are agonistic instruments" (Burke, *Grammar* 357), attempts to substantiate what people do, and as such they are rhetorical actions, "strateg[ies] for encompassing a situation" (Burke, *Philosophy* 109). They chart situations by realistically characterizing them (see *Philosophy* 6), but because there are infinitely multiple ways of characterizing such situations, there's no complete chart (7). So at best, policy and constitution provide a *sense* of the structure of actions that can and should (and cannot and should not) be taken, but the situations that face us aren't necessarily settled by reference to those policies. As Robert Wess puts it in his analysis of the "constitution" section of Burke's *Grammar*, the principles in the constitution come into conflict with one another just as the affiliations and identities in a neoliberal public do, and "no principle dictates how such conflicts are to be resolved in all cases" (23). At best, the principles expressed in a constitution or policy are "wishes generalized enough to be applicable in diverse historical situations" (23). "Principles as wishes are voluntary or arbitrary, inasmuch as men [sic] can meet in conference and decide how many and what kind of wishes they shall subscribe to. But once you have agreed upon a list of wishes, the interrelationships among those wishes are necessary and inevitable" (Burke, *Grammar* 375).

What Burke is talking about here are the decisions that must be made when conflicts arise: what happens when someone fails to observe their responsibilities, as outlined by policy or a constitution? What's needed is the intervention of some other body, and in the case of the US Constitution, that body is the Supreme Court. In the case of faculty governance, in which the rights and responsibilities of faculty are enumerated in whichever policy documents or statements, it is some combination of a faculty committee or an administrative body or a provost acting to understand the action's adherence or failure to adhere to policy and what to do as a consequence. But as an expression of wishes, of voluntary or arbitrary principles that are the result of Burke's "parlor" conversation, the constitution doesn't provide "direction" to that body so much as it forces that body to do *something* in relation, but not necessarily tethered, to those principles. "What is really mandatory upon the

Court is a *new act* . . . as partly an outcome that exceeds what may appear as prescribed by the law" (*Grammar,* 376). But as Burke makes clear, even these grand totalizing schemes will fall short in a context where any scheme is only a partial description. Policies enact what Foucault called "governmentality," the techniques or forms of relationality employed by institutional bodies, the partial freedoms individuals have in institutions, freedoms that, as Robert Nichols puts it, are not so much tactical and reactionary as they are "relational and creative," defined not so much by what we do as by how we do it. Freedom is "characteristic of a certain relationship between entities, not as a property of the subject (a free will), nor as a particular kind of action by the subject (an act of resistance)," a "freedom of *situations* not *subjects*" (Nichols 139). Policy enacts freedoms inherent in situations that are mobile, contingent, and precarious.

It's this idea of mutability—both the mutability inherent in the enactments of constitutions and the mutability or radical mobility inherent in the neoliberal context—that's often ignored in discussions of faculty rights and responsibilities and the policies taken to encode them. Freedom is "situated . . . , a superordinate relationship to the immanence and finitude of oneself and one's understanding of the world: a form of acknowledgement, acceptance, and care" (Nichols 15). There's no choice *but* to engage with others with whom we are bound to disagree and whose understanding of their obligations will conflict with mine. But to be free is to engage in the world as if we are not

> defined by what is given in our social, cultural, and historical condition (the actual), not only because we also possess the capacity to "stand out from" and reflect upon these conditions (suggesting we are in excess of them), but also because these conditions are always already a function of ongoing interpretation (i.e., potentiality is "in" the worldly conditions themselves). (32)

In higher education, this notion of freedom reflects the condition of a knowledge society in which "the conditions of knowledge production are no longer controlled by the mode of knowledge itself" because we live with the "challenge of . . . uncertainty and chaos . . . and supercomplexity"; in such a society, universities are hubs of just these kinds of challenges (Delanty 155; see 152–56).

The recognition of finitude doesn't mean that breaches of policy, abrogations of one's rights and responsibilities as a faculty member or as a member of a demos, cannot be addressed. It means, however, that addressing them requires an equally demanding examination not only of the policy violation but also of the urgency demanded by *justice.* The moment of urgency is reflected in Michel Foucault's idea of the "event." Freedom, Foucault writes, isn't a property of entities or subjects—we don't *have* the freedom to conduct ourselves, to exert our rights and fulfill our responsibilities—so much as an expression of "a field of possibilities in which several kinds of conduct, several ways of reacting and modes of behavior are available" (*Essential Works,* vol. 3, 342). It is this relationship, what Nichols calls the back and forth of actions upon actions, "that not only sets out a range of possible future actions, but also, over time, constitutes the *being* of the entity in question" (Nichols 152). Points of decision, instances of conduct and behavior, human action in Burke's terms, take place as moments of urgency, as *events*. An event is a "breach of self-evidence," through which the subject recognizes the "encounters, supports, blockages, plays of forces, strategies, and so on" that will make it possible to understand the moment of decision as something other than a crisis. It is "what allows us to step back from. . . . way[s] of acting or reacting, to present it to oneself as an object of thought and to question its meaning, its conditions, and its goals. Thought is freedom in relation to what one does, the motion by which one detaches oneself from it, establishes it as an object, and reflects on it as a problem" (Foucault, *Essential Works* vol. 1, 117). More than one possible response can be made in the face of this juncture, and all of them can be understood simultaneously (118).

In this model, policy isn't a guide for the direction of one's conduct; justice—characterized as a break in policy—is. In his writing on Levinas, Jacques Derrida wonders whether a constitution—a law or policy—can be deduced from Levinas's ethical theory. He calls policy "juridical content," and goes on to say that it

> remains undetermined, still to be determined beyond knowledge, beyond all presentation, all concepts, all possible intuition, in a singular way, in the speech and the responsibility *taken* by each person, in each situation, and on the basis of an analysis that is each time unique—unique and infinite, unique but *a priori* exposed to substitution, unique and general, interminable in spite of the urgency for the decision. (*Adieu* 115)

Of this passage, Diane Davis writes that there is "an *epoche* or hiatus [that] separates infinite ethical responsibility from moral and civic responsibility" (123). A decision that hews to policy may well fail to obey the ethical imperative to justice; a decision that abrogates policy may nonetheless be the just thing to do. To do justice is to recognize that freedom is always aporetic, an event followed by the rediscovery of "connections, encounters, supports," and—eventually, according to Levinas anyway—the regularization of it, in such a way that it can be brought under the law or made to adhere (or not) to policy. "Justice," writes Davis, "requires that I keep both the law and the laws," observe the mandate to obey the ethical impulse to engage openly with the other and at the same time obey the written law, which may foreclose that engagement, "which means simultaneously, that I break both" (135). Faculty members are thus responsible to observe and "obey" the laws of the country in which they reside as well as the principles of academic freedom and responsibility as outlined by the AAUP and their home institutions. But

> there is no way to *decide* without facing this impossible contra-diction, without first undergoing this experience of radical *un*decidability. Any decision aiming for justice would have to be taken in the face of this aporia, in a perjurious response to an infinite demand. (Davis 127)

Policy, by these lights, is only ever the expression of hope: the hope that one can obey the demand to navigate, by means of thought, the movements and aporias between the law and the demand to take the appropriate (the just) action. Policy is the hope that between polis and oikos and the communities represented by each, that when we respond to the event, we wind up doing the right thing.

RIGHTS AND RESPONSIBILITIES IN THE UNIVERSITY

The AAUP's statements on academic freedom from 1915 and 1940 and its statement on professional ethics describe rights and responsibilities as linked by the idea that faculty, as professionals (but not strictly employees) at their colleges and universities, are relatively autonomous by dint of their expertise and professional training. Those same statements, though, also make strong claims for faculty members' participation in the broader polis—beyond the 'family' structures in the oikos of the profession or institutional unit—setting up conflicting wishes that can't be easily reconciled in disputes about faculty members' ability to fulfill their responsibilities or assert rights that they don't have. What remains is to understand how these conflicts—and the aporias between oikos and polis and between adherence to policy and the adherence to what is just—play out in local circumstances.

Nearly all university statements outlining faculty rights and responsibilities share a constitutional quality: they are expressions of Foucault's "governmentality," the "techniques and forms of rationality" employed by the institutions, which is an expression of not what faculty do but how they do it, what Nichols calls "a kind of relationship to what one is doing" (139).[2] None of the statements, however, leave room for the kind of freedom that involves a relationship between individuals, and among individuals and entities, one that admits to the irreducibility of eventalization, the sense that events are breaks rather than concepts. The statements also share, either through explicit reference or implicit indication, an understanding of publicity that involves multiple constituencies: the community of scholars, which is more or less autonomous in its ability to police itself on matters of the ethical conduct of research or teaching or local governance; the community of institutional membership, which involves the faculty members' behavior in relation to students, colleagues, and administration; and the broader community of citizens, either of the state or beyond it, which involves all the associations described by Walzer in his analysis of the contemporary context. The policy documents set up, then, the same kind of impasse or hiatus described by Agamben between the oikos and the polis, between the regimes of power enforced hierarchically in local relations and the deliberative and more rational regimes enforced by the state but presumably granted by "the people." This aporia means that in individual cases, there will be the potential for uneven distribution of power and of consequence when faculty are deemed to have failed to abide by their responsibilities. These statements set up the rights of faculty—their freedoms—in more or less individual and local terms (they are free to write, to research, to teach, and to engage in their scholarly communities), whereas their responsibilities tend to be described in institutional or public terms. And finally, because rights and responsibilities are described as residing in different spheres—spheres that are more or less stable in their division between responsibilities pertaining to teaching, research, institutional conduct, collegial or interpersonal conduct, and conduct as citizens—there is little room left for the kind of mobility between and among these spheres. And it's just this mobility that is intimately connected, in Davis's Levinasian view, to the ability to achieve justice, insofar as achieving it requires us to become unmoored or deterritorialized from the structures of law, policy, and constitution to which we have become acculturated.

As we'll see in the following cases, policy and its accompanying procedure is often used as a framework not for thought but for *application*, as though the careful observation of university policies on a faculty member's rights and responsibilities could provide a clear guide for what to do when faculty fail to

---

2. The survey of university policies on faculty rights and responsibilities includes those from the University of Michigan, Michigan State University, the University of Wisconsin–Madison, the University of Texas, the University of North Carolina at Chapel Hill, the University of Illinois at Urbana-Champaign, and the University of California, Berkeley.

abide by their responsibilities, and as though by addressing the faculty member's conduct the university could achieve justice in the amelioration of conduct that has damaged the fabric of the university and its aims. Observance of "the law" fails to recognize the aporia between it and justice, the urgency of the demand to take appropriate action that may well run afoul of the law but respond to that urgency with care, even as it moves beyond the set of choices deemed legitimate—or even legible—by the university itself or by the public.

The "Need to Follow Procedure"

In the case I examine here, justice was deferred by reasons of strict adherence to *procedure*, the measures by which policy's governmental functions are curbed to ensure due process, one of the rights of faculty under most universities' statements of ethics.[3] While it was clear that a faculty member was almost certainly failing to abide by their responsibilities to conduct themselves according to policy and community standards of ethics, the threshold for making a complaint about the violations could not be crossed. In this case, it was the institution's failure to meet its obligation that forestalled its own ability to investigate what seemed an obvious instance of ethical failure on the part of an individual member of the community.

A staff member from a social science unit came to a representative from the provost's office to report possible faculty misconduct and to seek advice. The staff member described two problems: that the department had created an inhospitable climate for women by cultivating a "boys will be boys" culture (see DeFour) in which crude remarks about women and remarks of a sexual nature took place in public meetings of the faculty and that one of its members in particular was known to have engaged in acts that could be construed as sexual harassment and bullying over the course of a decade or more, incidents that had become particularly acute over the previous two years. The workplace climate issue had been going on for so long, she said, that it wasn't clear that there was any remedy that wouldn't take years to implement, but she was particularly aggrieved by the behavior of the senior faculty member, whose actions in the workplace were so egregious that they seemed to fly in the face of standards of human decency, let alone faculty responsibilities or

---

3. Events in this and the following cases are described with reference to notes taken by and interviews with faculty affairs representatives in the provost's offices at the corresponding institutions, along with material made available through open records requests. References to the notes, interviews, and reports and other internal documents are redacted to maintain confidentiality as required by institutional (IRB) protocols.

policy. Over time, the provost's representative discussed the options for filing a complaint at various levels: with the department chair, with the office of human resources, with deans, and with the Title IX office.

The accused faculty member resigned prior to the resolution of the investigation. But between the description of the initial report and request for consultation with the provost's office and the outcome—the faculty member's resignation under a cloud—nearly two years had elapsed, during which the faculty member's actions continued and those who were directly affected by his conduct were met again and again with requirements of university policy that were impossible to fulfill because the actual conditions of the events could not be thought of except in terms of the law. The university's ability to act on policies on sexual harassment and on bullying or hostile workplaces was stymied by the procedures of due process, which forestalled action—justice—compelled by the urgency of the faculty member's failure to act responsibly. The critical work of understanding necessary to determine the proper outcome, the proper conduct, in nudging the parties back to the path of their proper spheres of responsibility was used as a bar against implementing it.

It was "due process" that served as the bar to justice because, according to process, the first place to report concerns is to the employee's supervisor, which in this case was the department chair. According to an open letter to the university's leadership nearly two years after the initial concerns were raised and a month after a formal complaint was finally filed, rather than take immediate action to look into the concerns, the department chair "offered several alternative explanations for why this behavior might not constitute sexual harassment, including 'maybe he just needs his eyeglasses adjusted' (to explain [his] habit of staring at women's breasts'), 'he might be on the autism spectrum,' 'he might just be socially awkward like Albert Einstein was' and 'do you think maybe you're more sensitive than other people'?" (DeFour). While the chair did eventually address the allegations, it took months from the first reports to that discussion, and afterward a staff member reported that the faculty member became very hostile in his interactions with her. A year and a half into the matter, after having been told repeatedly about the continuing conduct of the faculty member, the department chair met with the faculty member, along with representatives from one of the dean's offices and from the provost's office, to set expectations for the faculty member—which included refraining from sexually harassing or bullying colleagues—and issued what university human resources offices call a "letter of expectations," which describes the conduct that falls outside the expectations for faculty as outlined in policy, makes clear the unit's expectations for the faculty member to hew to policy, and describes the consequences for failing to meet those expectations, which in this case included discipline or dismissal. When the faculty member once again violated the expectations that were set, the department chair issued a second letter of expectations rather than initiate the process that could lead to discipline or dismissal.

At the same time that the sexual harassment issue was playing out, the unit was undergoing a merger with another department, a process that involved significant oversight by the office of the dean. A program review undertaken by a university planning committee, which was supplemented by a response from the department and the graduate student organization in the department, noted problems of "sexism" in the unit, though it did not mention the specific instances of the faculty member whose conduct was brought to the provost's office initially for consultation. In this case, associate deans of both supervising colleges were aware not only of the pervasive sexism in the program review but also of the conduct of the faculty member cited by members of the staff. The associate dean of one of the colleges, when pressed by staff members and by a representative in the provost's office to forward the complaints he'd received to the dean of the college, responded that the staff members, and the dean, needed to follow procedure: those affected by the faculty member's actions had to officially make a report in which they would be named to the "respondent" (the faculty member), thereby making the reporters more vulnerable to the offending conduct, all the more because, among other conduct, the faculty member was known to have expressed a willingness to take to court anyone who made "false" allegations about his behavior. (The complainants were also told by the Title IX coordinator that filing a complaint in that office would require them to be named.)

The right of faculty to due process is a cornerstone of academic constitutions. Tenure assures faculty members that their sphere of responsibility in academic matters is more or less autonomous from institutional leaders (on matters such as tenurability of colleagues, setting of curriculum, and so on) and that as long as they observe the customary processes that are deemed sufficiently rigorous and ethical by their professions, and as long as they fulfill the responsibilities required by the institution—in this case, acting with honesty and integrity, and observing university policies and rules—they will be left alone to do their work. If a faculty member fails to act with honesty and integrity, or fails to observe policy, then their tenured status may be put in jeopardy, but only by means of due process, including knowledge of the source of a complaint and of the complaint itself, right to documentation, and right to hearing (see, for instance, "Faculty Policies and Procedure" chapter 9). But in this case, the faculty member's right stood in the way of the adjudication of their ability to fulfill their responsibilities. Because the staff members who were vulnerable to the conduct—conduct that included "staring at women's breasts, making inappropriate comments about appearance, and unwanted physical contact" (DeFour)—and who became even more vulnerable by bringing the matter to their department chair, were rightly fearful of litigation brought against them, they were unable to in good conscience tick one of the boxes in the requirements for due process under the university's policies, namely to file as a named complainant. As the dean of the college said in response to questions by a newspaper reporter about the events, in comments that appeared in print, "We have failed if colleagues or students must rely on a 'whisper network' to warn about harassment. We must create an environment where those who have complaints do not fear reprisal" (DeFour). In the words of one of the faculty member's colleagues in the unit, "due process cannot be a justification for inaction or a barrier to clear and confidential reporting options and tangible whistleblower protection. Without these, campus assurances that [faculty misconduct] will not be tolerated will continue to be meaningless and [those] who experience . . . demoralizing and damaging behavior will not feel safe coming forward" (DeFour).

Different from policy, seen as a framework for responsibilities that must be observed and enacted, procedure—in the form of the university's constitution—was seen as a rigid expression of faculty rights. The department chair, the associate dean, the dean, and the office of the provost knew for two years that one of the university's faculty members was making the climate in one of its units so difficult that staff members (and later faculty) were concerned enough for their well-being that they were bringing reports forward of sexual harassment and bullying. The university had clear policies holding that both sexual harassment and bullying were behaviors outside the bounds of the responsibilities of faculty members and were prohibited conduct, conduct that could get a faculty member disciplined or dismissed. But policies and procedures intended to create a pathway for the investigation and deliberation of instances of failures of responsibility weren't activated, because the critical engagement that ultimately leads to the analysis of events that in turn leads to justice—ethical action in the midst of others—was forestalled by the understanding of policy as an inviolable law, or by badly written policy, or some combination of the two. This is not to say that the urgency—and the hiatus—created by the vulnerability experienced by members of the unit was not felt. It is, however, to say that the rights of the faculty member as provided to him by the institution prevented the institution from recognizing that its parochial sense of responsibility—that is, a responsibility to itself—ignored that that vulnerability was not only institutional (felt as a worry about losing one's job or fraying relationships with co-workers) but also public (felt as a fear and mistrust of one's fellows and the precarity of being able to maintain one's job, and so one's ability to live). The boundaries of the oikos in this case were seen as impermeable (or were read as impermeable in policy), whereas the precarity felt by those most affected by the faculty member's failure to fulfill his responsibilities was very much at the interstices of the oikos and the polis, and the urgency produced by that precarity—an ethical urgency—seemed very much unfelt, or unfelt enough, by many of those whose institutional roles seemingly bound them more to policy and the law than to the personhood of their colleagues.

The Problem of Proportionality

In this second case, the dean of a major public research university's college of technology received a phone call from a parent of a doctoral student who worked in one of the faculty member's labs. The parent reported to the dean that he had a number of text and voice messages from their son that included evidence that his major professor—in whose laboratory he worked and who was acting as the student's dissertation director—had bullied him and that the behavior extended beyond this student to others in the laboratory. The parent forwarded the messages he'd received from his son and included a recording of the professor in a lab meeting, during which the professor unleashed an angry tirade at those in attendance, using profanity and deprecating terms to refer to some of the members of the lab, some of whom were international students. The dean was horrified by what was heard in the messages and recording and proceeded to turn the case over to the chief human resources representative in the college to look into the matter. At issue was whether the faculty member had failed to maintain his responsibilities to the university by bullying this student and others. The report from the human resources office—which included interviews with current and former lab members and faculty—confirmed that the behavior had in fact taken place and that others in the lab had experienced the anger of the professor as recorded by the student. At that point, the dean turned to the university policies on faculty members' rights and responsibilities, concluded that the faculty member had failed to meet his responsibilities, and filed a request for a formal investigation, pursuant to discipline or dismissal, with the Office of the Provost.

The focus of these investigations was whether the faculty member had violated the university's antibullying policy. That policy defines bullying as "unwelcome behavior pervasive or severe enough that a reasonable person would find it hostile and/or intimidating and that does not further the university's academic or operational interests" (University of Wisconsin–Madison, "Hostile") and links the prevention of bullying behavior specifically to the duties of members of the university community: the policy is "intended to address patterns of hostility or intimidation that impede persons from carrying out their duties to the University, ensuring that all, regardless of rank or status, may pursue their work and speak as they see fit." At the level of policy, then, the question of whether the faculty member had abrogated his responsibilities was more or less delimited to the faculty member's role in the institution rather than beyond it as a citizen in the public sphere. (There was never a question, for instance, whether the faculty member's failure to maintain his responsibilities to the student or to the institution was equally a failure to maintain his responsibilities as a citizen.) In the letter charging the investigation, the provost also asked the investigator to determine whether the faculty member had engaged in conduct that adversely affected his ability to perform his responsibilities to the university, which is tied to the university's policy on faculty rights and responsibilities. In part, this section of the "rights and responsibilities" statement reads, "The university faculty are responsible for teaching, research or other scholarly activity appropriate to the discipline, and public service. Furthermore, every faculty member has an obligation to maintain professional honesty and integrity, to seek knowledge and to share that knowledge freely with others" (see "Faculty Policies and Procedures," chapter 8). The professor was being charged with engaging in behavior that prevented him from doing his job. Per Walzer, the question was whether the faculty member impeded the mobility of his graduate student, and other members of the laboratory, requisite for the advancement of certain kinds of knowledge and the voluntary associative relations necessary for those individuals in the lab to become credentialed members of the profession they had chosen. The rights assumed by the faculty member—to direct members of the laboratory as he saw fit and to ensure that their research moved along a path he directed—were in direct conflict with those of the members of the lab and were protected by the institution, through its governmental function, by policing the boundaries of those associational and professional relations. In other words, the faculty member's responsibility to the institution was in definitional conflict with the faculty member's responsibility to organize his lab as he saw fit.

The investigator's report substantiated the charges that had been filed by the dean of the college against the faculty member: that he had "bullied" members of his lab and in so doing had prevented its members from carrying out their responsibilities to the university; that he had abused his authority by using threats of or actual retaliation in exerting his rights as a faculty member;

that he had directed abusive expression, beyond expression typically used in academic settings, at members of his lab and others; and that, having engaged in such conduct, he had impeded his ability to maintain his responsibilities as a faculty member. The report explained that the professor had produced a "toxic" atmosphere in the lab, so much so that members didn't want to attend lab meetings for fear of being reprimanded or publicly shamed, that members of the lab avoided the faculty member, that many members quit the lab over a period because of the behavior, and that while members had brought their concerns about the faculty member both to other faculty members and to the department chair, nothing changed, leading them to wonder whether those faculty or the chair had brought the matter to the faculty member's attention at all or had a plan for addressing conduct not just in this lab but in others in the unit. To the investigator, there was no question that the faculty member had abrogated his responsibilities to the university and, in so doing, had violated policy. The faculty member had. The investigator also found that in the conflict between the rights and responsibilities of the members of the faculty member's lab and the faculty member's own rights and responsibilities, those of the lab members had been violated in part because their vulnerability had been exacerbated. The question, then, became one of remedy; it became a matter of justice.

As is prescribed by the university's policies, the provost consulted with senior faculty to determine whether discipline should be levied or whether dismissal proceedings should begin. Up to this point in the process of sorting out faculty rights and responsibilities, the question had been whether rights had been violated and responsibilities had been shirked. Now, at the point of consultation, the question was one of justice: how, in the eventalization of the conduct in the laboratory and its troubling outcome, could the event be *thought* such that its complexity could be identified and the institution's responsibility, both to the individuals implicated in the event and the broader community, be made clear. In Davis's terms, how could justice be achieved by observing both the law, in this case policy, and the laws, in this case one's broader responsibility to engage as a member of a polis, while recognizing the aporia or caesura such an observance would produce? Because there was no record of the faculty member having been told to curtail bullying behavior in the past (there was nothing in the personnel file that reflected institutional action), it was considered a "first offense." Because the breach of faculty responsibility was limited to the oikos—to the laboratory and to the unit, if not more broadly to the institution—rather than more broadly public and entailing broader rights and responsibilities to what Levinas would call *witnesses*, the third parties in whose presence subjects engage with others (the *other* others), the outcome was also more limited to the individual agent (the faculty member) and to those with whom he engaged (members of the lab and the department). Dismissal of the faculty member, in other words, *did not seem proportional* to the misconduct as substantiated in the report or to the magnitude of the violation of faculty rights that would have resulted had he been dismissed (or the magnitude of the conflict between the wishes expressed by policy and that of the faculty member's conduct itself). The ratio of the institution's action with respect to the faculty member to the action taken by the faculty member did not seem large enough, apparently, to warrant dismissal. The decision was that the faculty member would be placed on a two-year period of unpaid leave, that he would need to be monitored on his return, and that he would have to be (re)trained in how to manage his laboratory employees.

What happened in this case, I would argue, was an instance of an unwillingness to recognize two hiatuses, one between the institutional (the oikos) and the public (the polis) and one between rationality and urgency (between the law and the laws, between the law and justice). What was missed in the deliberation or, more accurately, Foucault's "thinking," about the findings of the investigator was the extent to which the faculty member's responsibilities to the institution, to his students, and to his discipline were in *conflict* with his responsibilities as a citizen. It failed to consider how the faculty member's conduct in regulating the work of those in his lab interfered with their voluntary associations to engage productively with one another in their work and to associate not only as members of a profession but also as individuals themselves who had a public responsibility for, in the language of the university's statement on responsibility, "public service." The faculty member's rights trumped his junior colleagues' responsibilities, but those responsibilities also involve a responsibility to be free from harm, to occupy a workplace that is intellectually productive, and to engage in the mobilities inherent in the liberal (and, more radically, the neoliberal) public sphere. Institutional myopia on the part of the faculty member abrogated the ability of those colleagues to move, to associate, and to participate in the public project of higher education. Rather than allow the potential of the hiatus between institutional rights and public responsibilities to emerge and produce novel relations and engagements, the faculty member shut down that potential. Rather than recognize the need to open back up that potential in both institutional and public terms by taking action that would also recognize that need, the sanction proposed seemed instead to foreclose that potential through the creation of a ratio of potential that quantified the harm and vulnerability to the students with a corresponding sanction—and harm—to the faculty member.

In so doing, the decision also misrecognized a second hiatus—between the law and the laws—that resulted from the urgency of the matter itself. As described by the investigator, the laboratory led by the faculty member was toxic. Here the law, as manifested in the university's policies on bullying and on the rights and responsibilities of faculty members, took precedence over the laws, the modes of engagement between and among individuals in a broader forum (call it "the public," or "the polis," the liberal sphere in which its members form stronger and weaker, networked or individual associations, where those associations are open, mobile, and potential) that are not delimited by constitutions because they are not delimited by deliberation, argument, or reason. One of Walzer's principal arguments is that the mobility of association characteristic of the current conjuncture is not only rational and deliberative. Mobility is characterized by its susceptibility to influences that are beyond reason (what Walzer calls "passion"), that are, despite the requirements of thought and eventalization, not brought under a concept or understood as such. The result is that a response to such moments is demanded but also that any number of responses can be made; the recognition that multiple responses are all "simultaneously possible" is what creates the urgency to break with the law and to obey some other imperative in order to achieve an outcome equal to the urgency. Here the fairness of the law trumped the urgency of justice—policy trumped ethics; stasis trumped mobility—by means of a ratio. And as a result, certain "blockages" and "plays of forces" were also not recognized as significantly relevant, or at least not as relevant as they'd turn out to be once a newspaper reporter sought and received, through an open records request, the documents that reflected the policy and its outcome in this case and found that the faculty member who'd created such a toxic atmosphere in his lab would return to work in his lab in two years. In other words, what hadn't been adequately addressed, in the focus on proportionality in the matter of rights and responsibilities of the faculty member, was the role that was played by the institution itself in failing to observe its own responsibilities in maintaining a culture in which its members were free from situational vulnerability, harm, and damage. As we'll see, in the observance of faculty rights and responsibilities at times of crisis, this is not an uncommon failure.

CONCLUSION

In both instances above, the "right thing" was done—neither faculty member remained employed at their university. But in both cases, the urgency of the exigence, which was the failure of the institution's engagement with the mechanism of governmentality that grants its members the freedom to work without intervention, was not adequately recognized. So it's unclear whether the injustice identified in either case will lead to an examination of the injustice done by the institution to its responsibility to the broader public, Arendt's and Agamben's polis. Of course, the studies we have of faculty misconduct suggest that instances such as the two described above, in which a faculty member's abrogation of their responsibilities is so severe as to require investigation and discipline (or dismissal), are quite rare (see, e.g., Reisig et al.). They nonetheless highlight in stark relief the difficulties inherent in understanding faculty work in terms of rights and responsibilities. While neither of the faculty members in the case studies claimed that their rights as faculty members, and the accompanying autonomy, gave them the freedom to bully members of their labs or to peer down the shirt-fronts of their colleagues and students, it was the autonomy they assumed was theirs that provided the context in which these violations occurred. The freedom these faculty members understood they had, regardless of claims that we live in a neoliberal public, was a throwback to more traditional liberal notions of freedom and responsibility—a responsibility in which individuals "own" their behavior and are charged individually with responsibility for that behavior if it violates norms or policies and a freedom in which individuals are constrained only to the extent that the communities in which they reside say they are and communities themselves are more or less relatively autonomous. While examining violations of policy tells us much about the idiosyncrasies of faculty conduct in the context of faculty rights and responsibilities, it also tells us a lot about universities' assumptions about faculty rights and responsibilities themselves, the tensions between rights and responsibilities, and the difficulties in assessing just who or what faculty members are responsible to.

And this is a significant challenge. For one thing, the contemporary sphere in which public higher education is embedded is both highly associational and highly mobile. It's associational in that despite the separation that liberal and neoliberal subjects experience (from one another, from others' religious, political, or workplace communities), we are constantly associating, whether we realize it or not, with those in discrete communities and with those outside them. We associate voluntarily by extending our engagements beyond those discrete communities, and we associate involuntarily with those inside them by dint of social relations we didn't choose but into which we have been born or enculturated. It's mobile in that we are constantly moving between and among associational groups, and we join and separate ourselves from them with relative ease (notwithstanding the psychosocial disease that may result once a move is completed). And yet, these communities and associations aren't stable, and it's not always readily apparent when the movements between and among them are voluntary and when they're involuntary. Consider the spheres of work described in statements of institutional ethics at the University of California, Berkeley, as just one example of such statements. Responsibilities of faculty are enumerated in the areas of teaching, scholarship, the university, faculty members' relation to colleagues, and "the community," representing five distinct communities in which the faculty member resides: students (as their teacher), research colleagues (as a scholar), faculty members (as a member of the university), institutional citizens (as a colleague in a department and other affiliated departments and as a member represented in a governance unit, the faculty senate), and the broader polis. In which community, one might ask, were the faculty members in the case studies acting? It's not clear whether their relation of authority as a faculty member working with colleagues in their units (institutional citizen) trumped or was trumped by their relation to those colleagues as full persons who, by dint of their personhood, deserved respect not as an employee but as a co-equal subject. Spheres overlap, not because we deem them to but because we are born or socialized into them; they pre-exist us. Walzer's point—like Chad Lavin's and Robert Nichols's apropos Foucault—is that institutions and communities don't exist because we will them to; they are givens, as exigencies. The communities that are typically enumerated in statements of faculty rights and responsibilities, like the associational communities in liberal and neoliberal societies, are constantly on the move, and they intersect and overlap; like Agamben's understanding of the relation between the oikos and the polis, there are thresholds between and among them, thresholds that present aporias in need of engagement and action. This is not to say that the alternative to public universities' policy and rights-and-responsibilities statements is to eliminate them. It is to say that faculty members and members of their administrations and shared governance bodies must recognize that movement—and the thresholds and aporias that reside between spheres of responsibility that have been typically understood as relatively autonomous—and make judgments about faculty conduct, both before and after those spheres have been breached. It's also to say that we should treat faculty rights-and-responsibilities policies as constitutions—not a set of regulations to be observed but wishes to be enacted. We should also see them as rife with conflicts among those wishes that are to be adjudicated not (only) through the "application" of those policies but (also) by means of a critical engagement with those policies' *exigencies*. If we were to do so, then those policies would also be understood as equally exigent and, as Virginia Anderson says of Burke, as enacting a series of *peripeteia* in the life of the institution, "tracing shifts in the way

[it] has traversed its crises and concomitantly inscribed the unfolding tale of itself" (266).

Another important idea to bear in mind in the rights-and-responsibilities model of faculty work is that those rights and responsibilities are subject both to the law and to the laws, to both ethics and politics. Individuals are never only responsible for those with whom they engage immediately (ethics); they are also responsible for other others, those who are both close by and far off, witnesses, people who see and share—in community—the experiences and events that define an individual's responsibility (politics). The ethical relation is the one that forces itself upon the individual in the act—the engagement with the colleague, the moment in the office or lab or classroom, the moment just prior to speaking on the floor of the faculty senate—and in which the subject becomes a subject through the opening of the self to the other. The civic or political relation is the one that acknowledges Walzer's liberal association, those relations bounded by laws, constitutions, and policies, which are not static but also inevitably exigent. The civic relation involves the laws; the ethical relation involves the Law, the one that commits the individual to act in the face of the person with whom they engage from moment to moment (the student, the colleague, the lab worker). So while there's a difference between ethical and civic responsibility, there's also what Diane Davis calls "inescapable tension between the two" (122). It's this "hiatus" (123) that represents *justice*, the requirement that one keep both the law and the laws, knowing that they don't line up neatly and that to obey one may well be to abrogate the other. The space that resides between the civic and the ethical represents an *urgency*, a call to respond even in the recognition that doing so means something's got to give, that in expressing a constitution's or a policy's wish, we may be abrogating the law, reaching for some just action beyond its limits.

The urgency is at least twofold. First, there's the urgency to get it right, to obey the impulse to act responsibly and to do the work you're obliged to do, as a faculty member, in service to your students, your discipline, your profession, and your civic community according to law and to local and professional policy. It's easy to assume that getting it right is a simple enough matter if we maintain residence in our own sphere of responsibility, that getting it right as a teacher means observing our responsibilities, and our rights, as instructors in the classroom and our relatively autonomous control over academic affairs. But the second urgency, the urgency to act responsibly no matter the sphere of authority or the associational community, is often in conflict with the first, the knowledge that one's civic and ethical responsibilities don't line up neatly and that acting may well break the law or the laws, or both. This is the difficulty with policy that aims to express the desires of an academic community: it assumes that individual faculty members' understanding of those wishes will comport with their expression in policy and that even in those cases where adjudication is necessary—where some faculty body must sort out the conflicting wishes of the faculty and of the policy itself—a salutary, even if not a perfect, decision is possible. But what I'm arguing here is that faculty responsibilities will always involve these two urgencies, the need to get it right and the recognition that there's really no way to hew to the law or the laws (justice) when acting responsibly.

CHAPTER 3

Academic Freedom, Democracy, and Professional Rights

In January 2021, Iowa state legislator Brad Zaun, a Republican from the town of Urbandale, introduced a bill to prohibit any institution overseen by the Iowa board of regents from establishing or continuing "a tenure system for any employee of the institution" (Charis-Carlton and Petroski). His reasons for introducing the bill were straightforward: "I think the university should have the flexibility to hire and fire professors and then I don't think that bad professors should have a lifetime position guaranteed at colleges. It's as simple as that" (qtd. in Charis-Carlton and Petroski). He went on to say that as a legislator, his "job is to look out for the best interests of our college students and certainly for the people of the state of Iowa." This isn't the first bill introduced in state legislatures to eliminate tenure in the last couple of years: the Missouri state legislature saw a bill introduced in 2017 that would have eliminated tenure at all public universities in that state, though it did not reach the governor's desk for signature (Zamudio-Suarez), and in that same year, the Wisconsin state legislature passed an omnibus budget bill, which the governor signed into law, that included a provision removing tenure at the University of Wisconsin from state statute, forcing the board of regents (which was dominated by members appointed by conservative Republican governor Scott Walker) to create a tenure policy—which some faculty argue weakens academic freedom at the university—to replace it.

One of the arguments for eliminating tenure at public universities rests on the presumption that faculty members have an anticonservative bias; according to a piece in the *Chronicle of Higher Education* about the Iowa bill, "some lawmakers have linked the protections tenure affords with freedom to indoctrinate students with anti-conservative views" (Kelderman). Part of this argument also assumes that because members of the public pay the faculty in the form of taxes, the public should determine the extent of the freedoms held by faculty members whose institutions are supported by the public; and although the public university exists, at least according to the AAUP, to support and enrich the common good, it is the demos that determines the nature of that good, not the faculty members whose expertise has been honed institutionally and methodologically but not, or so the argument goes, democratically.

In chapter 2, I focused on faculty rights and responsibilities, the public university's attempts to balance those rights and responsibilities, and the threshold between them. Here, I focus on one of the rights, academic freedom, where tenure is understood as an instrument to protect a faculty member's work as a member of a profession and of an institutional community, a community that *resides* in a public but is not public as such. In fact, as we saw in chapter 2, the institutional milieu in which faculty members reside and in which they operate with academic freedom is not a workplace; instead, as the AAUP defines it, the faculty member is an appointee rather than an employee, whose appointment grants them relative autonomy to practice their "trade" according to the criteria laid down by their professional organizations, their fields, and best practices for teaching and research as expressed in the community itself. So while members of the faculty are members of the public by dint of their status as citizens, they are also—and in contradistinction—members of a profession autonomous from the public.

But this positioning of the faculty as citizens and members of the demos, as residents and members of an institution that is relatively autonomous from the demos, and as professionals whose expertise renders them even more autonomous from the public and to a certain extent from the institution, puts them in an odd place. The disciplinary autonomy provided by academic freedom so distinguishes faculty from the demos that while it secures their membership in the community of experts, it also places them at odds with the demos, the people (the taxpayers) in whose service they are working. It's this commonplace—that academic freedom is protected by tenure and in so doing functions as a public good—that I investigate in this chapter. As we've seen in the book's previous analyses of shared governance and the faculty rights-and-responsibilities pairing, the matter of the demos has been problematic because it is unstable or, maybe more accurately, in flux. According to Walzer, it is *defined by* its mobility. The public good—and the demos's willingness to abide the understandings of it provided by those in the demos most capable of defining it, experts—is also constantly in flux. So any understanding of academic freedom that does not also recognize the radical mobility of the demos, let alone of the nature of freedom itself, will fail to convince members of the demos who see the expertise at the foundation of academic freedom to be in conflict with the notion of the common good. What is necessary, in an account of academic freedom, is a recognition of the consequences of the *mobility* of freedoms both academic and democratic; such an account would recognize that tenure is an instrument to protect not an institutional safe haven in which academic freedom can be practiced but rather a more radical kind of freedom that would, ironically, threaten the very institutions and disciplines to which faculty members are attached.

Freedom, I argue, is closely related to mobility. Timothy Barouch and Brett Ommen argue that "conditions of liberalism demand that we take on varied social roles [and the attendant genres entailed by them.] Liberal individuals . . . take these forms as they find them and invent from within them" (170). In such a mobile system, "risk is an ever-present element" in the neoliberal context, so any defense of academic work would have to acknowledge that one of its aims is to address, if not ameliorate, these risks and asymmetries. Freedom (academic or otherwise) is not a characteristic or a right but a capacity, one that involves just such vulnerabilities and risks and that is mobile. Debra Hawhee argues by way of Kenneth Burke in *Moving Bodies* that mobility can be characterized as a capacity inherent in human subjectivity that serves as an engine for the rhetorical enterprise and that, as an "irreducible" aporia between action and motion, also has an unsettling effect (see Hawhee, *Moving Bodies* 166). Alessandra Von Burg's term—stochastic citizenship—points to how mobility, understood as a force, destabilizes the distinction between the institution and the demos, between the material circumstances that cause people to move and the broader potential of that movement that might be made more visible by rhetorical means (see "Stochastic Citizenship"). Nathan Stormer makes a similar case: mobility is the potential to be otherwise, aligned with what the Greeks called *physis,* linked to the Latin *potentia*: "a strange and crucial potential for inconstancy, . . . the expression of vitality, the changes that unfinished, distinct entities are impelled and/or compelled to undergo" (2). Mobility in these terms represents a "changeableness and inconstancy," because it serves as a "condition of betweenness that isn't physically measurable" (1). It results in a kind of epistemological homelessness that nonetheless serves as a way to mobilize the precarious location between the public space of the law and the lonelier space outside it without having to reach for the commonplace of democracy in order to do so.

So if faculty members are stochastic citizens, the capacity for movement—mobility—also comes with some risks. It's not only institutional and civic boundaries and intellectual and disciplinary conventions that determine where and when one can speak or that are constantly in flux. It's the very grounds on which conventions and boundaries are defined and understood that are constantly in question. Mobility, the capacity to be other, has as much potential to hinder rhetorical understanding as it does to make new understandings possible, because it puts those conventions and the institutions themselves up for grabs. The movement of people across national borders and the dispossession of noncitizens or of individuals who experience homelessness, to provide just a couple of common examples, are instances of mobility that hint at the vulnerability and potential violence that can be produced by mobility's material and discursive force. In higher education, this movement is often linked to what James Rushing Daniel has called the "precariat," a category of academic worker whose professional identity is insecure because their labor has been devalued and they have been forced to move from job to job and institution to institution without a sense of belonging, let alone a place where they hold tenure. Mobility can put useful question to some of those institutional verities like academic freedom, but it also opens the door to situational and institutional vulnerabilities that are just a part of stochastic citizenship. These vulnerabilities and potential violence trouble the commonplace of democracy and the public good which, as we will see, can sometimes stand as a bulwark *against* (academic) freedom.

To make this case, I outline the conceptual links between tenure and academic freedom as they have evolved in public higher education in the US since their inception in the early part of the last century, and I trace that evolution's dependence on a notion of the public good and of the democratic uses of public higher education, notions that have peculiar consequences for the freedom of faculty. In particular, I'm interested in how the contemporary understanding of academic freedom can be said to provide the mobility of thought, the critical capacity, and the movement between and among publics and between publics and institutions that seems to be required in a neoliberal context. The heart of my analysis is another set of case studies, in this instance an examination of the language of public universities' statements on academic freedom and tenure set against the efforts of some public universities to weaken those protections. In this context I also examine one of the more controversial cases of the abrogation of academic freedom—the unhiring of Steven Salaita at the University of Illinois in 2013–14—to see how the commonplaces of democracy and public goods can run roughshod over arguments about academic freedom. I conclude by suggesting what academic freedom might look like if faculty are willing to see beyond the idea of relative autonomy protected by tenure to a concept of freedom that does not so confine them to institutional or disciplinary criteria but rather allows them also to reside in the interstices of these communities.

TENURE, ACADEMIC FREEDOM, AND MOBILITY

There was no concept of academic freedom as such in the early American university. As I noted earlier, and as Laurence Veysey puts it in his study of the emergence of the American university, "the idea of academic freedom was brought to the United States [in the late nineteenth century] by professors who had studied in German universities. In Germany the concept contained two major aspects: *Lernfreiheit*, or freedom of the student to choose his own studies in an elective system, and *Lehrfreiheit*, the freedom of the professor to investigate and teach the results of his researches without governmental interference" (384). *Lernfreiheit* became transformed, in the years between the Morrill Act and the Second World War, into a question of who *owns* the curriculum, the administration or the faculty; *Lehrfreiheit*'s focus moved away from the subject of governmental control over a faculty member's research and closer to the control exerted by administrators, and—through the board—the public, on those matters that faculty turned their attention to for their research and their public engagement. By the beginning of the twentieth century, the faculty began to understand their work, and the associated freedoms, as a means of serving the public.

As Robert Post and others explain (see also Reichman, Whittington), academic freedom became clarified by the AAUP in its statement of 1915 on academic freedom and tenure. It was that statement that formally tied the concepts of *Lehrfreiheit* and *Lernfreiheit* to what the AAUP called a "public trust." "Rights of academic freedom," Post writes, are "designed to facilitate the professional self-regulation of the professoriate, . . . to ensure that the faculty within the university are free to engage in the professionally competent forms of inquiry and teaching that are necessary for the realization of the social purposes of the university" ("Structure" 64). The landmark 1940 "Statement of Principles on Academic Freedom and Tenure" by the AAUP makes clear that tenure is the instrument by which such freedom is secured and that tenure offers protection to faculty from being disciplined or fired because of positions they have taken (either consistently with or apart from their expertise) on matters of public interest, matters that faculty members have not only an expertise in—by dint of their training—but also a moral obligation to speak about. The AAUP Committee A "Statement on Extramural Utterances" makes clear that "a faculty member's expression of opinion as a citizen cannot constitute grounds for dismissal unless it clearly demonstrates the faculty member's unfitness to serve." In fact, the overriding principle in these statements is that academic freedom must be protected by the institution of tenure and other attendant policies precisely because it has a singular and supremely important role in ensuring that the public is organized, deliberative, educated, and engaged.

The adoption, in public higher education, of the concepts of academic freedom and tenure coincided with the Progressive politics that emerged in the first few decades of the twentieth century. The Progressive movement's trust in democratic principles of an engaged and educated citizenry contributes much to American higher education's commonplaces that link tenure, academic freedom, and democratic values. But Hans-Joerg Tiede notes that the rhetoric of democratization is a double-edged sword. "The rhetoric of democratization had previously been employed to advance popular control of state universities, which at times restricted academic freedom" (28). This is particularly true when speaking, as Tiede does, of "political influence on state universities." So while tenure may protect the academic freedom to pursue one's research in an area of expertise that contributes to the public good, the public itself may see tenure as protecting faculty whose opinions on matters they hold dear vary widely from their own and as an unwarranted form of job security that neither they themselves nor their family members hold.

This is the tension that Henry Reichman describes in his book on academic freedom. The faculty, according to AAUP founding documents and statements, have a special obligation in their roles as stewards of expert knowledge. They have secured the right to practice their expertise and to have authority in those areas of university work that are directly related to that expertise. Academic freedom and tenure protect those special responsibilities. But faculty also, according to the AAUP, have rights as citizens, and inasmuch as a university is not a democracy—it has delimited spheres of authority, each having designated leaders—it resides (in the US, anyway) inside of one, and faculty members are members of the demos. While the public good is enhanced by the special responsibilities of members of public university faculties, the rights and responsibilities of faculty members, as delineated by principles of academic freedom and the protections of tenure, can reasonably conflict with those of citizens. As I've noted, some scholars have tried to resolve this tension. Robert Post, who was AAUP's general counsel and serves on its Committee A, insists on academic freedom's protections as local, but he wants to ensure that the freedom of faculty to engage on public issues—and to be protected by the institution of tenure in doing so—is also protected. To do so, he distinguishes between democratic legitimation and democratic competence. For Post, democratic legitimation "requires that the speech of all persons be treated with toleration and respect; democratic competence requires that speech is subject to disciplinary authority that distinguishes good ideas from bad ones" (*Democracy* 34). To resolve the impasse, he argues that while academic freedom protects speech "only when it complies with 'professional norms,'" and while these norms and standards "cannot be determined by reference to public opinion" (67), "First Amendment coverage is extended to faculty speech regardless of whether it involves matters of public concern" (85) and "whenever the publication of research in the classroom is inhibited for reasons that do not depend upon ensuring disciplinary competence as determined by disciplinary experts" (90). The novelty of Post's argument is that while academic freedom does not extend beyond the institution—to actions taken by faculty outside the bounds of professional expertise and ethical principles—faculty are nonetheless covered by First Amendment protections because of the democratic *purposes* of those actions.

Post's argument founders, however, on democratic commonplaces because it sets up two relatively autonomous spheres, one that is informed by expertise and one that isn't. In his book on the value of free speech in the university, Keith Whittington devotes a chapter to exploring the evolution of the concept of freedom of speech, and he later links that tradition to the value of academic freedom. He argues that in order to prevail against the tyranny of the majority, the development of an expert class was important to "discipline free speech" by tempering the free-wheeling debate in the demos with the careful accumulation of knowledge. The creation of separate spheres sets up "a tension between the value of democratic egalitarianism in which everyone should get a fair hearing, and the value of meritocratic expertise, in which those who are thought to have something to add to the scholarly conversation should take priority" (Whittington 49). Academic freedom is meant to protect the latter; the First Amendment is meant to protect the former.[1]

---

1. It's worth considering how donors fit into considerations of the public and its tyranny. I would argue that the problem of donor pressure on the academic direction of universities is not a distinct issue but a subset of the tyranny of the majority. The only difference between donor influence and the larger issue of majoritarianism is that—at least in terms of the *Citizens United* case decided by the Supreme Court in 2010—donor wishes are accompanied by dollars, which have a distinct and additive power but differ little from speech in the public sphere. In short, the voice of donors and their attempts to pressure universities to adhere to their wishes are no different from the voices of other members of the public; they're just maybe a little louder. And as I note later in this chapter, it's not altogether clear whether the amplification of those voices makes much of a difference in how the university makes decisions about, say, the hiring and firing of one of its faculty members.

In practice, the relative autonomy of these spheres breaks down in the face of the tyranny of the majority, trumping any defense of academic freedom as marshaled by faculty members. As I argue, this is because no argument for academic freedom based in the commonplaces of democracy allows for the possibility that democracy itself relies on static principles of belonging, or spheres of interest and authority, and of *work* (Aristotle's notion of the ergon) and as a result fixes the membership of the academic republic, distinguishing it from membership in the democratic republic and preventing the possibility of movement between and among those publics that is more consistent with the neoliberal context in which public universities—and publics more generally—reside. It doesn't, in other words, allow for the mobility inherent in a (post)liberal public sphere, in which an autonomy dependent on fixed identities runs into and founders upon the constant change inherent in the contemporary university.

Toward the end of this chapter, I suggest an alternative notion of (academic) freedom that, while recognizing the unavoidable democratic commonplaces on which higher education is founded, is also consistent with principles of mobility. To begin with, one would need to consider, along the lines of Burke and Von Burg, (academic) freedom as a kind of power, a capacity working against fixity that involves a notion of vulnerability. As I noted in earlier chapters, Giorgio Agamben describes a notion of human activity—it would be too much to call it democratic, let alone civic—that provides ethical direction in a world characterized by flux and potential. Freedom resides in the tension between what Vico would call *civis* and *hostis,* in the aporia between motion and action, pure exteriority on the one hand and the interiority of affect and logos on the other. Agamben calls the force of human activity *stasis,* "a threshold of articulation" between the two terms and between the related terms oikos and polis, the purely private realm of the home and family and the social realm associated with publicity and engagement with other citizens. This isn't the same thing as passivity or the cessation of activity; rather, *stasis* makes work inoperative, pure potential, and makes possible activity that is otherwise unimaginable. To put it in terms of academic freedom, the faculty member is neither entirely autonomous—as an expert—from the demos nor entirely encumbered by it; the work of the faculty member, insofar as it is (academically) free, resides between the demos and the institution and as such has no proper sphere of work at all, liberated from the economy of the democratic commonplaces that adhere to notions of faculty governance and academic freedom and serving as a capacity rather than as a characteristic. One who is destituent is all mobility, all potential, and rather than finding a kind of unison between motion and action, she finds herself "think[ing] anarchy" and in doing so finding herself "in aporia and contradictions without end" ("Elements" 14). This mobility—this kind of freedom—is intense, troubling, and potentially violent, and any agency that derives from it, whether in the public or the private sphere, whether institutionally or democratically, calls the individual speaking subject into question, making the subject vulnerable. The crucial questions are whether and how the potential (and potential violence) of such power—mobility—deployed by us as academics leaves us vulnerable to the very depredations of higher education that we're scrambling to protect against and how vulnerability, at the threshold of oikos and polis, provides a way to engage more actively than we have so far to remake higher education.

We'll see some of the perils of understanding academic freedom in these terms in the chapter's next section. Robert Post writes that even healthy disciplines and universities are sites of conflict over notions of faculty work—their proper ergon—and where those freedoms reside (in the institutional family, the oikos, or the broader demos, the polis). This is especially true in cases where there's institutional or state intervention in inter- or intradisciplinary controversies, and in such cases "it may be difficult for a court to determine whether the value of democratic competence is truly at stake." This is because, Post goes on, the "more divided the community of disciplinary expertise, the greater the leeway for political control. . . . Knowledge-creating professions and disciplines have their own dynamics of power" (*Democracy* 97) and, I would add, mobility and capacity. Saying much the same thing as Post, but couching their argument as a disagreement with his understanding of academic freedom, Judith Butler writes that we should understand the profession—whatever that is—not as a static entity that, as an institutional family (an oikos), is at odds with the broader demos (a polis). We should see it instead as "a community that is fundamentally a venue for debate and disputation in which norms are scrutinized, revised, invoked, in evaluative judgments, reconsidered, and subjected to innovation" (Butler, "Academic Norms" 112–13). The nature of academic work, and the freedoms through which that work is done, is constantly in flux, has the capacity for change, and is defined by its inability to remain embedded inside of one polity or another. It's better to see professional norms as emerging "from a realistic understanding that there is significant disagreement about which norms ought to be invoked [to protect academic freedom] . . . and that new disciplinary innovations have made these questions the norm, rather than the exception, in such deliberations" (116). The work of faculty, in the context of academic freedom, is an ethical problem not of "how to best apply a pre-given norm (fabricating its stability in the moment of its use) but how to be open to a clash of norms while making the best possible judgment in the fray" (122). As I describe in the conclusion of this chapter, such a view of academic freedom—constantly vexed, never residing in one place (oikos) or another (polis), and continuously threatening the stability that tenure is supposed to provide—involves the risky business of recognizing the field of possibilities in following out any train of thought and of saying things that, even with the protections of tenure, could get us fired because there is no necessary outcome but only "a field of possibilities."

CASE STUDIES: THE PRECARIOUSNESS OF ACADEMIC FREEDOM AND TENURE

The principle of academic freedom as outlined by Robert Post, Keith Whittington, Henry Reichman, and the AAUP is only as useful as it is elaborated in statements and policies at the public universities where it becomes operational (that is, in their constitutions). As public research universities reached maturity in the US in the middle of the twentieth century, they adopted statements on academic freedom that in most cases mirrored, and in some cases diverged from, those devised by the AAUP in their 1915 and 1940 documents on the topic but in all instances provide openings for antidemocratic leverage and consequent erosion (if not undermining altogether) of the principles themselves. And it's just these non- or antidemocratic strands running through the principle of academic freedom and the protections of tenure that have led not only to drives to weaken tenure protections (through the creation of post-tenure review policies) but also—and regardless of the tenure protections provided by universities—to the dismissal of faculty *on the grounds of* academic freedom, or of violations thereof. To that end, I also discuss in more detail the moves at the Universities of Tennessee and Wisconsin to create new post-tenure review policies and the extent to which those policies were meant to undermine tenure *in the name of* academic freedom, highlighting the specific case of a faculty member—Steven Salaita—who was essentially drummed out of the academy because of statements he made as a citizen that were seen as evidence of his unfitness as a scholar.

In my examination of statements on academic freedom at a number of public research universities, what becomes clear is that, despite their differences, they explicitly link academic freedom to the establishment of democratic competence (see University of Wisconsin System, "Commitment"; "Faculty Legislation"; "Faculty Policies and Procedures," ch. 8.01; "Tenure"; University of Michigan Senate Assembly, "Senate Assembly Statement"; University of North Carolina Board of Trustees, "UNC Policy Manual"). Faculty members are to have the freedom to pursue their scholarship according to the principles, ethics, and methodologies established by their profession, and thus those programs of research and teaching are meant to provide the knowledge, both new and established, necessary for the public to deliberate on matters of the day, knowledge that is more robust than public opinion. So while the purposes of academic freedom are democratic, the determination of the faculty member's legitimate pursuit and observance of the principles of that freedom are made not by the institution writ large or by members of the public but by the profession and its well-earned expertise. They all establish tenure as an instrument to secure the protections of academic freedom, though the explicit breadth of those protections differs from institution to institution. In all instances, tenure protects faculty (in the terms used in the UW-Madison statement on tenure) to "pursue a bold research and teaching agenda." Tenure secures broad public rights of expression, or more narrow rights of academic expression and activity, or both, but because of the ways in which the democratic underwriting of these statements is expressed, it's not always clear just which is protected: one's right to speak as a citizen or one's right to speak as a faculty member. And because tenure's protections of academic freedom are secured at the divisional level—which is to say, by colleagues who share expertise in similar departments or in a similar or the same discipline—rather than at the level of the polis, the ability of faculty members to promote democratic competence is (perhaps ironically) secured in disciplinary or departmental enclaves rather than by broadly democratic means. Furthermore, the constitutions, as we saw earlier, that govern institutional communities are themselves fraught with tension and inconsistencies. In other words, tenure may well hold fast the distinctions between and among institutional, disciplinary, and "customary" communities and maintain distinctions between those institutional and broader democratic realms, while preventing mobility between and among those communities. If academic freedom, and the democratic competence it fosters, is maintained by tenure, a protection that is itself established by locally governed disciplines and expertise, and if the statements by universities cannot clearly define the relation between democratic and institutional or expert engagement, then it's no surprise that when academic freedom is threatened, some of these institutions are hard-pressed to defend it on democratic, let alone expert, principles.

Post-Tenure Review

The tensions between the democratic principles bolstering academic freedom and those that undermine it are visible in two states' impositions of post-tenure review of their faculty members. Such policies are sold to the public as a kind of "quality control" measure given to university deans and other administrators, justified using tropes of democracy and expertise: post-tenure review is simply a means by which faculty are periodically assessed on the currency of their expertise, which is required to inculcate the critical consciousness necessary for full participation in democratic self-governance. The University of Tennessee post-tenure review changes were made in the context of its board of trustees' initiation of a review of its tenure criteria and the process it had been using for several decades, apparently with some success. The board created a joint committee of faculty members and administrators in 2017 to examine the process and made recommendations, in early 2018, for strengthening the processes for tenure and for post-tenure review. In addition to regular annual reviews of faculty performance, Tennessee's board—and its ad hoc committee—recommended some years earlier that it create what it called an enhanced post-tenure performance review (EPPR), which would give extraordinary discretion to campus administrators to "target individual faculty members or programs" (Lyons, "Message"). But what gets lost in the arguments over board control of faculty work, or about shared governance overreach (the focus of much of the press coverage of the Tennessee PTR debate), is that it was not clear from the very beginning why such a change was necessary. Were faculty members slacking off? Were they teaching courses and conducting research that were not providing the democratic competence that academic freedom and its protections through tenure were supposed to afford? University of Tennessee president DiPietro's letter to the university community, sent after Colleen Flaherty's article in *Inside Higher Education* about the controversy had hit print, describes things this way:

> Periodic post-tenure review of all tenured faculty is not uncommon in higher education, and I am convinced that requiring it will enhance academic excellence, accountability and transparency at the University of Tennessee. Additional rationale for doing so is that it will recognize faculty accomplishments and achievements, rejuvenate underperforming faculty, identify inadequate annual faculty evaluation procedures and support removal of faculty who are performing unsatisfactorily. (DiPietro, "Truth")

DiPietro's justification for the introduction of the EPPR, and for the review of tenure policies more broadly, is a version of the democratic competence argument: university faculty are tasked with creating knowledge characterized by excellence and accountability to university stakeholders, in this case the citizens of the state of Tennessee as vouchsafed by the members of the university's board of regents.

A faculty senate report on the proposed changes pinpoints "accountability," a key component of democratic competence, as one of the signal weaknesses of the Board's PTR policy: in order to be accountable to the public as faithful and rigorous stewards of the university's public mission, the faculty must be accountable to tenure and rank criteria that "are discipline specific" and that take account of teaching, research, and service judged as competent by "a committee of faculty peers." The only way to ensure that faculty, even those with tenure, are capable of discharging their public duty to ensure that their students are well-informed and critically engaged citizens is to bring them before a jury of their peers—experts—in order to assess their work. But that isn't how the University of Tennessee regents define democratic competence. In the Tennessee regent policies on academic freedom and tenure, there is a force that lingers at its edges, one occluded by the language of professional rights and responsibilities and of academic freedom and its protection by means of tenure. While the board "recognizes and affirms the importance of tenure in protecting academic freedom and thus promotion the University's principal mission of discovery and dissemination of truth through teaching, research, and service," it also recognizes "its fiduciary responsibility to students, parents, and all citizens of Tennessee" (University of Tennessee Board of Trustees, Committee on Academic Affairs and Student Success, 11). The university's faculty, under the new PTR policy, can be dismissed not because they have failed to be accountable to their peers, their discipline, or their institution's mission but because they've failed to be responsible to citizens: not those citizens who've had the benefit of an education, presumably a good one, in those areas of the curriculum deemed necessary by the faculty to inculcate those characteristics necessary for democratic self-governance, but any citizen, all citizens, regardless of the level of their democratic competence. The public interest here is not one that is tempered by the competence provided by the work of faculty in their fields of expertise but one closer to the idea of public opinion, which in the words of Robert Post is constantly in motion but which also "does not possess the internal consistency of integrity that is characteristic of agents who must decide and act" (*Democracy* 20–21). The University of Tennessee's post-tenure review process is contextualized first and foremost as a means by which to temper the freedoms of the faculty to inculcate the competencies necessary for public deliberation through the exertion of public opinion, opinion not necessarily informed by expert judgment but wielded by the board by means of its fiduciary duty to the broader polis (if not the demos). Here the language of democracy is used as a cudgel to suppress the very means by which that democracy is supposed to be fostered.

At Wisconsin, which underwent its own PTR battle with its board around the same time as Tennessee, the rationale for the creation of the policies was based on public opinion in a much more explicit manner. At the board of regents' initial meeting with the Madison campus's task force charged with creating its own iteration of the regent policy, regent member John Behling and board president Regina Millner made clear why such a policy was needed.

> "If we don't add post-tenure review to the policy, I fear we will get forced into a policy that is unlivable," said Behling, chairman of the Tenure Task Force.... It's not just state Legislators who think faculty don't work much, Regina Millner, president of the Board of Regents, told fellow task force members. "It's in the zeitgeist of the general public." (Schneider, "Regent John Behling")

Faculty members' academic freedom comes at a cost—tenure is "an enormous investment of university and societal resources"—and taxpayers, through their representatives in the legislature, want to be sure this cost is worthwhile. Post-tenure review policies curb the academic freedom of faculty members in the name of public opinion, an opinion that holds that faculty "don't work much," particularly when the faculty themselves determine the nature and value of the expertise required to ensure that their work is done in service to the promulgation of democratic competence.

While assessment of faculty is done, at least theoretically, by other (expert) faculty, the accountability cited by the governing boards confers the authority for accountability, ultimately, to members of the *public* by means of opinion—Millner's zeitgeist—and public sentiment about the nature, value, and credibility of faculty work. There are two god terms, in Richard Weaver's sense, at play in these policies, and each is at considerable odds with the other: disciplinary expertise and competence on the one hand and the primacy of public opinion on the other. In Post's argument, and Butler's extension of that argument, *both* intellectual and disciplinary work *and* public opinion, in order to establish democratic competence, are understood to be mobile, constantly in flux, and capable of dislocating or unmooring the paradigms that make for stability; what is necessary for freedom, as a capacity for thinking, is the capacity for each of these locales to dissolve one into the other, destabilizing both. But in the argument of the governing boards, which required a system of post-tenure review to serve as a check on the freedoms of faculty members to do their intellectual work, the latter—public opinion, not necessarily informed by the expert judgment necessary to "communicating knowledge that is professionally regarded as *true*" (Post, *Democracy* 53, emphasis added)—trumps the former. If there are two god terms operating in the justification for criteria for faculty work within the bounds of academic freedom, one—public opinion—is more powerful than the other.

Academic Freedom and the Oppressiveness of the Demos

If ever there was a case that demonstrates the oppressiveness of the demos over academic freedom, and the weaknesses of the argument for academic freedom based on the commonplaces of the democratic competence and the public good, it's that of Steven Salaita, a faculty member at Virginia Tech who was offered and who accepted a position on the faculty at the University of Illinois in 2014. In some ways, Steven Salaita could be considered a unique case: what he did to invoke the ire of the governing board at the University of Illinois took place in a particular context (recent violence in Israel's occupied territories), and he was not technically a faculty member at either Virginia Tech or the University of Illinois (he had resigned his position at the former institution to take a position offered by the latter, only to have the offer be withdrawn before he could begin teaching). But these circumstances suggest the paradigmatic nature of the Salaita matter: his freedom, as an academic and an expert, was challenged by both the institution and members of the public, and his status as a faculty member was ended *in the name of the public*. And yet it was Salaita's role as an academic—one in which he exercised a freedom that, in the terms I've used earlier, challenged the boundaries between the disciplinary and the democratic or public *in the name of potential*, the capacity to collapse borders and create novel and potentially disorienting ethical and intellectual positions—that was seen as a threat by those who didn't want to see him hired. His case shines a light on the thinness of arguments for higher education and academic freedom based on public and democratic commonplaces, and it suggests that Salaita's actions, and those of the University of Illinois, are at loggerheads: dynamism and stasis versus community standards, public ideals, and majority rule.

In the 2012–13 academic year, the Department of American Indian Studies at the University of Illinois at Urbana-Champaign ran a search for a senior faculty member in their department, and Salaita, then a tenured faculty member at Virginia Tech, applied for, and in the fall of 2013 accepted, the position. Salaita, who identifies as being of Palestinian origin, was known for a book comparing the colonialism in the American political approach to, and violence against, Indigenous peoples with that of Israelis in their approach to the occupation of Palestine. Between October 2013 and the middle of the summer of 2014, Salaita was negotiating his course offerings, his computer needs, and his orientation to the department where he would hold tenure, and he had resigned his position at Virginia Tech on the well-placed assumption that he would begin his teaching and his other scholarly work at the University of Illinois at the beginning of the fall semester. During the summer of 2014, Salaita's attention, like that of many people, was drawn to Israel's two-month incursion into Gaza and its violent attacks on Hamas forces there, an incursion sparked by the kidnapping and murder of three Israelis that June. Salaita's horror at the violence of the incursion, and at the continuing Israeli violence against Palestinians in Gaza and the occupied territories (including Israel's expanding and illegal settlements), led him to issue a number of posts on social media, posts that were defiant, in some cases profane, and that compared the Israeli prime minister and Zionists to savages and racists.

As Salaita was preparing to move to the University of Illinois and issuing posts on social media, the chancellor at the University of Illinois's flagship campus in Urbana-Champaign, Phyllis Wise, began to receive email messages protesting Salaita's appointment, which she began forwarding to the office of the U of I board of trustees. On July 21, the associate chancellor for public affairs issued a statement to the local newspaper, saying, "Faculty have a wide range of scholarly and political views, and we recognize the freedom of speech rights of all of our employees" (CAFT 33). But apparently this statement touched a nerve somewhere, and the assistant to the chancellor asked the office of the dean of the College of Liberal Arts and Sciences whether Salaita had officially accepted an offer of employment in the Department of American Indian Studies; the chancellor's assistant was told that he had. At some point around this time—exactly when isn't clear—there was a question of whether Salaita's appointment had been approved at all levels, and it became clear that because the beginning of his appointment was delayed from January 2014 to August 2014, so was the University of Illinois board of trustees' vote on his hiring, the final step in formalizing his appointment. On July 24 the board of trustees met in executive session to discuss Salaita's appointment; one week later, he was issued a letter—signed by the U of I System vice president for academic affairs and the campus's chancellor—stating that while he had been offered a position by the dean (a position he had accepted), the recommendation to hire was subject to board approval. The letter read, "[Your] appointment will not be recommended for submission to the Board of Trustees in September, and we believe that an affirmative Board vote approving your appointment is unlikely. We therefore will not be in a position to appoint you to the faculty" (CAFT 61, Document 7). After the decision by the board not to make the offer of employment, the news spread quickly across the university community, resulting in calls for Chancellor Wise to reverse her decision and for the board to do the same, calls for the chancellor's resignation, and a fair and perhaps equal number of faculty and community members defending the chancellor and the board for their decision not to bring Salaita's position to a vote.

From nearly the moment that Salaita's posts came to light, internal discussions at the University of Illinois office of the chancellor suggested that there was a battle underway between the principles of academic freedom and free speech and the rights and responsibilities of faculty members. In late July, about three days after the social media posts and the beginning of the email deluge protesting the hire, the chancellor sought the counsel of her provost and her associate chancellor for public affairs about how to react to the controversy. The provost sent Wise a note on July 24, in which he writes, "Decency, collegiality and mutual respect are at the core of our institution. We have to continue to appeal to these values and make sure that our University maintains its integrity and societal impact over the long term" (University of Illinois, Emails 2). At this point, apparently one option on the table was to accept that Salaita would become a faculty member and to meet with him early in the fall to essentially reprimand him by reminding him of the university's "core values." In an email exchange on the same day between Chancellor Wise and Professor Nick Burbules, a faculty member in the U of I's College of Education, Burbules writes that the Salaita case is "NOT [an] academic freedom (or free speech) issue[ ]. I will defend those principles to the hilt. But having the right (and privilege) of these protections also comes with certain responsibilities as a professor and as a representative of the institution (and not just an individual saying whatever he or she likes)" (University of Illinois, Emails 24). And Chancellor Wise was thinking the same way: in a message to a colleague, she writes, "The real question for me is when does freedom of speech cross the line into hateful, harassing, unprofessional speech and action." On the same day, she wrote to both Burbules and her colleague, "The hateful, totally unprofessional and unacceptable Twitters have appeared mainly since July. . . . It reveals a side of the person that I believe makes it difficult for him to contribute to the culture of respect, collegiality, collaboration that we hold so dear" (University of Illinois, Emails 5, 7). By August a consensus was beginning to form that what Salaita had engaged in was neither free speech protected by the First Amendment nor the academic freedom "to present scholarly opinions and conclusions both in and outside the classroom" but some other form of utterance that isn't protected.

On August 22, just about a month after Salaita's tweets, Chancellor Wise posted an essay entitled "The Principles on Which We Stand" on her official blog, which was intended to outline the rationale for refusing to bring Salaita's case to the board and, hence, to hire him. The essay included this:

> What we cannot and will not tolerate at the University of Illinois are personal and disrespectful words or actions that demean and abuse either viewpoints themselves or those who express them. We have a particular duty to our students to ensure that they live in a community of scholarship that challenges their assumptions about the world but that also respects their rights as individuals. As chancellor, it is my responsibility to ensure that all perspectives are welcome and that our discourse, regardless of subject matter or viewpoint, allows new concepts and differing points of view to be discussed in and outside the classroom in a scholarly, civil, and productive manner. (Wise)

Just over a week later, in part because of campus outrage over her "Principles" blog, the chancellor finally brought the matter of the Salaita hire to the board of trustees; in its meeting, the trustees voted not to offer him employment. Presumably the board agreed with the chancellor's argument and in so doing voted against the hire: the board president issued a statement arguing that "disrespectful and demeaning speech that promotes malice is not an acceptable form of civil argument if we wish to ensure that students, faculty and staff are comfortable in a place of scholarship and education. . . . There can be no place for [such speech] in our democracy, and therefore, there will be no place for it in our university" (CAFT 8). Oddly, in the Committee on Academic Freedom and Tenure's interview with Chancellor Wise in the aftermath of the Salaita affair, she was asked to distinguish between professional and extramural speech—effectively, between academic freedom as expressed in the University of Illinois statutes and freedom of speech as protected by the First Amendment—"the Chancellor stated that in this matter she saw no clear distinction. . . . 'The manner in which you speak reflects on how welcoming you would be as a faculty member,'" and she "expressed her conviction that in a small community such as Champaign-Urbana, there was little distinction between 'faculty members, community members, and bloggers'" (CAFT 9–10).

What's beginning to occur here is a shift from a set of core values of the university that are directly related to the academic freedom afforded by faculty members to one that involves a kind of democratically justified understanding of those values, values that place the idea of civility and welcome above the open and free exchange of ideas in the service of democratic competence. It's telling that in her interview with the CAFT, the chancellor is at pains to distinguish between academic freedom and freedom of speech, not because it's an easy matter to distinguish—it's not—but because of the statement that follows her inability to do so. It's not possible to distinguish between academic freedom and freedom of speech, because in a community like the one where the University of Illinois is located, there's no easy way to distinguish between who's a faculty member and who's a citizen (or a blogger), and so—at least according to Wise's "The Principles on Which We Stand" blog—community values trump academic ones. If the community believes that what Salaita has to say in his public pronouncements about Israel's activities in the occupied territories, and Israeli colonial politics more broadly, is uncivil and demeaning and thereby is made uncomfortable (something the hundreds of emails coming into the chancellor's office from community members, university alumni, students, parents, and others clearly showed), then Salaita has effectively ceded his academic freedom in the face of this democratic outcry.[2]

In an email to Wise, a colleague sent scanned copies of a portion of Matthew Finkin and Robert Post's book *For the Common Good* that focused on freedom of extramural expression and professional responsibility of faculty. One passage from the book that was underlined and is particularly relevant here is the following: "Extramural speech cannot be disciplined unless it bears on professional competence, and judgments of professional competence, for reasons we have discussed, are primarily reserved for faculty determination" (Finkin and Post 148; cited in University of Illinois, Emails 50). This is in reference to a portion of the AAUP's Committee A statement on extramural utterances, a comment on its original 1940 statement: "The controlling principle is that a faculty member's expression of opinion as a citizen cannot constitute grounds for dismissal unless it clearly demonstrates the faculty member's unfitness for his or her position. Extramural utterances rarely bear upon the faculty member's fitness for the position" (AAUP Committee A, cited in CAFT 25). The Committee A statement also makes clear that judgments about whether extramural statements demonstrate unfitness should be conducted by a *faculty committee,* consistent with the idea that academic freedom is to be

---

2. The CAFT report examined whether donors to the university represented a significant number of these messages of concern and whether the action taken by Wise and the board of trustees resulted in their fear that unless such action was taken, they would withdraw donations to the university. CAFT found that while some messages did refer to donations—future or current—to the university, they were not at all sufficient to suggest that donors exerted inordinate pressure (or any pressure at all, really, different from that of the overwhelming number of expressions of concern from nondonors, alumni, and citizens of the state of Illinois) on Wise or the board.

maintained, because it involves matters of expertise and disciplinary convention, by members of those disciplinary and expert communities, not by the community at large, let alone by chancellors or governing boards. But this isn't what happened; instead, the Committee A standard—one clearly intended to protect academic freedom of the faculty, a protection against institutional punishment for utterances issued by faculty as citizens—was used as justification to punish Salaita for his speech on the grounds that as an expert, his speech undermined his ability to maintain a "safe" and "civil" environment for his students.

The CAFT report in the aftermath of the affair puts its finger precisely on the problem here: both the University of Illinois statutes and the 1940 AAUP statements on academic freedom "draw a distinction between speech in one's professional capacity and speech as a citizen on matters of political, economic, or ethical concern to the larger community. In other words, [the statements] are more categorical than the Chancellor was willing to recognize" (CAFT 23), particularly her insistence that you can't distinguish between academic freedom and freedom of speech. The report goes on to say that "there are circumstances where political speech can legitimately trigger inquiry into professional fitness, [but] the question, however, [is] one of professional fitness, *not* political acceptability" (23). In a piece on the AAUP's "Academe" blog, John K. Wilson goes further to suggest that the CAFT is simply wrong about political speech's ability to trigger an inquiry: even speech that, as the CAFT describes Salaita's social media posts, is "devoid of facts," "obdurate" in refusing contrary points of view, or "single-minded in pursuit of the speaker's personal agenda" is protected by the principles of academic freedom (Wilson, "What's Wrong").

The report understates an important point: it notes that "the line between the political and the professional can blur," that academic freedom and freedom of speech are *not* easily distinguishable. But there's an important point that Wise, in her interview with the CAFT, gets exactly right, though Wilson sees this as a weakness in Wise's assessment: academic freedom and freedom of speech aren't clearly distinguishable, at least in instances like Salaita's. Of course extramural utterances are different from faculty members' discussions of their academic subjects, though both are protected. The problem is that when a faculty member says things that will get members of the public exceptionally angry and when that anger causes a crisis at the institution where the faculty member is employed, the power of public opinion swamps the distinction. (The matter of employment status here, much discussed by the university's administrators and, later, the CAFT, is not at issue: Salaita was *acting as a faculty member*, with the expectation that he was or would soon be employed by the University of Illinois.)

This is the crux of the Salaita affair: the posts on social media that so angered those whose emails flooded Chancellor Wise's and board of trustee members' inboxes in the summer of 2014 resided precisely in the threshold between academic freedom and free speech. They sat squarely between the institutionally protected spaces where expertise and disciplinary authority and custom are understood to operate autonomously (the oikos) and the broader community whose members are charged with self-governance as a democracy (the polis). Salaita was unleashing the kind of destituent power—the capacity, described by Foucault and Nichols as *freedom*—that, because it resides in the threshold between the professional and the public, has the capacity to undo and unmoor both. In so doing, he was exhibiting "inconstancy," in Nathan Stormer's terms, the stochastic movement that is necessary in a (neo)liberal public context where everything, including the disciplinary and methodological customs inside of which faculty members do their work and determine the criteria of performance necessary for, say, a successful post-tenure review, is put into question. Of course, as reported by the CAFT, "it was not the political content of Dr. Salaita's tweets, but their emotive content that caused [the chancellor's] concern" (CAFT 26). It's precisely the power of Salaita's utterances on social media—and almost certainly his academic work and his classroom teaching—that made it nearly impossible for members of the community, academic or public, to determine whether what he was saying should be granted First Amendment protection or the protections of academic freedom under the U of I's or the AAUP's statements on the subject. And it was that power that made it necessary for the university, and the public, to find a justification—any justification—to distance themselves from the oscillation, the *inconstancy*, of it all. That the ultimate justification for doing so and for barring Salaita's employment at the university was made on democratic grounds—that the power of what he had to say was so intolerable to the public that the public was obliged to remove him from a position where he was able to exert that power—shows the deep danger of using the language of democracy to justify academic freedom for members of university faculties. While Salaita himself may not have been able to maintain his position as a member of the U of I faculty and in the profession—most recently (as of fall 2019), he's employed driving a bus in suburban Washington, DC (Pettit)—he so destabilized, if even momentarily, the assumptions about academic work at the University of Illinois at Urbana-Champaign that its chancellor resigned, its board turned over, and both its faculty and the AAUP had to reconsider just how democratic its principles of academic freedom and of faculty rights and responsibilities are.

CONCLUSION

If our current understanding of academic freedom in democratic terms is inadequate in the current context, characterized by constant movement, social instability, the jettisoning by the public of orthodoxies such as the formation of consensus (let alone the existence of facts or truths), what are we to do? Is there a way to safeguard faculty work that will allow it to proceed untrammeled by the predations of state legislatures that represent a public more interested in accountability than in engagement with ideas and unimpeded by policies whose blind spots and inconsistencies open the door to administrative interference? Clearly there's a need for it: academic freedom is crucial to the work of faculty in universities, at least in some form. We live in a time when faculty members are seen as hopeless dilettantes by members of the public because of their expertise, when their rights to speak as citizens on those controversial issues are curbed by their institutions despite those very institutions' statements about the public value of those rights and of taking positions on just those controversial issues, and when legislators and governing boards see the protections of tenure as "job protection for life" for highly paid service-sector employees who, once they've secured this "perk," can draw a paycheck for thirty years without doing an honest day's work. (Wisconsin Assembly Speaker Robin Vos, during the debate over a bill proposing to restrict universities from taking positions on controversial issues, sarcastically referred to faculty members' research on "the ancient mating habits of whatever"; Schneider, "UW-Madison Researchers.")

One way to rethink the idea of academic freedom is to do so in the context of freedom as theorized by Michel Foucault and elaborated by Robert Nichols, a concept closely related to the idea of mobility explored earlier. Debates about academic freedom, as we saw in the work of Post, Reichman, Whittington, and Wilson, to cite only four examples, tend to think of freedom as "freedoms from" and "freedoms to," fitting comfortably in the rights-and-responsibilities model of faculty work. But if Foucault is right about freedom, then academic freedom can be thought of as opening up a relation to the institution, to one's colleagues, and to one's subject matter. It's an opening that doesn't necessarily involve the observance of methodologies appropriate to one's field or the recognition of lines of authority or autonomy, a faculty member's appropriate ambit, that of academic affairs. Academic freedom can be thought of instead as an approach that allows for the possibility that those methodologies and lines may be abrogated or broken. Academic freedom, in this view, is certainly an engine of critical engagement—and quite possibly of some version of

Robert Post's democratic competence—but also a kind of eccentric, or destituent, force. It is a kind of techne that can suspend direction in favor of intensity—in Rosi Braidotti's terms, a "going without destination," or in Alessandra Von Burg's, stochastic—that undoes fixity. Freedom, and in particular academic freedom, can be understood as the "alarming possibility of being able" (Kierkegaard qtd. in Ahmed 30), alarming because it *does* involve fear and a vulnerability resulting from the recognition that going without destination is breathtaking. As Ahmed puts it, "the potential to fall into the abyss of the not yet becomes the requirement that the subject stop itself from falling . . . [by] negat[ing] the potentiality the will names, understood in negative terms, as the potential to compromise the very ground of one's existence" (30). But it also requires a kind of itinerancy, insofar as it means that faculty members absolutely recognize that the risk of this breathtaking freedom means that— like Steven Salaita at the University of Illinois, or like faculty members subject to post-tenure reviews such as those at Wisconsin and Tennessee (policies implemented by legislators who were channeling the public's deep distrust of the destabilizing possibilities inherent in critical engagement)—faculty members may themselves become deterritorialized.

Faculty work takes place at the interstices of disciplinary expertise and the broader organization of the demos. Public university statements and policies on academic freedom describe tenure as protecting the ability of faculty to work in their areas of expertise *as understood by those who hold that expertise.* While academic freedom, as defined by the AAUP and most if not all public research universities, also prevents administrations from sanctioning faculty members who take positions on controversial issues (regardless of their relation to their academic work), those protections are sometimes fragile. They're so fragile that if a faculty member's speech as a citizen is curtailed by the university in some way, those abrogations of AAUP statements may lead to sanctioning of the institution, as they eventually did in the case of the University of Illinois in the wake of the Salaita matter, but faculty members will still need legal protection *as citizens.* The arguments over post-tenure review at the Universities of Tennessee and Wisconsin illustrate the conflict: the PTR policies were justified by their boards and legislatures as a way to ensure that the faculty who teach at those institutions continue to be productively and intellectually engaged in their work—that they continue to meet the standards for that work as established by professional norms and institutional policy—so that they can be in service to the publics that in part fund their operations. And yet as those promulgating the policies also made clear, governing boards have a fiduciary duty—and more specifically a financial one—to the citizens of the state to guarantee that the work of public universities as conducted by faculty is worth the money. If it isn't, they have an obligation to create policies to eliminate those aspects of the institution—faculty working on the ancient mating habits of whatever—that aren't cutting it. There is, in this understanding of academic freedom and the protections of tenure, a discernable distinction between the oikos, the professional sphere in which faculty members operate and the institutional and methodological regulations that govern those operations, and the polis, the public sphere in which faculty members consider themselves to be citizens and to be free to engage with their fellows to deliberate on how best to govern themselves.

But academic freedom described in the context of the work of someone like a Foucault or an Agamben is a potential that resides on *the threshold between* the oikos and the polis, the professional and the public. It recognizes that faculty members don't just reside in one or the other depending on the kind of work they do or in what context they're doing it. As I noted above, despite John Wilson's incredulity, Phyllis Wise wasn't far off when indicating that it was hard to distinguish between professional and extramural speech. It's not that they both don't merit protection; it's that the protections afforded by the AAUP and by university policies on academic freedom and the protections of tenure aren't necessarily helpful when faculty members are seen to traverse their responsibilities as faculty members at the very time when they are speaking out on controversial matters as is their right under the First Amendment as citizens. Salaita's actions should have been protected, but because they were seen in the context of institutional politics and policies rather than as residing at the crux of the institutional and the political (in the space of disciplinary work rather than in the space of the demos), they were understood to be covered by institutional action rather than by social or political (that is to say, democratic) action. The University of Illinois, like many universities, was trying to have it both ways—Salaita has the right to say what he wants as a citizen, but those pronouncements are breaches of professional decorum and ethics—as, I think, the governing boards of the Universities of Wisconsin and Tennessee are trying to have it both ways when they promulgate post-tenure review policies that narrow the circumstances for faculty to develop their research and teaching programs by means of professional standards but do so not because of their desire to up the game of their faculty members but because the public doesn't trust the very professionals whose standards are meant to be observed. Democratic competence only works as a justification for academic freedom if the demos is interested in its own competence. Perhaps Post's concept should give way to the concept, as expressed by Agamben or Foucault, of radical engagement, the refusal to occupy any single position in the pursuit of understanding, where events are seen as breaches of self-evidence, the paradigms inside of which we tend to recognize what we see (an object of research, a controversy), and where it's possible not only to discover those inconsistencies, idiocies, surprising facts, and aspects of reality that might be seen as other than how they appear but to give voice to them, to step back from them in order to extend one's relation to others—both institutional others and others in the political or social domain outside the institution—openly and knowing the risk that such openness entails. Say what you will about Steven Salaita's tweets about Israel and Zionism, but his engagement was of just such a nature—it so confounded the institutions of tenure and academic freedom at the University of Illinois that it threw into question, and crisis, the institutional boundaries around which we understand faculty work, our relation to our institutions and our publics, and how risky those relations and engagements really are.

CHAPTER 4

Expertise, Discipline, and Faculty Autonomy

The American public research university came to prominence in the late nineteenth and early twentieth centuries by means of the development and maturation of the academic disciplines and their cultures of expertise (see Veysey 293–349; Loss 91–164). Roger Geiger, among others, points to the years immediately after 1945 as the period in the development of the American university when the proliferation of scientific discovery, fueled by exponential increases in funding by the federal government during the Cold War and (later) the partnership between the government and private industry, led to a concomitant proliferation of disciplinary and subdisciplinary development in the university. The research university essentially became the hub of the "knowledge economy" (Geiger xvii). Federal policy changes, led by the Bayh-Dole Act of 1980, encouraged technology transfer, leading universities to seek funding from the federal government to make up for the decreases in funding coming from the states that had traditionally supported them and to pursue research into societally "wicked problems" that require multiple perspectives for their solution. As a result, universities began to embrace the *interdisciplinary* work that some of their faculty members had begun to pursue individually by expanding the number of interdisciplinary centers and institutes located on their campuses to initiate new research agendas in order to address thorny scientific and social issues. The turn toward interdisciplinarity was intended also to address the deteriorating ethos of the expert, the university faculty member who was traditionally seen as an individual expert who works on their own to solve problems in isolation. And that individual's disciplinary expertise was closely tied, both institutionally and culturally, to an academic department, contributing to a "deification of the disciplines" in which academic departments "continue to dominate the modern university, developing curricula, marshalling resources, administering programs, and doling out rewards" (Duderstadt 120–21). The drive—and institutionalization—of interdisciplinary faculty work was meant to work against the tyranny of the academic discipline (and department) by bringing together experts working together on matters of public concern, and by so doing reaffirming the expert's ethos and restoring some of the respect that experts, and the universities in which they worked, had lost.

That interdisciplinary revolution can be seen clearly in the recent proliferation of interdisciplinary faculty hiring initiatives, frequently called "cluster programs," whose aim is to hire three to five "faculty members in emerging fields of what [former president of The Ohio State University Kristina] Johnson called 'leading-edge research, where [the university] can and should be world-class—and where we should, without question, be educating the next generation of leaders'" (Flaherty, "Hiring Booms"). Other cluster hiring programs have been initiated at the University of California, Riverside; the University of Illinois at Chicago, and (in a reboot of a program begun in the late 1990s) the University of Wisconsin–Madison. As I describe in this chapter, such interdisciplinary programs have shown some significant positive effects. They've proliferated new research, burnished the ethos of expertise at the university among legislators and the broader (taxpaying) public, and created new lines of research and research funding as well as courses, public programming, and access to expertise. But this drive toward interdisciplinarity also sometimes ignores the history of the development of disciplinary knowledge as one of the primary engines in the development of public higher education in the US and works against the faculty's role in fostering a culture of independence and in governance, not to mention academic freedom, at those universities. In fact, some of the most innovative interdisciplinary efforts—at places like UC-Riverside and Arizona State University, to mention those that have garnered the most attention in the higher education press and which I explore in some detail—have eroded the confidence among faculty members in their universities' commitment to academic freedom and faculty governance.

What follows is an examination of the social and historical dynamics of the "disciplining" of American public higher education through the establishment of academic expertise and its role in the professionalization of faculty work and the robustness of academic autonomy, in which I trace the effects of the interdisciplinary revolution on knowledge creation, faculty autonomy and governance, and the confidence in institutional protections of academic freedom for faculty work. The test cases in the analysis will be the establishment of interdisciplinary cluster hiring initiatives at several major public research institutions in the US, cases that demonstrate clearly the trade-offs necessary in their creation and promulgation. These trade-offs significantly challenge the practices and cultures of faculty autonomy that have served the development of public higher education in the US. Toward the end of the chapter, I suggest an alternative to the current interdisciplinary model of faculty work that recognizes the need for "disciplining" faculty work which emphasizes the rhetorical mobility of the intellectual capacities of faculty expertise, cuts against the grain of the centripetal forces of academic disciplines, and capitalizes on the revolutionary, centrifugal force of a relatively autonomous and mobile faculty.

EXPERTISE AND DISCIPLINARY AUTONOMY

The growth of, and distinctions between, academic disciplines is a fairly recent phenomenon, both in the history of ideas and in the evolution of the American public university. As noted by Veysey and by Oleson and Voss, the rise of science and scientific knowledge in the middle of the nineteenth century caused a restructuring of the classical college curriculum—in the ancient languages, in metaphysics, in natural philosophy—giving rise to discrete new fields, not only in the sciences (chemistry, biology, physics) but also in the arts and humanities (the contemporary languages, including English, and their literatures and what would, by the early twentieth century, become sociology, among others). The move toward the formation of discrete forms of knowledge, and the accompanying methodologies, led to the need for specialized (graduate) training, which in turn contributed to the formation of expertise and professionalization among the faculty. It is, as Jack Schuster and Mark Finkelstein put it, "the emergence of the discipline [that serves] as the central organizing principle of academic life and the university as [its] dominant organizational form" (27); the formation of academic disciplines in the nineteenth century, in this view, leads to the professionalization of the faculty and, with the autonomy that comes with it, academic freedom.

By the middle of the twentieth century, research in the American university had been fueled by massive infusions of federal funding: the GI Bill, direct funding to research programs spurred by Cold War competition between the US and the Soviet Union, and programs meant to export and otherwise disseminate American ideology through language, exchange, and other cultural programs such as the National Defense Education Act and the International Education programs funded under Title VI of the 1965 Higher Education Act. While research funding proliferated, and as the relationship between universities and the federal government continued to grow closer, it became clear that there were some risks to this relationship. Geiger puts it this way:

> By 1968 a new consensus had emerged. The principal focus had now shifted from what governments had done or might do to universities to what they were doing to themselves. The active agent behind these developments was none other than the research process itself, stimulated as it had been by federal largesse. The very proliferation of research, specialized academic knowledge, and graduate education seemed to have overwhelmed the organizational and financial ecology of those institutions. (201)

This characterization of American universities carried away by their disciplinary overspecialization is jarring when one considers the degree to which the disciplinary expertise won by faculty members during the Progressive Era also granted them professional status and a prominent role in "public service on a scale heretofore unknown" (Schuster and Finkelstein 32). But with the growing specialization of the faculty, their roles on campus also began to shift. Charles Kidd's study notes that the expansion of research led to adverse consequences for, and lack of attention to, undergraduate students at many major research universities (a point echoed by Kerr in his assessment of the "multiversity"). It also meant that other roles for faculty were augmented, including faculty members' claim to an enhanced role in decision-making about aspects of the university that involved its educational mission. The narrowing of disciplines and the growth of the research programs on their campuses led faculty, according to Jencks and Riesman, to shape graduate education, departmental organization, and the lines of research pursued in both so narrowly as to constrict the conversations that could occur between and among scientists, social scientists, and humanists, as well as between and among the students who majored in the different disciplines that had departmental homes in different corners of and buildings on the campus. It was against this backdrop that interdisciplinarity appeared to be a remedy to the fragmentation of knowledge and of the university in which such knowledge was created.

One of the conclusions to be drawn from the narrative of disciplinary specialization provided by Geiger, Jencks and Riesman, and Veysey is that the formation of expertise around disciplinary conventions advances knowledge at the expense of a relation between and among those who serve as principal researchers (the university faculty members), between their departmental and disciplinary units and their universities, and between and among the discrete ways of knowing and the languages intended to convey them. As a result, what we learn about the world by means of disciplinary research and expertise becomes opaque to anyone but the specialist. Bryan Turner, in an essay attempting to provide some coherence to the idea of academic disciplines, points to the ecclesiastical connotations of the term *discipline,* the order maintained in an organized religion, and to references to medical regimens imposed by a physician to maintain a patient's health. And much of the secondary work on academic disciplines suggests that they share a number of characteristics (see, e.g., Bridges; Goodlad), one of which is a set of social or microcultural practices, beliefs, and affiliations that provide the disciplines' "policing" function. This last characteristic is the ethical glue that holds the discipline together centripetally—the responsibility to be accountable not only to the general public but to the discipline itself (and in some sense to the institution that sponsors the discipline's research). Maybe even more than the shared methodologies or specialized languages of a discipline, the ethical reinforcement of shared practices is the (rhetorical, and sometimes extra-rhetorical) force that resists the chaos and subjectivity that would otherwise prevent institutions from organizing themselves coherently and which also prevents more radical orientations of knowledge.

As Steven Brint puts it in his study of expertise and its role in the public, the characteristics of the disciplinary professions "are based on the link between tasks for which a demonstrable market exists, training provided by the higher educational system for the performance of those tasks, and a privileged access of trained workers to the market for the demanded task. Professionals are, therefore, people whose ties to the skills and cultures of an organized occupational group provide structure for markets for professional labor" (23). The value of disciplinary work, and the training necessary for its promulgation, is its ability to serve the marketplace's demand for expertise in certain areas of thought. Discipline perpetuates a set of practices that are useful for the economic sustenance of the public, by means of a "naturalization" of those practices through language, culture, concepts, and research practices. But disciplines also serve to maintain a degree of autonomy from the economy itself, maintaining a kind of self-governance, discipline by discipline, in which experts police one another, establishing and at times adjusting their disciplinary boundaries, and maintaining compliance with the conventions of work, language, practice, and associational culture.

The emergence of the relative autonomy of the disciplines mirrored that of the professions more broadly. To paraphrase Brint, because the professions relied on higher education to provide access to markets, the development of the professions created conditions in higher education that allowed for discretion as to who merited inclusion in the economy, and *autonomy* is one of the most notable conditions. As he puts it, "Each profession was understood to work on a single important sphere of common life—such as conflict resolution, health, design, education—and the whole of the realm of socially essential knowledge could be realized only through the aggregation of these many spheres" (7). The disciplines carried with them authority: those working in the disciplines had authority to set social policy; experts would *not* be judged as successful, let alone as morally or professionally right, by those *without* such expert knowledge, only by those who had it (see Brint 7).

Eventually, the sense of the collective benefit of disciplinary expertise and the autonomy that accrued to it gave way to a more technical understanding of autonomy. What this meant was that the public good or larger social purpose toward which expertise and disciplinary specialization centripetally aimed gave way to a more inward-looking, or centrifugal, understanding of the work: "Here the fundamental concept was of intellectual training in the service of the purposes determined by organizational authorities or market forces. . . . [More and more] those who claim knowledge-based authority increasingly eschew any claims to representing vital social or public interests" (Brint 7, 15). The autonomy of the disciplines is no longer justified in terms of the social benefit of describing ways of knowing in different terms or in creating citizens whose shared expertise in those disciplines will serve the public; rather, it's justified on its own terms for what it "earns" for the professionals themselves. But this kind of autonomy is beginning to erode too, as evidenced by the public's distrust of experts, in particular experts whose disciplinary niche is narrow and whose ability to describe their work in lay terms is thin. And it's also evidenced by "university scientists and researchers [who] say they are now less likely to pursue high-risk basic scientific inquiries and prefer instead to stick 'to research in which an end product is assured, or in fields they feel are favored by funding agency officials'" (125).

Trevor Pinch, in the context of his study of the micropolitics of knowledge production—which for him are as valuable as disciplinary distinctions are for research practitioners in carrying out their work—notes that professional and cultural affiliations forged by disciplines are even more valuable *rhetorically* for the purposes of self-identification and of defending academic and disciplinary work itself. "Reference to a particular discipline in the sense of an *academic subject* is a common way in which identities are established, especially in the context of universities" (Pinch 299). Describing yourself as a sociologist when discussing academic affiliation doesn't tell the person with whom you're speaking much about the research you're doing or the methodologies one turns to when doing it. But it does work to maintain one's status *as an expert*, both in institutional settings and in more public ones. Pinch calls these self-descriptions a type of language game, in which the disciplinary expert uses a term that best describes their output as serving the widest institutional or public goal. Disciplinary expertise matters as a descriptive term that stands metonymically for a range of methodologies or objects of knowledge with which its practitioners describe their work to one another. But it matters more as a means of justifying expertise than as a means of solving problems to begin with. As Pinch describes, the greater the certainty attached to the knowledges established under the name of a discipline, the more authority that discipline has in defending itself in the court of institutional or public opinion. "Different assessments of the certainty and uncertainty of disciplinary knowledge indicate the existence of a rhetoric of claims of certainty and uncertainty" (301), yet that certainty is context dependent. It's unlikely that a scholar will admit to the uncertainty of the boundaries of their discipline when making a case to a dean that the unit in which their discipline is located merits the establishment of another professorship in that unit. It's more likely that they're willing to make such an admission when they're writing a grant application to a federal agency that requires an expertise in adjacent fields, fields that may be outside the disciplinary boundaries of the scientist but close enough to make certain knowledge claims about it.

The rhetorical work of disciplinary naming is also important in the disciplining of the institution itself. This point is integral to Foucault's understanding of the formation of knowledge. As Charles Rosenberg has indicated, insofar as disciplinary identity shapes scholars' tasks of work—setting problems and defining the tools used to solve them—it also structures their relationships to institutional and economic contexts. Disciplines function as "ordered procedures for the production, regulation, distribution, circulation, and operation of statements" (Foucault, *Power/Knowledge* 133), statements that operate institutionally. They exert a power at the institutional level that operates alongside that wielded by, for example, the federal government and other agencies by way of the funding that is available from them. What this means, as Timothy Lenoir writes in his analysis of the relation of disciplines to scientific work, is that disciplines generate

> credit [that] comes from symbolically appropriating others' work, incorporating it into one's own work, and going beyond it (Bourdieu, "Specificity" 23).... Laboratories and other institutional settings ... become themselves instruments for generating credit. Beyond the resource requirements for

conducting science is the obvious point that since the beginning of its professionalization in the nineteenth century, as an institution situated in universities and state bureaucracies . . . the organizational and managerial skill necessary for assembling and maintaining such productive credit-generating instruments can itself become a resource for acquiring authority. (78–79)

Disciplines marshal resources and help establish departments, centers, faculties, and the internal and external (grant) funding necessary to achieve not just the knowledge production inherent in scientific and other kinds of disciplinary work but also the organizations, affiliations, credentials, and authority (that is, the *ethos*) necessary for the establishment and propagation of university work. As Steve Fuller puts it, "the degree of objectivity or realism [demonstrated by scientific and disciplinary expertise] is closely tied to the degree of control that the [discipline's] practitioners have had over the circumstances under which they displayed their expertise" (146). Such organization and rationalization of the institution is a disciplinary—but not necessarily a *research*—program, and this understanding of the institutional function of disciplines has a lot to do with the administrative attraction to interdisciplinary programs: it challenges the credit-generating authority of the disciplines, and hence the autonomy of departments (and their faculties), in institutional governance.

And disciplinary expertise plays a significant role in governance. It's crucial because it provides the people or their representatives the knowledge necessary to move forward (Post, *Democracy*). On this model, power—represented by politics—and knowledge—represented by expertise—are separate, though inextricably intertwined, forces. As Mark Brown aptly put it, "experts are in politics but not of it" (9); they remove themselves from the political arena in order to become trained in the methodologies and practices that serve as the tools for knowledge formation, and then they return to the polis to convey the results of their work for the public benefit. It's this division of labor that serves as the foundation to Robert Post's notion of democratic competence, a division that sees disciplinary expertise as necessary to the operation of democracy. "The creation of reliable disciplinary knowledge must accordingly be relegated to institutions that are not controlled by the constitutional value of democratic legitimation," namely the universities, and must "shield from unchecked political control the authoritative disciplinary practices that produce expert knowledge" (Post, *Democracy* 29, 31, 35). Faculty governance depends on the recognition that faculty themselves have the best ability to judge the competence of their peers and the curriculum and research programs at the university. "The effectiveness of the [AAUP's statement on academic freedom and its] reliance on peer review . . . depends on the willingness of faculty to assume responsibility for judging the scholarly work of other faculty, and doing so fairly. The [AAUP's 1915 statement] somewhat ominously warns that unless the academic profession is willing to 'purge its ranks of the incompetent and unworthy,' then others will assume that task" (Areen 961). I'd argue that the link between institutional autonomy and the integrity of the academic disciplines begins to come apart if expertise—and the disciplines that form the basis of that expertise—is not as clearly demarcated as we think it is or if the certainty that the disciplines' methodologies presumably warrant is not quite as firm as we'd like to think (even if, in making the argument for certainty effectively in a public context, that argument isn't as successful in an institutional one).

THE ATTRACTIONS OF INTERDISCIPLINARITY

Because research in both the dynamics of disciplinary work and the social contexts of disciplinary certainty has led to questions about the value of maintaining firm disciplinary distinctions in the work of experts employed by research universities, interdisciplinarity has become attractive over the last couple of decades. It's one of the main reasons why universities have rushed to implement interdisciplinary initiatives to hire faculty members whose work challenges boundaries or works at their interstices. In much of the secondary literature about the nature of interdisciplinary work, very few authors suggest that the contextualization and social construction of the academic disciplines has so undermined their usefulness that a recommendation to eradicate them is warranted (as if such a possibility were even available). Andrew Pickering, in his essay bemoaning the current state of the literature in the history of science, notes that interdisciplinary work takes place all the time. It includes instances where scientists resist the centripetal, centralizing dynamics of legitimation and peer review forced by the twin tyrannies of professional organizations and federal funding. And it includes instances where radical contingency—where a material dynamic and the work necessary to explain it just doesn't fit any of the current models available to the existing disciplinary arrangements and tools—forces an entirely new approach to problem-solving, only to have a discipline or subdiscipline grow up around it. What he recommends, in opposition to the idea of discarding the idea of disciplinary rhetorics altogether, is to adopt instead a notion of circulation, in which "technique is an actor that *circulates*" (114), produced by one group of experts in a particular field, say physics, and then moves to another arena, say the infrastructure of military R&D or a civil engineering lab. The techniques remain more or less the same but the context where they are used shifts. In the case of circulation, it's not the disciplinary boundaries that are crossed; it's that the actors that use the techniques move around the university.

As Angela Brew puts it in her analysis of the disciplinary and interdisciplinary self-identifications of experienced researchers, individuals don't so much cross disciplinary boundaries as they describe their disciplinary affiliations in terms of relations. In the metaphors scholars use to describe those affiliations, she sees "a shift of emphasis away from viewing disciplinary identity as presenting academic distinctness or separateness, to an emphasis on relationships" (433). This is consistent with work that analyzes the gap between the way interdisciplinary scholars describe themselves to one another and their colleagues and the work they actually do in the lab or in the archive. Julie Thompson Klein writes that "the substantive problem at the core of interdisciplinary work [is] the fundamental need disciplines have for each other as checks upon the validity of their own generalizations and theories. Hence, the most important obligation is knowing what concepts have to be borrowed and what transactions are necessary to insure the validity of disciplinary formulations" (37). Klein points to the model of disciplinary and interdisciplinary relations provided by Nicholas Rescher. Rescher contrasts the axiomatist with the coherentist researcher. The axiomatist sees disciplines resting on a foundation of knowledge whose movement toward discovery is linear, evolutionary, and representational (or at least able to account for Pickering's radical continency). The coherentist, by contrast, sees the work that takes place among experts as enmeshed, networked, nodal, and cyclic, in which scientists and other researchers are constantly moving back and forth and in relation to one another's knowledge-building and where there is no necessary home or direction. Klein sees the model for this kind of coherentist approach to disciplinary work in area studies, where the work is "a pattern of zigzags . . . [in which] specialists sought to gain skills and concepts from the disciplines . . . [while] combin[ing] their own advancing theorist, sophisticated knowledge of areas and culture" as well as other areas of knowledge, then "shifting tacks" and questioning what they'd come up with and then starting again (57). The coherentist model of interdisciplinary work is founded on movement, a willingness to discard the names under which the work takes place if not the orthodoxies of those locations, and contingency on its own terms.

But there is also an argument to be made about the transgressive potential of expertise. Helga Nowotny identifies a transgressive quality that provides an opening for the kind of relational paradigm suggested by Klein, Rescher, and others. She writes that "to have any predictive value at all, expertise must be able to understand the interlinkages that bind diverse practices, institutions, and networks of diverse actors together" (152). As such, expertise must be understood to be vulnerable to contestation: "By definition experts speak about matters that transcend their competence as defined in purely scientific-technical terms[, . . . transgressing] the boundaries between specialized knowledge and its multiple, many-layered (and often unforeseeable) context of implication" (152). By recognizing the need to engage in relational practices that involve insights from multiple disciplinary perspectives, Nowotny argues for what she calls "socially robust" disciplinary expertise. It's an expertise that understands itself as vulnerable to contestation by nature and that involves what she calls a "technology of humility" (154), where disciplinary knowledge is "challenged by a larger community that insists its voice should be heard and that some of its claims are as valid, on democratic grounds, as those of more circumscribed [disciplinary] communities" (155). The results of socially robust knowledge would be open to contestation by nonexperts in and outside of the institution.

I would argue that this view of interdisciplinary work—as relational, coherentist, and socially robust—is *alloiostrophic*, a term used by the materialist rhetorician Jennifer Clary-Lemon to describe an approach to acknowledging otherness in humans' relations to nonhuman animals and their material circumstances. The term is derived from the work of Jane Sutton and Mari Lee Mifsud, who note that it isn't among the rhetorical tropes canonized in the classical rhetorical lexicon but can be found instead in the adjectival lexicon used to describe that which does not appear as the self-same. The term is derived from *alloio-*, meaning otherwise or differently, and *strophos*, a turning, twisting, or bending. The alloios orients toward the strange, toward change and alteration. Alloiostrophos, according to Sutton and Mifsud, operates outside the logic of the sequential telos; rather, its telos, if it has one, is of possibility, contingency, aggregation rather than assimilation, the principal naming function of metaphor and metonymy. Alloiostrophos "wishes for a contact that would recognize and attend to the complexity of other possibilities as well as diversity and difference" (Sutton and Mifsud 228). In this understanding of disciplinary expertise, the relation among disciplines recognizes the extent to which their methods and social practices are hybrid, that the distinctions between them (and between the departments in which they are located) are permeable and dependent on the exigence that they're addressing, that the work frequently proceeds in an iterative fashion rather than directionally, and that the narratives of progress that are forged within them—whether to justify their projects to federal or private funders, or to justify their aims to a sometimes skeptical public or legislature—sometimes occlude instances of success or failure that fall outside that narrative because they look odd, anomalous, or just wrong.

The implications of interdisciplinary work on these terms are significant in at least two ways: first, for the authority granted to academic expertise, particularly along disciplinary lines, that has traditionally served as the justification for academic freedom and faculty autonomy in universities and the public more broadly, and second, for the closely related argument that disciplinary expertise, because of its integral role in the advancement of the public good, grants faculty members, as experts, a role in the governance of the university and in the direction of the academic mission of the university at which they work. The relational, alloiostrophic understanding of disciplinary knowledge may serve to weaken the faculty's claims to autonomy, insofar as that autonomy derives from boundedness of their disciplines, and also weakens the legitimacy of those disciplines' claims to knowledge creation in their respective domains. The credit-bearing instruments of the disciplines, in Lenoir's terms, are legitimated by their discrete methodologies and the specialized training needed to master them. The institutional administration of those instruments is justified by a recognition that only those who are fluent in the practices, discourses, and habits of mind in those disciplines have the capacity to manage them. As we've seen, those practices and credit-bearing instruments are more useful in specialists' self-descriptions of their work than they are in describing the work itself—even in work that takes place squarely in a single methodology or discipline—which is often iterative, hybrid in its use of techniques borrowed from other areas of the institution, and multidirectional. If university faculty members were to more fully recognize the degree to which their work is inter- or multidisciplinary by definition, and named it as such, it would be harder to justify the bureaucratic accretions of distinction (between discipline, department, or area), and as a result their claims to autonomy would be harder to justify as well. This diminishment in disciplinary autonomy doesn't undermine claims by faculty members to autonomy from the administration of the nonacademic areas of the university—disciplinary specialists, even insofar as their claims to specificity of area of methodology are reduced, are nonetheless specialists in a way that members of boards of trustees (unless, of course, they are themselves members of a university faculty) are not. But it would make it harder to justify separate departments of, say, sociology and community and environmental sociology, or of economics and agricultural economics, or of communication, life science communication, rhetoric, and business communication. And it would also make it harder to fend off claims that only experts in a single discipline are competent to judge grant applications, tenure dossiers, or nominations to professional societies when the lines drawn between those disciplines are permeable, when the expertise derived in one discipline depends on an understanding of methodologies employed by another or several others, and when that discipline's claim to certainty may be rhetorically sound in the laboratory but far less so when subjected to public scrutiny.

The implications of an alloiostrophic model of disciplinary knowledge formation for governance—both institutionally and more broadly democratically—also tend to sharpen, though in opposite ways, the argument that places expertise in relation to its role in the formation of the public good through deliberation. If Helga Nowotny is right, and the transgressiveness of disciplinary work demands that it be socially robust in a way that acknowledges both its vulnerability to public engagement and critique and the need for that knowledge to be iteratively tested, then disciplinary expertise becomes all the more accountable to its results in the public sphere. In this way, turns to interdisciplinarity—recognizing the permeability of departments and disciplines and the social practices through which experts in their domains of knowledge production interanimate one another by definition—actually *enhance* the role of expertise in what Post calls democratic competence, the knowledge necessary to make decisions in a constantly moving and sometimes vexed public and political sphere while also subjecting that expertise to much greater public scrutiny, not just when it gets things wrong but also—and maybe more importantly—when it gets things right. But because expertise, in interdisciplinary contexts, is interdependent—where experts borrow the language and the methodological instruments for knowledge creation from one another, regardless of their own self-identification as linguists or botanists—it also suggests that, with the autonomy of the disciplines giving way to the centrifugal forces of multidirectional approaches to academic work, scholars may be less accountable to the conventions of the professional organizations, departmental practices, and disciplinary conventions within which they (presumably) work and more accountable to the institutions (the universities, granting agencies, and private industries) that sponsor that work. And that greater institutional accountability makes it even more important for those faculty to push back on the imposition of administrative burdens associated with university work, including bureaucratic reach-in and the scrutiny of deans, provosts, and governing boards.

THE INSTITUTIONALIZATION OF MULTIDISCIPLINARITY: FACULTY CLUSTER INITIATIVES

All of these dynamics—the burden of history on academic disciplines as the organizing structures of research universities, the relative autonomy of those disciplines in the organization of knowledge, the disciplines' role in faculty members' understanding of their responsibility to govern their institutions and in determining the quality and (social and financial) value of their and their colleagues' research—have played out in one of the signal manifestations of the institutional turn to multi- or interdisciplinary research programs: the cluster hiring initiative. Typically these programs are launched by a university president or provost as a way to boost the research productivity of their universities by increasing the number of research-active faculty. In so doing, they also increase the likelihood that those faculty will succeed in writing large grants for their work, grants that in the best cases are in the tens of millions of dollars and last over the course of several years (with the indirect costs, often 60 percent or more of the face value of the grant, returning in some combination to the faculty member's departmental, school or college, or university budget for uses beyond the faculty member's research project). But the initiatives are not billed as principally focused on hiring; rather, they're described as bringing together faculty members from different (usually, but not always related) disciplines to solve a society's "wicked problems" or to focus in an area of work defined by its exigency rather than its disciplinary home. In some cases, the initiatives are launched for other purposes, such as to increase the proportion of the faculty who come from backgrounds that are otherwise underrepresented (women in science, people of color) or who work in areas of research for which there is either a workforce demand (engineering) or a moral demand (studies in race and ethnicity, research on disparities in health care).

In every instance where I've explored the nature and consequences for a campus of interdisciplinary cluster hiring initiatives,[1] no matter the reasons

---

1. Universities whose cluster hiring initiatives are examined in this chapter include the University of Illinois at Chicago; the University of California, Riverside; Purdue University; North Carolina State University; The Ohio State University; and the University of Wisconsin–Madison. I participated in the creation of a white paper on cluster hiring initiatives issued by the Urban Universities for HEALTH (Health Equity through Alignment, Leadership and Transformation of the Health Workforce), a partnership that includes the Coalition of Urban Serving Universities (USU) / Association of Public and Land-Grant Universities (APLU), the Association of the American Medical Colleges (AAMC), and the NIH National Institute on Minority Health and Health Disparities (NIMHD), which involved conversations about cluster hiring initiatives with faculty and representatives from the provost's office at several other universities, including Rutgers University, the University of Hawaii at Manoa, the California State Universities at Fresno and Los Angeles, Florida International University, and the University of Cincinnati.

given in a strategic plan or media launch, these programs have several features in common. Those features are directly related to the challenges of American universities' disciplinary orientation—their continued reliance on distinctions between and among disciplines partly because of the intransigence of both the structures of their organization around schools and colleges, departments, and units, and partly because of the durability of the cultures and practices that have accreted in the disciplines over time—and their difficulties in moving toward a more truly interdisciplinary focus. The first of those features is that all the programs emphasized the initiatives' goal of increasing research funding, ideally by capitalizing on federal agencies such as the National Institutes for Health (NIH), National Science Foundation (NSF), Department of Agriculture, Department of Commerce, the National Aeronautics and Space Administration (NASA), and others that announced funding projects that cross disciplinary lines. Depending on the university, this goal was announced not so much as a way to solve wicked problems but, at least in internal documents, as a way to boost the university's research funding. All the initiatives took as one if not the single principal aim the de-siloing of the university, fostering research that crossed departmental lines and encouraged faculty members to participate in teams rather than engaging in single-person or single-lab research projects.[2] Second, the programs wrestled with a number of common issues in implementing the initiatives, not least of which was the tension between departmental units on the one hand and cross-departmental or cross-college hiring and evaluation (promotion-and-tenure) committees on the other, from the initial phases of the process. These included defining the cluster and the exigencies it would address, hiring the faculty members for the cluster, orienting new faculty members to departmental and cluster cultures, and evaluating cluster faculty prior to and after earning tenure, including retaining them when other universities attempted to hire them away. Third, the clusters presented governance challenges: cluster faculty were unsure of where their governance rights originated (the department or the cluster), and departments were uncertain about their roles in evaluating faculty members' interdisciplinary work, given that in some cases an external committee was charged with evaluating the success of the clusters and their members. University administrators often ran into problems initiating the clusters and coordinating their management (and funding) because

---

2. In the only report created to assess the effectiveness of cluster programs in increasing research funding of faculty members, the University of Wisconsin–Madison (the cluster hiring program that's been around the longest, over twenty-five years) reported that among faculty with extramural research funding, the average award per faculty member was actually *smaller* for faculty members hired in clusters than it was for faculty members hired outside of clusters (lower by as much as 10 to 15 percent). See "Report of the Cluster/Interdisciplinary Advisory Committee" 26.

there was a lack of clarity about just who, institutionally, was accountable to whom. Taken together, these issues make clear the consequences of attempts to institutionalize interdisciplinary faculty work for the principles of faculty autonomy and its implications for university governance. Though this section of the chapter includes information gleaned from research on a number of cluster hiring initiatives, I focus on one—a new program launched by the University of California, Riverside, in 2014–15—which brings into high relief the complexities of organizing faculty work along disciplinary lines and the intransigence of those complexities when university faculty and their administrations attempt to reorient those complexities in favor of what they call interdisciplinary work.

In late 2009, the chancellor of the University of California, Riverside, announced a strategic plan, UCR 2020. The plan landed on the campus just as the worst of the Great Recession was also landing, and so implementing the plan was put on hold while, over the next four years, working groups appointed by the chancellor's office, which included university faculty, staff, and students, created initiatives that it saw as fulfilling the promises made in the plan. Among those initiatives was a hiring plan, to which significant financial resources would be devoted. According to a report on the cluster hiring initiative issued in 2017, the university would hire, by 2020, 300 new faculty members (which included 50 new clinical faculty members in the medical school, 19 new teaching professors, and 231 "ladder" or tenure-track and tenured faculty members), "a significant percentage [of whom] would be hired through a centrally-funded 'cluster hiring' initiative that would aim to build critical mass of expertise in priority areas of research and creative activity" ("UC Riverside Cluster Hiring Initiative" 1). The hiring plan was announced by UCR's new chancellor, Kim Wilcox, in 2013 (Timothy White, who had served as chancellor as the plan was being formulated, was replaced in 2013 by Wilcox), and in the late fall of 2014, after a new provost—Paul D'Anieri—arrived on campus, the "cluster" portion of the hiring initiative was announced. One of the features of UCR's initiative was that the funding for the positions would be provided centrally in its entirety; schools, colleges, and departments would not have to provide a portion of newly hired faculty members' salaries, and new faculty start-up funds would be handled in the same way that other, non-cluster-faculty's start-up packages would be provided. Needless to say, members of the faculty were encouraged at the announcement of the program, and no doubt they were particularly heartened that their home units would not be responsible for paying for the new faculty but would have those positions essentially added to their departments without financial consequence (McMurtrie).

Faculty began to be concerned when the call for proposals was issued by the Office of the Provost in December 2014. The objectives listed in the call were "to advance towards the goals of the UCR 2020 plan, including enhancing UCR's performance on AAU metrics." These included "(1) Hir[ing] scholars with promise for excellence in both research and teaching; (2) Build[ing] nationally visible programs; [and] (3) Diversify[ing] the UCR faculty" (UCR, "Provost Announcement"). These objectives struck faculty as vague, but they *were* consistent with the AAU metrics that could be found in the UCR 2020 announcement. The criteria for evaluating proposals, however, did not appear to foreground the interdisciplinary nature of the program itself. Those criteria were the "Potential of attracting exceptional recruits; Likelihood of increasing performance on appropriate competitive metrics (e.g. prestigious fellowships, federal funding, etc.); Potential to bring programs into the top quintile nationally; Potential to put UCR at the leading edge of emerging fields; Likely contribution to faculty diversity; [and] Synergy with existing programs" (UCR, "Provost Announcement"). The only criterion listed by the provost that is related to the stated goal of UCR 2020 is to take up initiatives that "provide invaluable means of enhancing research and creative activities by cutting across departmental boundaries and unifying faculty with common interests" (UCR Office of the Chancellor, "UCR 2020" 12). According to the 2017 report issued by the provost's office, however, the criteria used by the committee evaluating the actual proposals were different and included—in addition to those listed in the call for proposals—"bridging or enabling research in multiple areas; creating a new focus that crosses traditional school or department lines . . . [or] within a department or school; moving from good to great; [and] retaining strengths that will retire within a few years" (UCR, "Provost Announcement"). These criteria were not visible to faculty who submitted proposals in response to the December announcement.

The other issue with the initiative was that the exigencies—the interdisciplinary areas of research that the new hires would address; the "wicked problems" that interdisciplinary research is, according to many scholars in the area, best poised to respond to—had already been decided by the time of the announcement. You could easily make the case that in the middle of the 2010s, these problems were at the very forefront of those most clearly needing to be addressed (genomics and food scarcity, new information technologies, human well-being, sustainable development of energy and the environment, development of education and social policy, and including new voices in the creative and performing arts). But the areas of focus had been developed by a strategic planning committee, not by faculty whose expertise in disciplinary (and, presumably, interdisciplinary) research and creativity would give them a purchase on the kinds of (new) knowledge that could be brought to visibility outside of disciplinary or departmental boundaries, let alone by faculty in those units whose experience in hewing (or not) to disciplinary lines would be suggestive of other, just as urgent, problems to be addressed. The priority areas were already four years old by the time of the provost's announcement—the racial unrest in Ferguson, Missouri, took place in the summer of 2014 as the result of a police officer shooting an unarmed Black man in connection with a minor traffic infraction, unrest that gave rise to the Black Lives Matter movement—and had been established, at least according to some faculty (see UCR Faculty Senate), by administrative fiat.[3]

The call for proposals raised alarms for another reason: not only were the criteria unclear, and the cluster areas predetermined, but the process of evaluating the proposals also appeared to violate the principle of shared (faculty) governance, governance that is predicated on faculty members' disciplinary expertise granting them the ability to determine matters pertaining to a university's educational mission. For one thing, the committee charged with evaluating the faculty proposals called for in December was convened by the vice chancellor for research and economic development; someone had to convene the committee, and charging the vice chancellor with the university's research mission was not a bad decision. The identity of the committee's members, however, was not initially disclosed to proposers (see McMurtrie), making it hard for them to understand how committee members' areas of disciplinary expertise might affect their application of the RFP's criteria. The other step in the evaluation process involved "campus leadership" ("UC Riverside Cluster Hiring Initiative" 2), which turned out to be the university's deans (McMurtrie). Deans are, of course, academics, who—before and sometimes

---

3. In a survey conducted in 2015 by the UC-Riverside Faculty Senate seeking responses to the levels of satisfaction with the cluster initiative, one faculty responded as follows:

> I was a member of the steering committee. I felt my input, as a humanist and faculty member of color, doing work in multicultural studies and, more particularly in black studies[,] was discounted and dismissed by the non-humanists on the committee. Not a single one of the proposals in African, African American or Afro-diasporic studies was given serious consideration, the result of which is that not a single one of the proposed searches for the current cycle is devoted to the field of black studies in its broad, global and interdisciplinary dimensions. This is, quite simply, unconscionable and intellectually indefensible. I am extremely disappointed and am led to wonder, quite frankly, if the current administration has any commitment whatsoever to my field of study. This, combined with the near-silence that has accompanied the precipitous decline in black student enrollment, leaves me profoundly pessimistic regarding the future role of black studies and black students on this campus. (UCR Faculty Senate 12)

while serving as administrators of their unit—pursue research programs of their own, programs in which they trained rigorously. But deans' disciplinary orientations shift *as* deans because not only must their evaluation of their schools and colleges recognize the successes of individual faculty members and the units that serve as their homes, but they must also assess the financial consequences of those successes and move the schools and colleges in directions that have the best chance of acquiring the financial resources that will allow those faculty members the greatest success. The way that a dean assesses a cluster proposal's chances of bringing their program "into the top quintile nationally" (one of the posted criteria) or "increasing federal funding" (one of the criteria not posted in the RFP) might differ substantially from a faculty member's assessment; the five-point rating that the committee members (and presumably the deans—it isn't clear that they used the same measurement) used to assess the strength of the proposals on each of the criteria was impossible to understand because those committee members remained anonymous, and their understanding of those criteria was not posted, and so it was unknown to the faculty making proposals. According to a piece in the *Chronicle of Higher Education* that got a great deal of attention in national higher ed circles, Timothy Lyons, a UCR professor of biogeochemistry, noted that his and many of his colleagues' initial optimism about the program—"I was thrilled about it. It immediately made sense" (McMurtrie)—gave way to deep dissatisfaction. The piece goes on to say that Professor "Lyons challenged the provost in a town-hall meeting [in] May [2015]. He said the provost was not getting 'a full sense of the level of dissatisfaction' among faculty members concerning perceived biases by the administration, which were thought to have led to a number of the best proposals being overlooked, including some 'rising stars of excellence' on campus" (McMurtrie).

The provost's response to Lyons's caution was interesting. D'Anieri noted that while it's possible that some of the proposals for interdisciplinary clusters were "rising stars of excellence" that had been overlooked, the program itself—and the clusters that had been selected from the 128 proposals received—"could make Riverside a 'star nationally'" (McMurtrie). While it's possible to read too much into this response, I believe it reflects a conflict of accountability: while faculty proposers, each of whom has a disciplinary orientation that would presumably allow them to have a view of the problems that are best solved through interdisciplinary collaboration, wish to bring those areas of research into visibility nationally (and as a result seeing themselves as accountable to the fields in which they work and to the research problem itself), the provost, in his response, suggests that he was making his recommendations on which clusters to fund based on the national visibility of the campus itself and on the campus's ability to—according to the posted criteria—"bring programs into the top quintile nationally" and "increase[e] performance on appropriate competitive metrics." At issue was a disagreement between Lyons and the provost about which entities are owed accountability and by which measure. In the provost's response, there is every indication that with interdisciplinary research comes a broader accountability than simply to faculty expertise or to faculty governance of the university. That accountability is to the institution, not to the problems laid out by the disciplinary communities formed to solve them. This was also reflected in survey results that showed that of over three hundred faculty members who responded (nearly 40 percent of tenure-track faculty on the UCR campus), 85 percent disagreed or strongly disagreed that the cluster hiring strategy was consistent with their department's strategy for hiring, and 80 percent agreed or strongly agreed that the strategy interfered with their department's hiring strategy. Faculty wanted at least some sense that the program acknowledged their department's disciplinary practices and approaches to their mission and how that mission is accomplished through hiring; apparently the cluster program itself, at least according to the survey respondents, is accountable not to those local cultures but to the campus and its rankings.

As the tumult about the initiative's rollout continued, the program was to enter into its first full year of hiring in 2015–16. That fall, the provost's office created a steering committee that would "provide coordination and oversight to the hiring initiative across the academic units," a committee that included an associate provost and an associate dean or some other dean appointee from each college and school. That committee named a "lead dean" in a single school or college who would coordinate the searches assigned to them, and the dean would identify a faculty chair of a search committee, who would in turn assemble the members of that committee, who were themselves recommended by the lead dean. All the work associated with the hiring—including the creation of a job announcement, the creation of a search process, the coordination of the cluster search committee with the departments in which prospective faculty members would have their academic homes, and the approval of "campus visits" for finalists in each of the cluster positions—would be cleared by the steering committee. Again, I would argue that the heavy administrative oversight of the search process in UCR's cluster program was due to the assumption that because the hires would be made as cross-disciplinary, rather than as appointments to any single discipline or department, it was incumbent on the campus, and not those disciplinary cultures, to devise and carry out the processes that would lead to the hires. Because there was no single disciplinary expertise whose cultures and practices would lead the hiring process, the need to observe the traditional distribution of authority through faculty governance—that is, allowing departments to devise their own "credit generating instruments" to determine the most meritorious or potentially effective person to serve as a faculty member in their units—was deemed unnecessary.

This conflict between disciplinary and cross-disciplinary interests and values continued throughout the 2015–16 academic year. In a report issued by the vice chancellor for research and economic development (VCRED)—under whose purview the hiring process was coordinated—addressed to the chair of the UC-Riverside academic senate in the fall of 2017 (which had issued the survey results to the provost and requested a response in early 2016), a section was devoted to what the VCRED called "persistent challenges." One of the first listed was the conflict between departmental hiring plans and priorities and the process outlined for the cluster program. The next two issues are worth citing in their entirety:

> Second, some cluster committees have struggled to reach consensus on candidates, both within their own deliberations and with potential home departments. Part of this is a welcome challenge: too many highly qualified candidates in the applicant pools. But there also have been cases where departmental preferences have differed so substantially from committee preferences that searches have failed despite the high caliber candidates brought to campus. This leads to frustration among all involved and delays the arrival of the fresh ideas and energy that new hires bring to our campus.
>
> Third, we must acknowledge that the desire for cross-departmental collaboration in the current cluster hiring process can be at odds with the realities that our campus remains largely department-based and that our resources are limited. While most search committee members have brought with them a spirit of cooperation to the committees, it is sometimes hard to escape the tendency of faculty to put our departmental interests first. This tension has been another source of frustration that in some cases has undermined the search process and in others has caused some committee members to become detached from the search. (UCR Office of the Vice Chancellor for Research and Economic Development 3)

The concern about conflicts between the cluster search committees and the departments in which faculty members would be hired could easily be chalked up to disagreements over faculty autonomy: members of a department, when discussing who they'll hire and tenure as colleagues who'll be with them for a several-decade career, will certainly bristle when presented with candidates for positions by a search committee appointed by vice provosts and associate deans who aren't as familiar with their departmental cultures, the disciplinary conversations taking place inside them, or the department's own priorities in hiring. But the concern is also over governance: who ultimately has the authority locally to determine hiring. You could make the case that, as the memo makes clear, the disagreements over whom to hire resulted in failed searches rather than the ramming-through of the search committee's preferred candidates over the objections of the faculty in the units, which is a preferable outcome. But the result is that the exigency that drove the hire in the first place—one that, according to the announcement of the initiative and the criteria for successful proposals, is urgent and in need of expertise that can't be found in any single department—is now one year further away from being addressed successfully.[4]

The concern about the conflict between disciplinarity and cross-disciplinarity is at the foundation of the concern about authority over search outcomes: sometimes the cultures of disciplinary expertise are so intransigent that any program that attempts to circumvent or breach them will cause institutional anxiety, upheaval, and a sense of disenfranchisement. This is a governance problem insofar as campus leadership should recognize the difficulties inherent in overcoming a several-centuries-old organizing principle not just of universities but of knowledge formation in general. It's also a problem of infrastructure, insofar as the processes designed to guide the campus through the transformation required making several hundred faculty hires outside of the usual practices of departments. But it's also a cultural problem: the university's forward movement on the matter of interdisciplinary research was highly successful rhetorically (see Professor Lyons's statement that the announcement of the program was well received by many of his colleagues) but far less successful as a matter of institutional or cultural practice. The dynamics involved in disciplinary self-identification are simpler than the dynamics of the work itself, and the question of who a department will hire—a person doing a

---

4. This same dynamic plays out not only in hiring but also in tenure, promotion, and post-tenure evaluation. At UW-Madison, whose cluster program has been in place for a quarter of a century and evaluated over that time, interdisciplinary faculty chafed at being evaluated by senior colleagues whose training was disciplinarily more "myopic" or conventional than theirs, and many cluster faculty had trouble finding mentors during the probationary period because few people were trained in the same combination of fields. There were also arguments about how tenure and promotion would be evaluated: by the department in which the interdisciplinary faculty member had their "tenure home" or by a broader, cross-unit group, thereby raising arguments over governance. While resignation rates for cluster faculty were similar to those for conventionally hired faculty, many cluster faculty reported resigning because the disciplinary tensions in service work, governance, and career advancement were simply too burdensome. See UW-Madison "Cluster Report" 10–13.

specific kind of work using particular methodologies to respond to specific material and social circumstances—is far more complicated that crafting the language for a job advertisement. A relational approach to disciplinary work—in which steering committees, search committees, and departments had the opportunity to understand how prospective hires would form relations with one another and their publics, respond to those extradisciplinary colleagues' objections to their methodologies and approaches, and form allegiances with other units and adopt others' approaches—might well have ameliorated, if not resolved, the tension between disciplinary and interdisciplinary approaches. But it would have done nothing to get past the fact that you're hiring interdisciplinary faculty members into a university whose organizing principle is by discipline and department.

CONCLUSION: INTERDISCIPLINARITY, RUIN, AND NOMADISM

What would a more robust notion of interdisciplinarity look like, and what would its consequences be for faculty work? I would argue that one of the reasons cluster programs like the ones at Riverside and elsewhere have less than robust effects—and seem to have negligible effects on the overall structure of higher education and, hence, faculty work—is that it's difficult to undo the epistemologies of knowledge and power that Foucault wrote about fifty years ago by nibbling at the edges of those structures. Attempting to superimpose an interdisciplinary structure on top of a university administrative complex that owes its shape to a couple of hundred years' worth of enculturation isn't going to work out easily. A prime example of this can be found at Arizona State University, which over the last decade has overhauled its administrative shape under the leadership of its president, Michael Crow. In a bid to become a leader in public higher education, ASU has attempted to undo the "rigid" structures of departmental and school/college orthodoxy and reconfigure the relation among scholars, expertises, and disciplines to create new schools—such as the School of Sustainability—out of old departments and to reconfigure departments into new divisions, such as the School of Evolution and Social Change, previously the Department of Anthropology, and the School of Global Studies and the School of Social and Family Dynamics (whose faculty, together, formerly composed the Department of Sociology). But as some of the higher education press has noted, and as interviews with some faculty and administrators at Arizona State University suggest, it's not clear that this restructuring has had much effect. Speaking of the newly configured field of anthropology, Geoffrey Clark—in a piece in the *Phoenix News Times* about the ASU "experiment"—says, "Things are incoherent. It's not that people aren't collegial. It's the nature of the way this was done. Autonomy is important to us pencil-necked academics. I fear that, down the line, anthropology will be just part of a blob of social sciences that have nothing to do with each other" (qtd. in Irwin). But what the university calls "forcing faculty out of silos and making them work together for the greater good" (Stripling) appears to others as simple rebranding. As several faculty members at ASU noted in interviews with a reporter for *Inside Higher Education,* the history of disciplinary work is more than a matter of renaming or of being comfortable with shifting one's self-identity while doing one's work more or less the same way. As I noted earlier, there's a long history of disciplinary work, let alone organization, in higher education, one that includes a mutual understanding of what departments and disciplines mean, how they are governed, what the relation between disciplinary autonomy and institutional autonomy means, and, not least, the value of work created by disciplinary means. Without disciplinary conventions at ASU, some faculty worry that tenure bids by their faculty and the worth of the doctorates received by their graduate students will be undermined because the criteria that reflect methodology and culture remain more or less unchanged in higher education despite how ASU is reconfiguring itself. "Doing away with departments has not meant doing away with degrees. The [newly reconfigured] Fulton Schools [of Engineering] still offer all of the ABET-accredited programs they did before reorganizing, because [the dean] felt it was important for [the] engineering graduates to have identities and qualities that are recognized by employers'" (Stripling). Reconfiguration of disciplines still faces the material reality of the complex relation between private industry, the federal government, and higher education, one that has evolved, in the "golden age" of American higher education, anyway, over the course of a century.

Nearly twenty years ago, Bill Readings, writing mainly about the humanities but thinking more broadly, described the neoliberal American university as being "ruined," and the American higher ed press, as well as publications like the *New York Review of Books,* the *New Yorker,* and others, took notice but badly misunderstood his point, which was also taken up by the neoconservative press as evidence that pencil-necked academics were burning the place down. But Readings was describing something else entirely, which goes part of the way toward suggesting what interdisciplinary work could look like and what it would mean for faculty members. He ends his book by describing "institutional pragmatism," by which he means understanding the university as an institution that doesn't have to make grand claims for its purpose. He writes, "The non-ideological role of the University deprives disruption of any claim to automatic radicalism, just as it renders radical claims for a new unity susceptible to being swallowed up by the empty unity of excellence" (168). He wants, in other words, to let the university keep moving, not only directionally but also stochastically, and to allow its organizing structures to be temporary, joining together and breaking up as needed by the faculty who are doing the work. This is what he means by "ruin": not a state of decrepitude but a state of un-built-ness, where change—between and among disciplines as much as in administrative structure—is permanent.

> The argument has to be made to administrators that resources liberated by the opening up of disciplinary space . . . should be channeled into supporting short-term collaborative projects of both teaching and research (to speak in familiar terms) which would be disbanded after a certain period, whatever their success. I say "whatever their success" because of my belief that such collaborations have a certain half-life, after which they sink back into becoming quasi-departments with budgets to protect and little empires to build. (176)

He advocates for the abandonment of disciplinary grounding, but as "an abandonment that retains as structurally essential the *question of the disciplinary form that can be given to knowledges* . . . [which provides] the opportunity for the installation of disciplinarity as *permanent question*" (177). It's not that disciplines have served their purpose and are, at this point, unnecessary or to be seen as obstacles to faculty work by definition. It's that disciplinarity must be understood as a matter of power, and faculty members should be ever vigilant about the dynamics that shift, centripetally and centrifugally, the force of those disciplines. The university in ruins simply means that the university "is a contradictory place where the [knowledge elite class, the disciplinary experts] seek alliances with business or with apolitical culture or with political subversion," where "openness to contradiction" is a given, and where "intellectual knowledge becomes free of traditional ties," though also recognizing that these new arrangements might also be configured as instances of domination (Delanty 24, 80–83). Note that neither Readings nor Delanty wants to do away with the knowledge elite or disciplinary expertise; what changes is their relation to knowledge itself, to power, and to the publics to which they are (centrifugally) accountable.

This kind of rearrangement of disciplinarity isn't so much interdisciplinary as it is *transdisciplinary*, by which I mean stochastic and mobile. In his book on the relation between experts, expertise, and democracy, Mark Brown examines Bruno Latour's understanding of the inextricable relations between science and politics, and in particular he takes up Latour's arguments against fixity. He points to Latour's distinction between "science," which is "characterized by 'certainty, coldness, aloofness, objectivity, distance, and necessity,'" and "research," which is "uncertain; open-ended; immersed in many lowly problems of money, instruments, and knowhow" (Brown 181). Regardless of the stability of the institutions in which "research" takes place, the actors—the scientists, the researchers themselves—are unconstrained by sociotechnical practices and concepts, a lack of constraint that may not look very democratic but which is nonetheless apt to let loose practices, languages, and cultures that have been heretofore marginalized. Whether these loosenings remain permanent or not is an open question for Latour (see Brown 182–83). Hence Latour's preference for assemblages rather than institutions and boundaries, because they allow for anarchic and unconventional modes of organizing among humans (and nonhumans) without doing away altogether with establishing clear lines or relations between and among the entities doing the assembling. When faculty members engage in research, they are reiterating, actively becoming-other, repotentializing both the object of research and the act of researching. "There is always the possibility that the event will be carried far enough afield that it will fall from its accustomed framework" (Massumi 19) and that the focus of research becomes (and we ourselves become) something else. And this becoming-other results in a kind of vulnerability, one whose consequences are potentially liberatory but also potentially paralyzing.

The model of this kind of postdisciplinary work—in fact, more an orientation than work—is available in Deleuze and Guattari's idea of the nomad and the methodology—if it can be called that—of the "nomad scientist." Their work offers an alternative understanding of the unmooring of research and the researcher-subject that doesn't depend on methods but functions as a capacity for upheaval and radical change. Nomadism is not descriptive: it doesn't outline the features of movement exhibited, for example, by stateless persons or undocumented national residents or the movement between social or ethnic categories. It's an alternative epistemology characterized by "absolute movement, in other words, speed; vertical or swirling movement is [the nomad's] essential feature" (381). Nomadism refers to the "in-between [which] has taken on all the consistency and enjoys both an autonomy and direction of its own.... The nomad goes from point to point only as a consequence and as a factual necessity; in principle, points for him are relays along a trajectory," one that is distributive rather than directional, indefinite, and that is both *unspeakable* and compelling further movement (380). The concept of nomadism disturbs orthodoxies and renders subjects vulnerable.

But nomadism doesn't provide an anchor for institutions. If it does provide a sense of direction, it's one that works against sedentariness, a refusal to be fixed or pinned down, to be always moving even if one doesn't go anywhere. Nomadism serves as a collective and heterogenous multiplicity that inhabits and passes along nodes in a network, moving randomly, exhibiting "lines of flight," the potential movement between points, making the potential of movement the focus of attention. The epistemology of mobility—its "method" if it can be described this way—is "eccentric science," which involves understanding material reality not as static or definitional but rather as flux and which sees the real—the concatenation of natural and human—as a model for becoming rather than being, instability rather than stability, inconstancy rather than eternality, not unlike stochastic citizenship that emphasizes randomness, probability, and the assumption that mobility is simply part of the conundrum of human agency. It doesn't involve theory and practice, hypotheses and conclusion, but rather is *problematic,* in which the variables in an equation are "themselves in a state of continuous variation . . . irreducible to the algebraic form and inseparable from a sensible intuition of variation" (Deleuze and Guattari 369). Whereas royal or normal science attempts to reproduce its findings, eccentric science consists in following out lines of thought, involving "itineration," mobility.

A transdisciplinary university would be one that functions in terms of discipline, expertise, and specialization while recognizing the need for iteration and reflexivity. It would involve, as Gerard Delanty notes, a shift in orientation in faculty work, which would emphasize the problematizing of expert knowledge—with expert knowledge maintaining its central function in solving problems, wicked and otherwise—as well as the need to press on disciplines' and expertises' "intersubjectively shared assumptions" enough to prize them open through "open-ended discourses." It *articulates* crisis and social construction rather than overlays disciplinary construction with interdisciplinary arrangements. So while the university may at certain moments "lose some of its functions, for instance its exclusive role in the production of knowledge . . . its role will increase in the communication of knowledge. Reflexive communication . . . involves the inclusion of as many voices as possible in the construction of knowledge. . . . The future of the university lies in preserving [a] relatively non-institutional space," in which we *live* and *work* with (disciplinary) uncertainty (Delanty 154–55). This would mean, then, that the struggle in, say, evaluating interdisciplinary faculty members' work for tenure, and for grants, is a feature, not a bug, of inter- (or trans)disciplinarity, and the extent to which it challenges disciplinary lines of authority is a positive development in the contemporary context because it potentially shifts the movement of knowledge from a linear to a stochastic—or alloiostrophic—one. And it has the potential, on those terms, to reshape governance by acknowledging that disciplinary knowledge, as something more than autonomous and apolitical, grants faculty more, not less, authority. But it's an authority vested not so much by expert-granted tenure as by the potential to unmoor them from institutional shared values and—while making them more vulnerable—make them more open to forging solidarities, and politics, across units, employment categories, and communities.

This kind of mobility, and the power to deploy it, has as its aim—at least potentially—to unsettle us and the disciplinary and institutional conventions that tend toward fixity, in a way that recognizes both our mutuality and the extent to which that mutuality is threatened by *situational,* as opposed to constitutive, vulnerability. This is not to say that mutual recognition just happens; it doesn't. In fact, one could argue that in the current configuration of higher education, in which tenure and shared governance (attempts to normalize intellectual mobility and mutuality) are threatened, it's easy to understand the tendency for academics to push back with both hands to protect them. But the alloiostrophic work of the faculty member has a critical dimension that identifies situational vulnerabilities and rediscovers the connections, encounters, supports, blockages, and plays of forces that have the potential to reconfigure institutions and to open new modes of action.

CHAPTER 5

The Vulnerabilities of Institutional Diversity

In the mid-winter months of 2021, the faculty in the University of North Carolina at Chapel Hill's School of Journalism voted to offer a tenured professorship and the Knight Chair in journalism to Nikole Hannah-Jones, a UNC alumna, a MacArthur award–winning investigative journalist of race and racial inequality, and the creator, as staff writer at the *New York Times Magazine*, of the *1619 Project*, which won a Pulitzer Prize. Hannah-Jones's hire languished for months in UNC's administrative offices, and she was eventually offered a five-year, nontenured position in the journalism school (all other Knight Chairs had been offered tenured positions). In the spring, once students and faculty members understood what had happened, the Hannah-Jones affair reached the national media, and investigations revealed that the UNC board of governors had refused to offer her a tenured position because some of its members objected to the *1619 Project*'s aim of understanding the structural racism that had underwritten the national project since its inception. Only after the efforts of the lone student board member and faculty and students on the UNC-CH campus did the board finally vote on offering Hannah-Jones a tenured position, which passed 9–4. But by then the bitterness on the campus, and the dismay caused to Hannah-Jones herself, was too deep, and in July of that year, Hannah-Jones very publicly declined the UNC offer and took the Knight Chair to Howard University, which had offered her a tenured professorship. In a letter explaining her decision to take her talents to Howard, she wrote that she wanted to "go where you are valued, not where you are tolerated," and she urged the boards at UNC and at Chapel Hill to make necessary reforms so that the university and its board "reflect[ ] the actual population of the school and the state, [and] to ensure that the university leadership lives up to the promises it made to reckon with its legacy of racism and injustice" (Hannah-Jones).

It would be easy to see the Hannah-Jones fiasco at the University of North Carolina as an instance of the legacy of racism at a southern public university, but there's more going on here. While this chapter does not focus on the Hannah-Jones episode, it investigates the structures that more broadly undergird the diversity and equity efforts at public universities like the University of North Carolina at Chapel Hill. I want to understand how initiatives to attract and retain faculty like Nikole Hannah-Jones work, how they are framed rhetorically, and how they founder on the complexity—and vulnerability—of the lived lives of those who are the "targets" of faculty diversity hiring initiatives. Hannah-Jones's expression that she felt "tolerated" and not "valued" speaks to the mismatch between the university's stated reasons for making the hire—that her focus on race and racial justice would be valuable for her students and her colleagues alike—and the affective economies at work in a process (such as the hiring and tenuring of faculty members) that so often fails to acknowledge the situational vulnerabilities that such hires create in the lived lives of faculty members themselves.

One reason for this mismatch, as I lay out in the first part of this chapter, is due to two related shifts in the orientation of universities in the last sixty years and to how a permutation of the rights-and-responsibilities commonplace described in earlier chapters plays out on campuses in their drives to diversify their faculties. The first shift, traced by Christopher Loss, began in the 1950s and reached its height, if not its culmination, in the early 1970s. In this shift, inasmuch as knowledge creation serves a public good, it was also understood to have a *personal* dimension: "education . . . offered access to one's historical self and identity," and "higher education was of inestimable financial benefit to individuals and society" (Loss 210). This shift initiated a *rights-based* idea of public higher education for the students enrolled in colleges and universities, where going to college on a campus with a diverse student body and faculty was a right that enabled those on the campus to thrive as citizens in a more diverse nation. This shift then created an additional responsibility for institutions and their faculties: to ensure that the ideas of right reason and deliberation that underwrite the institution's democratic goals did not exclude those whose ideas about themselves and about deliberation differed from the institution's and whose exclusion led to greater situational vulnerability. In other words, it included a responsibility to give students and faculty a sense of their *felt location* in history along with a demographic and historical sense of belonging.

The second shift, which occurred at more or less the same time and which came about from very similar dynamics, was administrative more than ideological: a challenge to the idea of the university as a guardian of reason and reasonableness. The agitation by students and some faculty for a larger role in critically evaluating the university's collusion with the state and its traditional ideas about reason and (self-)deliberation which created the exclusions noted above, led to reassessments of university curricula. These shifts, along with federal regulations and guidelines such as Titles VII and IX of the Higher Education Act and the federal protection of student records, led to a backlash from students, parents, and legislators against the university's overregulation and "social engineering" of institutions of higher education. State legislatures, in the three decades since the initial shift to an emphasis on students' rights in higher education, have often "reacted vindictively to punish universities" for their students' and faculties' excessive demands, a reaction that is clearly visible in the UNC board's reaction to the student agitation over its refusal grant tenure to Nikole Hannah-Jones (Geiger 263).

It's against the backdrop of these two shifts that I trace, in this chapter, how initiatives to attract and retain faculty from historically underrepresented groups at public research universities have both succeeded and failed. They have succeeded in increasing the numbers of faculty who identify as people of color, women, LGBTQIA+, or as members of other previously marginalized people who teach and are tenured at public universities, often meeting the numerical thresholds established by the universities in their "diversity plans." But they have failed to recognize, as Hannah-Jones recognized, that those who are hired are often more "tolerated" than "appreciated" and that their lived lives on majority-white campuses where their experiences as historically marginalized people are frequently unrecognized involve more, not less, situational vulnerability. Part of my argument is that in traversing the often complicated political and legal landscape of diversity (still called, in legal terms, "affirmative action"), universities are careful to ensure that their programs and initiatives successfully navigate constitutional and ethical hurdles but in so doing make the lived lives of faculty—and especially faculty from historically underrepresented groups—more difficult. These faculty members find it hard to, in Butler's terms, "give an account" of themselves and their experiences to their colleagues and members of their administrations in a way that makes visible their place in entwined (vulnerable) relations with others, their *felt location*. This difficulty, in turn, has effects on the institutions, making it reasonable to ask just how *free* faculty are, given that their constitutive vulnerability is heightened by institutionally created, situational vulnerabilities. This chapter, then, examines how programs designed to increase the presence of historically underrepresented faculty members, often called "target of opportunity" programs, are rooted in historical paradigms—in a diachronic mode—which often lead to a failure to recognize the *vulnerabilities* that such programs sometimes create and sometimes simply exacerbate.

INSTITUTIONAL DIVERSITY, RIGHTS, AND RESPONSIBILITIES: A MICROHISTORY

By the late 1950s public universities in the US had been irrevocably changed by the Second World War. The GI Bill greatly expanded the number of students who attended colleges and universities, and the technological advancement of the postwar Soviet Union led the federal government to fund scientific and other projects at universities to ensure that the US could successfully compete for scientific, technological, and cultural supremacy. Two things happened that were systematically at odds. The vastly greater numbers of students entering higher education expected not only an education but, as the civil rights and women's rights movements gained headway in the 1950s and 1960s respectively, also a means by which to explore their identity in the context of the social and historical changes taking place around them. At the same time, the university, by dint of its increased bureaucratization, was becoming more "siloed," with faculty members needing to confine their attention to their responsibilities as researchers to honor the terms of their federal contracts. The result was that as "different groups battled it out" for resources (Loss 165), "research ruled, not teaching, and increasingly 'fractionalized' disciplinary lines" meant that faculty shared fewer social and outward-facing concerns, which meant, for administrators, "continuous intergroup conflict" that required "constant oversight and attention" (166).

With President Lyndon Johnson's signing into law of the Higher Education Act (HEA) in 1965, the widening of educational access for "instrumental purposes" (168) became not just policy but law. The legislation's eight titles extended federal oversight over all aspects of the nation's higher education system, providing funds for land grant institutions to pursue urban antipoverty programs as well as funding for building projects, faculty development programming, a teacher corps to train teachers to work in impoverished areas, student financial aid, and the support of historically Black colleges and universities (HBCUs). As more and more students took advantage of the provisions of the HEA's titles, more and more faculty were hired to teach them. These new students were determined to engage in the social problems that the HEA was intended to address, which also meant that they intended to explore their own identities in the context of their social realities. The changes hastened by the HEA were also supported by case law: in 1961, in *Dixon v. Alabama Board of Education,* the Fifth Circuit Court made clear that students were rights-bearing citizens, and ten years later the Twenty-Sixth Amendment gave eighteen-year-olds the right to vote. Taken together, these developments made the need to diversify higher education—not just who attended and who taught at public colleges and universities but also *what* was taught, with what emphasis, and taking into account which social contexts—absolutely crucial. Consistent with the commonplace that public higher education was part of the engine of democracy, through the inculcation of knowledge and critical acumen by forming engaged citizens, the GI Bill and the Higher Education Acts made it impossible to ignore the extent to which diversifying the student body and the faculty was very much a part of the drive toward democratization.

By the 1990s a consensus had been reached that diversity had not only social benefits but also educational ones. "Diversity was more than an idea; it had become a lived experience of millions of Americans and a core value of large-scale public and private organizations, especially colleges and universities" (Loss 232–33). And with the recognition of diversity as a "compelling interest" in higher education came the acknowledgment that alongside the responsibilities that inhere in the mission of public colleges and universities—to create critically engaged and well-educated citizens—came equally important rights *for students* to pursue subjects that didn't so much have a pecuniary value as they did an ethical or a social one. This shift to an emphasis on identity in public higher education didn't come easily, however. Though the increase in funding for higher education during the Cold War led to the hiring of greater numbers of faculty members, those hired were initially not especially tuned in to the shift that was occurring around them. "Accustomed to their traditional posture as guardians of reason and reasonableness, universities were repeatedly unnerved to find themselves morally outflanked" (Geiger 231), and faculty members often felt disoriented by the changes. With "university administrators [resorting] to coercion" to manage the changes, sometimes violently as in the Dow Riots or dismissively as in the Black Student Strike at the University of Wisconsin in the mid-1960s and early 1970s, respectively, "their moral ascendancy was lost" (233). Many members of the public who saw the student demonstrations during those years also became concerned, and their representatives in the government did too. As a result, the 1970s brought a backlash to university diversification in the form of federal regulation of everything from intercollegiate sports and DNA research to the confidentiality of student files and other aspects of university life. Members of the public were worried that the focus on students' identities and their concerns about redressing social inequities would unleash a cheapening of higher education that saw less value in the traditional verities of reason, citizenship, and a common core of knowledge.

The disenchantment with public universities was also reflected at the state level. As Geiger puts it:

> Although policies varied enormously across the fifty state systems of higher education, three kinds of developments affected research universities adversely. In a few states legislatures reacted vindictively to punish universities for their failure to control the student rebellion. Second, and more widespread, changes in state control over higher education lessened the autonomy of flagship campuses. Third, constraints on the funding of universities were commonplace, whether related or not to the two other developments. (263)

These developments have only become more pronounced since the 1970s and 1980s. What this all reflects is that in reaction to the development of the importance of students' rights and a focus on identity in public higher education, there arose a countervailing discourse of responsibility (the word most frequently used is *accountability*), which sought to rein in what appeared to its critics to be the excesses of the egalitarian orientation of public colleges and universities.

One of the regulatory changes on university campuses that has had a most lasting effect has been in the diversification of the faculty. Over time, while universities initially resisted diversity hiring because of a fear of lowering standards, the goals of affirmative action were eventually internalized and universities began to go to great lengths to hire women and minority faculty (see Geiger 260–63). "The result was the outcome that prevailing egalitarian values had sought: greater ethnic and sexual diversity on university faculties. But what was not achieved, however, was the original liberal ideal of color-blind and gender-blind evaluation of accomplishments and provisions of subsequent awards" (263). And this failure, I argue, is related to the failure to recognize that in the tension between acknowledging the rights and identities of students and faculty and the public's demand for institutional accountability to observe the traditional model for higher education, what got left behind was sustained attention to the lived lives of those on its campuses, in its classrooms, and working in its labs, libraries, and offices. In her book *Free Speech on Campus,* Sigal Ben-Porath makes the point that the expansion of diversity on university campuses makes it necessary for universities to "create an environment in which [its residents] do not find it necessary to hide their identities, because of the harm to their well-being as well as the resultant loss of a valuable opportunity . . . to engage with a diverse set of perspectives they may not have considered" (36). Ben-Porath develops a concept of inclusive freedom which recognizes the central value of vulnerability, in the two senses that I've used it in this book so far: the general openness to others (constitutive vulnerability) and the susceptibility to harms that result from the exploitation of that openness (situational vulnerability). What often gets lost in university efforts to hire and retain faculty from groups that are historically marginalized and underrepresented is precisely what Ben-Porath calls the "aggregate accumulation of small harms," the experiences of lived life on campus and in the community that, according to Ben-Porath, represent "a blind side in the search for knowledge" (45), experiences that don't fit neatly into the rights- or responsibilities-based models of higher education and its democratizing aims.

THE LEGAL LANDSCAPE OF FACULTY DIVERSITY INITIATIVES: DIACHRONY AND SYNCHRONY

One can begin to see *why* vulnerability is omitted from faculty diversity initiatives at public universities because of how the cultural and legal discourses of such programs—initially understood in terms of affirmative action—evolved. One of the most significant reasons why the hiring of historically underrepresented people on the faculties of public universities takes the shape that it does is that the notion of vulnerability was itself shaped by the language of affirmative action, which is founded on a commonplace of numerical representation, of a kind of democracy that has to do with one's proportional visibility in the demos. This commonplace recognizes that vulnerability has a historical or diachronic dimension that requires remediation but doesn't clearly recognize its synchronic dimension, which has as much to do with one's *felt location* in the contemporary institution as it does with one's place in history. The idea behind affirmative action, as established by the Civil Rights Act of 1964, is to redress past discrimination against historically underrepresented groups by maintaining that "no person in the United States shall, on the basis of race, color, or national origin, be excluded from participation in, be denied the benefits of, or be subjected to discrimination" under programs funded by the federal government (US Department of Labor). The passage of the law had a significant effect on the inclusion of people from historically underrepresented groups in the years immediately after, though it also raised a series of legal questions about how to implement it, because it was explicitly designed to redress *historical* discrimination.

At colleges and universities, the uncertainty about how to implement the Civil Rights Act can be seen in the way the questions themselves were posed during the first twenty years after the act's passage. As Loss and Geiger note, higher education was one of the places where the impetus to deploy egalitarian values and a drive toward openness was most prominent. This included an openness both to previously underserved populations, including women, LGBTQ people, and ethnic and racial minorities, and to an array of disciplines that provided a means to explore matters of identity, belonging, and social justice. And yet even at universities, by the 1970s, the question of how to make good on those values was fraught. In a letter to the White House in 1974 questioning an executive order on diversity hiring, the authors (which included prominent academics) cited "the ineffectiveness and injustice of the quota programs" as a "numbers game." In fact, the letter argues that the implementation plan developed by the Department of Health, Education, and Welfare would be imposed "in gross defiance of the Civil Rights Act of 1964 and Executive Order 11246" issued by President Kennedy as an "unjust and discriminatory quota program" (Maeroff). A *New York Times* article a year later about equity hiring at Northern Illinois University quoted professor of philosophy emeritus Sidney Hook as saying that "no one would argue that because many years ago blacks were deprived of their right to vote . . . that today blacks and women should be compensated for past discrimination" through affirmative action policies or hiring initiatives that favor people from historically underrepresented groups. "Equal opportunity yes; special preference no" (Fields). According to critics, even hiring goals were problematic, since universities were "fearful that employers [would] use goals as rigid quotas they must fill, even if they hire[d] female and minority applicants who [were] not as well-qualified as available white males" (Fields). In a *Times* article published in 1983, the reporter notes that the University of California, Berkeley, had pledged to hire 31 minority and women faculty members by 1986 in order to remedy a pattern of discrimination in its hiring practices ("Affirmative Action"). Taken together, these reports and many others from the 1970s and 1980s make clear that the remedy of past discriminatory practices is most often described in numerical and diachronic terms. The situational vulnerability experienced by individuals who were either hired as faculty by colleges and universities and then discriminated against or not hired because they were passed over in order to hire a white or male applicant is understood as diachronic—it was experienced in historical or comparative terms—rather than as synchronic, as a susceptibility to harm, or an actual harm, that was sui generis, was experienced materially by the individual subject, and hampered their freedom as individuals and affected their felt location as members of a university faculty.

The constitutional law surrounding faculty hiring practices at colleges and universities follows this same pattern. In the *Bakke* case, the University of California argued that the rejection for admission of the named white plaintiff was justified on the grounds that its admissions system, which reserved sixteen of its one hundred places for qualified minority applicants, was meant to redress past instances of discrimination. The argument was in response to a lower court order that deemed the dual-track admissions program at the UC-Davis medical school a violation of the Constitution's equal protection clause. In its decision, the US Supreme Court established, by an 8–1 majority, a framework for initiatives in higher education, in which the justices asserted that such initiatives were constitutional if they were subject to, and met, strict scrutiny. The court wrote that the five justices who upheld the notion of affirmative action did so because "the goal of achieving a diverse student body is sufficiently compelling to justify consideration of race" in decisions such as whether to admit students and that race could be considered "a factor"—but not the only factor—in such decisions (see *Bakke*). *Bakke* ruled out any initiatives that would have established quotas or numerical goals for the admission (or hire) of historically underrepresented people but made clear that redressing patterns of previous discrimination or exclusion was constitutional if there was a "compelling state interest" in doing so.

What was meant by a compelling state interest became clear fifteen years later in *Grutter v. Bollinger*, an admissions case that came to the Supreme Court in 2003. In a 5–4 decision, the court held that Michigan's law school admissions process was constitutional, and in so doing it clarified the criteria that could be used in initiatives designed to create more open access to higher education: that the program was time limited, that it was the least restrictive means to achieve its aim, and that it fulfilled a compelling state interest. In *Grutter*, that interest was described as *educational*, specifically that the state had an interest in protecting initiatives that created an "educational benefit[ ] that flow[s] from a diverse student body." In the majority opinion, Justice O'Connor wrote that "universities occupy a special niche in our constitutional tradition" and that Justice Powell, in *Bakke*, had thus correctly argued for the "freedom of a university to make its own judgments as to education [which] includes the selection of its student body" on the grounds that "cross-racial understanding'" helps "break down racial stereotypes and 'enables [students] to better understand persons of different races'" (all quotes from *Grutter*, section III.A). The *Grutter* decision subtly but crucially introduced a shift in the notion of vulnerability from a diachronic to a synchronic register. If *Bakke* eliminated—or at least curtailed—the idea that a past injustice could be addressed in mathematical or numerical terms by a mathematical or numerical approach—what its critics had called a "quota system"—it also complicated the question of what would take the place of such a diachronically oriented approach. *Grutter* upheld the idea of diachrony in both examining past discrimination and describing its effects in higher education: under two of the criteria for strict scrutiny—that initiatives needed to be time limited and that they had to be the least restrictive of all possibilities—programs could only be in place until instances of past discrimination had been addressed and the principle of openness and access in higher education had been achieved. But the compelling *educational* interest in *Grutter* introduces a synchronic element to the diachronic ones upheld in *Bakke*; it suggests that it is the very vulnerability and marginality of those who join the university that enriches the education of all those who attend, in effect arguing that the foregrounding of the vulnerability of those who have experienced—historically or in the present—harm through discrimination or racism makes the institution itself more vulnerable but, also, richer. As O'Connor writes in the majority opinion, "We have never held that the only governmental use of race that can survive strict scrutiny is remedying past discrimination" but that enrolling "a 'critical mass' of minority students" is of direct benefit to them, to their majority peers, and to the institution (*Grutter*, section III.A). In *Fisher v. Texas II* (a case that, like *Grutter*, involved a challenge to an admissions policy, in this case at the University of Texas–Austin), that notion of synchronic vulnerability was expanded: compelling educational interest includes the "destruction of stereotypes," "cross-racial understanding," and the need for students to actively and intelligently participate in an "increasingly diverse workforce" and to cultivate "leaders with legitimacy in the eyes of the citizenry" (see *Fisher v. Texas*, section IV). It is the very situational vulnerability of those who have been marginalized—the extent to which they are, in the present, stereotyped, minoritized, and denied legitimacy as leaders and citizens—that justifies the creation of initiatives designed to better include those individuals.[1]

---

1. I want to briefly address the question of whether cases on student admission (*Bakke, Grutter, Fisher,* and others) apply to faculty hiring initiatives. One line of argument, advanced by L. Darnell Weeden, is that because of O'Connor's argument in *Grutter* about the compelling educational interest in diversity, what holds for students also holds true for faculty: namely, that by having persons on the faculty who have experiences that differ from those of the (majority of) students, those students will have an educational advantage once they have graduated from the university. In a second line of argument, Suzanne Eckes makes the case, two years after *Grutter*, that if universities wish to create faculty hiring initiatives to address diversity, then

The validity of initiatives to ensure equity in university hiring decisions is also caught in the tension between arguments based on the rights of students to be afforded an education that addresses matters of identity and those based on the responsibility of the institution and its faculty to be accountable to public demands on the institution. There is compelling educational interest by the state to pursue diversity hiring initiatives because the members of the educational community have a right to an education that represents the experience of the greater demos. Understanding the experiences of those who have been historically excluded from a higher education requires that individuals who have undergone those experiences must be present in the classrooms, the laboratories, and the offices of colleges and universities. But universities also must justify those initiatives based on their responsibilities to their students, to their faculties, and to the institutions and the broader public, and they must justify them, too, as a way to remedy past injustices and exclusions. Both arguments—those based on the rights of community members to an education that reflects the historical (diachronic) experiences of those who have been marginalized and those based on the responsibilities of the institutions to represent the broader communities—are meant to bolster the case that universities' efforts in diversity serve all members of the public. The state's compelling interest in regulating colleges and universities to ensure the inclusion of underrepresented faculty (and students) is based on those institutions' responsibilities to their students and faculty; those responsibilities are in turn vouchsafed by a recognition that those students and faculty have a right to learn, and teach, about the experiences of those who have been previously marginalized. But caught as they are between these two impulses, what is missing is a sense of the (situational) vulnerability of those faculty who are hired to ensure that the state's responsibility is met. Those who provide the education, and create the (new) knowledge that accounts for the experience of that vulnerability, live and work in institutions that define those faculty members as historically underrepresented and that as a result continue to operate

---

Grutter suggests that it's not so much the advantage it provides to students as it is the advantage it provides to faculty members hired under those initiatives. Eckes analyzes employment laws and Supreme Court decisions that upheld those that were "race-conscious" and finds that in nearly all, "evidence of past discrimination [was] provided in order to meet the compelling state interest standard," suggesting then that "when a university uses a race-conscious hiring plan to remedy past discrimination, the institution needs to have concrete evidence" (45–48, 50–51). Jonathan Alger and Cordelia Glenn argue that initiatives in the public sector, like those in the private sector, must be based on evidence of past discrimination; in summing up a justification for the *Fisher II* decision, law professor Michael Olivas, writing for *Inside Higher Education* in 2016, notes that the "numbers" belie any claims by the appellant in that case that white applicants are at a disadvantage in applying for places in a class at a university.

as institutions that "contain" those faculty members, and their experiences, *as institutions*. What's missing, in other words, is attention to those faculty members' experiences and to how they suffer the harms inherent in the situational vulnerabilities that result from their status as marginalized, as a kind of "undercommons" (a term I describe more fully later; see Harney and Moten) that functions by means of numbers, but numbers—a critical mass—quite different from those used to justify the hiring initiatives themselves.

Situational vulnerability, as I've suggested in earlier chapters, is the uneven distribution of constitutive vulnerability—our general openness to others, an openness that renders corporeal subjects susceptible and at least potentially subject to violence or deprivation but that ultimately makes us who we are, a being-in-relation. It is often exacerbated by institutional or state power. One's identity is bound up in vulnerability—one becomes who they are by means of that (open) relation to others. Rosalyn Diprose writes that our existence is best thought of "as 'uniqueness' or 'potentiality' open to a world and to ongoing transformation and renewal" (186). That interrelatedness and that potential openness confirm that "there is an irreducible *singularity in the experience of vulnerability,* one that belies any categorical account of how it is that vulnerability and dispossession are lived" (189, citing Ann Murphy). But identity and a commitment to diversity rooted in vulnerability also mean having to recognize the "multifarious commitments and entanglements" (190) that dwelling in a community such as the public university entails. It also means that individuals are vulnerable not only because of their status as a member of a historically underrepresented group but also because that marginal status and its complexity provide a perspective that has the potential to radically destabilize that institution and community. The norms, institutions, laws, and legal precedents, the "counting" and accounting for, say, faculty of color in proportion to white faculty, are to some extent the very causes of the deficits inherent in situational vulnerability. The institution itself is responsible for what Catherine Mills calls "the injurious risk of *misrecognition,* which has as its consequence the failure to fully appear as subject within the social" (137). Those "norms are internally and necessarily violent, insofar as they bear a direct world-making capacity, and moreover, because that world-making capacity necessarily entails exclusion of that which does not accord with the norm or does not fall within the grid of intelligibility established by it" (140).

One way to think about the gap between identity and responsibility in the landscape of diversity in university faculties is to consider it a "break in the conditions of its production" (Mills 151), the production, namely, of the ethics and norms in relation to which university faculty operate in the first place. The break to which Mills refers is the recognition that beyond a notion of who we are and to whom we are responsible—as a matter of accountability—is the motivation both to engage with others and to resist the deprivations inherent in situational vulnerability. Of course the numbers—accounting—by which so many faculty diversity initiatives operate (the demographics of a state, the percentages of minority faculty in proportion to majority faculty, dollars spent, persons hired) seem difficult to resist. It's easier to recognize historical wrongs, wrongs perpetrated by others, and to remedy them than it is to acknowledge current wrongs, wrongs for which I may be personally responsible. And it's easier to quantify individual members of the faculty—how many white, how many Black, Indigenous, or people of color (BIPOC), for example—than it is to quantify the affective labor required to *be* a faculty member in one's institution, their felt location. And yet, as Sabsay, Harvey and Moten, and others note, it's the numbers—the critical mass—that provide a kind of disruptive power. It's a power founded on the affective unruliness resulting from lack, from situational vulnerabilities, from feeling not quite at home, making faculty feel, even on the most welcoming campuses, like a minority. "One could understand [Judith] Butler's claim," writes Sabsay, "that 'when the body "speaks" politically, it is not only in vocal or written language' to suggest that, in certain circumstances, bodies could produce political articulations" (294). She goes on to wonder whether the assemblage of bodies, particularly those placed at the margins of institutions or states, will ultimately have the effect of changing those institutions. But even if they don't, the marginality of those bodies, argues Sabsay, can "expose[ ] vulnerability" and, in so doing, "question how vulnerability is extremely ill-distributed" without necessarily questioning the outer limits of the "we" (297). It's this power that is most often ignored when universities develop initiatives to enhance diversity, navigating between an ethics of identity and an ethics of responsibility, failing to understand that this in-between-ness is not an elision but a catalyst for recognizing the marginalized other in very different terms.

DIVERSITY HIRING INITIATIVES IN PUBLIC UNIVERSITIES

Initiatives to address the diversity of public universities have become more extensive since the federal directives of the 1970s and 1980s and have more frequently been authorized by the universities themselves than by legislative fiat. The social movements of the 1960s and 1970s created more open universities and more demands by students and faculty alike that their campuses' classrooms and research agendas be more closely oriented toward the concerns of the students who were in the classrooms and laboratories. As this opening occurred, the institutions recognized that the state's compelling educational interest in creating a diversity of experiences could only be achieved by intentionally executing a plan for their campuses to bring the principles of diversity to all aspects of their operations. To do so, they ended up addressing opposing tendencies: the *rights of students and faculty to explore and test* the ways that *their identities* and critical concerns took shape amid the material realities whose properties they were also learning by means of disciplinary and methodological testing and the *responsibilities of institutions to their publics* to ensure that the education created on their citizen-funded campuses would support and maintain the public good and create new knowledge that would benefit those citizens.

What's clear through an examination of the diversity, equity, and inclusion (DEI) statements and plans created over the last twenty years by some of the leading public research universities in the US is that navigating this tension is fraught with peril.[2] This is particularly true in those parts of the universities' DEI plans that are meant to address the diversity of the faculty, who are charged with creating knowledge and the courses of study that make that knowledge available to the university's students and to the people of their states. What I have found in these plans, and in the ways they are executed through faculty hiring initiatives, is that it's in the lacuna between faculty members' (and students') rights to critically engage with their own histories and experiences as an integral part of their work on campus and the faculty members' (and universities') responsibilities to their students, citizens, boards, and legislatures where the vulnerabilities of those faculty members reside. I observed four consistent patterns in an analysis of DEI plans and the initiatives in them designed to attend to faculty diversity.[3] First, nearly all diversity

---

2. Diversity initiatives are referred to by a number of acronyms and titles; recently, the term "belonging" has been added to these initiatives—DEIB—though in the remainder of this chapter, I use the shorthand DEI to refer, generally, to campus diversity initiatives, as this acronym is the one the universities themselves tend to apply.

3. The public research universities whose DEI plans I examined include the Universities of Connecticut, Iowa, Missouri at Columbia, Nebraska–Lincoln, Oregon, Texas at Austin, Michigan, North Carolina (its system and its campus at Chapel Hill), Illinois at Urbana-Champaign, California (both its system and its campus at Berkeley), and Wisconsin–Madison (I do not cite documents from all of them.) In addition to system and campus diversity plans, I also examined DEI plans from specific colleges and schools within the universities and progress reports issued by presidents, provosts, chief diversity officers, and chancellors to campus stakeholders and governing boards. I also looked at faculty diversity hiring initiatives, often described as "target of opportunity" initiatives, at the Universities of Illinois at Urbana-Champaign, Michigan, Minnesota, Nebraska–Lincoln, North Carolina at Chapel Hill, and Wisconsin–Madison and at Penn State, Rutgers, and Ohio State. I also interviewed faculty affairs officers in the provost's offices of most of these universities, in whose portfolios faculty diversity hiring initiatives fall; references to those interviews have been anonymized to comport with the IRB protocols for this study.

and inclusion plans were specifically connected to universities' statements of public mission or, in a more explicit nod to the constitutional legal cases over admissions, to a compelling educational interest. Second, while DEI plans referred both to the rights of students to an education that addressed their identities as individual subjects with diverse experiences and to the universities' responsibilities to those students and other stakeholders, the language of responsibility most frequently trumped that of rights and of identity. Third, one of the major justifications for affirmative action and diversity programs cited in legal history of such programs—the need to remedy past discrimination—was sometimes but not often cited, and that language often elided or was distinct from acknowledgment of current instances of racism, discrimination, and marginalization that occur on those very campuses. Fourth, the vast preponderance of the material used to justify the diversity of universities was based on quantitative data—numbers, proportions, comparisons with other universities—rather than on qualitative descriptions of the lived lives of the individuals whose very vulnerability was most at issue.[4]

---

4. For all the language in the plans based on the university's responsibility to provide its *community members* the right to pursue an education in a hospitable place where they can safely explore the significance of their identities and the histories of those identities in the context of the academic disciplines that form the core of the university, the vast majority of the efforts, as reflected in the language of the plans, seem to focus on the responsibilities of the institution to the state, or to some vague notion that the state's citizens or its legislature or—more likely—its peers and competitors will pounce on the institution should it not meet its goals. The assessments called for by Oregon's plan include the evaluation of campus efforts at diversity and the "establish[ing of] appropriate and measurable opportunities for improvement" to do so, establishing measurable goals and outcomes, and aligning existing resources with "programs and initiatives that have a proven track record of success and impact" (Alex-Assenoh 4). Like Oregon, the University of Michigan makes "measures of accountability" a central part of its plan (Schlissel et al. 3), as do the Universities of North Carolina and California.

These accountability reports are interesting because, for all their complexity—and some of these plans, particularly Michigan's and Oregon's, are laudably rich, extending to nearly every corner of the university and community—they boil down to numbers. The success of diversity efforts is often based on numerical comparisons between a university's current "headcount" (of students, faculty, staff), reflecting demographic data, and the surrounding community, the state, or regional or national peers and on tracing those comparisons over time. North Carolina's diversity report (Clayton et al.) in 2014–15 includes a number of initiatives to recruit and to support diverse students and faculty and staff, and it goes on to list programs in the university's various units that achieve these goals. But just what a "critical mass" amounts to is never defined, and what compelling educational interest such a "mass" might create is also not explained. Instead, reading the first section of the report, which employs an array of colorful pie charts and graphs, was the closest I could come to understanding what critical mass might look like if plotted on an asymptotic curve. The University of California's report on diversity to its governing board in 2016 doesn't use the term *critical mass* but instead notes that its diversity goals as stated in a regents policy document include the need to "achieve diversity among its student bodies and among its employees" (UCR Regents 2). Nearly a third of the report to the regents is an appendix that lays out, in bar graphs, data on students, faculty,

What's missing in these and other reports of the progress these universities have made in diversifying their campuses, and their faculty in particular, is a sense of the lived lives of the faculty members who live, work, and do their teaching and research there. This is an especially glaring omission when one also considers the extent to which—in the terms outlined in Supreme Court decisions and in these universities' responsibility to their publics—some of them refer to the need to ameliorate instances of past discrimination of historically marginalized groups. The University of Oregon's 2020 report on the implementation of its IDEAL Framework explicitly calls out the state's history of racism, including the expulsion of its Indigenous people from the area where the Eugene campus is located, and notes, for example, that the state "distinguished itself as the only State in the union to ban Black people from settling within its borders with a series of Black exclusion laws starting in 1844" (Alex-Assenoh 6–7). The University of North Carolina's reports in the years following campus demonstrations over the removal of its memorial to students who served the Confederacy during the Civil War cite the state's history of racism and the university's refusal to admit Black students until 1951 and restrictions on women students through the 1960s (see Chancellor's Task Force 5–6). Some reports and plans even go so far as to cite current instances of racism, discrimination, and other structural issues that create an inhospitable campus climate for members of its student body, staff, and faculty. Examples of the inclusion of contemporary instances of exclusion are part of the UIUC's Diversity Strategy Task Force's report, which includes a survey of women faculty, and the University of Wisconsin–Madison's climate surveys, conducted every three to four years by its Women in Science and Engineering Leadership Institute, which report that women and faculty of color are among the least satisfied with the climate in their units and the university overall (WISELI 3–5).

---

staff, and leadership by ethnic, racial, and gender categories. The University of Illinois at Urbana-Champaign is explicit about its goals for diversity being numbers-driven. In a diversity proposal for the campus as part of its Strategic Plan for 2018–23, the "Diversity and Inclusion Goals and Actions" document lays out ten recommendations, one of which is the following:

> Meet affirmative action placement goals for staff who are from URM groups, women, individuals with disabilities and veteran representation across the board in hiring, salary, and staff representation at all job levels on our campus. Foster and maintain a staff that reflects the diverse composition of our state and contemporary society, and demonstrates the University's value as an agent of economic growth and upward mobility. (Zerai 7)

In a chart reflecting the diversity of the faculty in racial and ethnic terms (for Black and Hispanic faculty in particular), the UIUC compares its percentages of faculty in those groups with those at its peers in the Big Ten Academic Alliance.

Taken together, the diversity initiatives on many of these campuses, and the reports they make to stakeholders on the progress of those initiatives, reflect an inability, or an unwillingness, to fully recognize that there is a gap, a tension, between the imperatives of responsibility to the public and their students' and faculty members' rights to work in a community that supports their capacity to critically engage with their concerns and the ethical imperatives to address their place in just such a fraught public space. It is a tension in which their vulnerabilities, as students and faculty members, was at least in part *caused* by the institution's divergent aims. For all the language of democracy, public mission, and the compelling educational interest to create a "critical mass" of diversity on their campuses in order to better enrich the educational experience, the universities' focus on numbers, and on the resources that make it possible to further the aims of diversity, eclipses the ability to recognize the situational vulnerabilities that these institutional aims often cause and the affective economies that result. This is nowhere clearer than in universities' diversity faculty hiring initiatives.

Such programs, frequently called "Target of Opportunity" (TOP) initiatives, are found at nearly every public research university and are very frequently noted as a key aspect of their DEI plans. Most TOP initiatives provide central funding—either through the provost's or some other central office—to departments for a period of one to three years (in some cases longer) that allows them to hire faculty from historically underrepresented groups. Such hiring can take place separately from the regular hiring cycle (that is, even departments that don't have authorization to make hires can apply for and receive such funding in order to make a targeted hire) or through the regular hiring cycle (if, for example, a department posts an authorized position and has, in its pool of candidates, a qualified applicant from a historically underrepresented group whose profile is not a perfect fit for the position or who is a highly but not top-ranked finalist).[5] At the University of North Carolina at Chapel Hill, its TOP program, called the "VITAE" hiring initiative (Valu-

---

5. There are important variations to the TOP approach to diversity hiring. At the University of Texas at Austin for a number of years, a "Thematic Faculty Initiative" provided funding lines to colleges and schools "for the hiring of faculty members who bring more diverse scholarship and course offerings to campus" (UDIAP 17), thus avoiding the targeting of individuals from historically underrepresented groups in favor of targeting academic areas of expertise. And at the University of Nebraska–Lincoln and Penn State University, there is no TOP initiative focusing specifically on faculty underrepresentation; instead, there is a process whereby departments identify individuals who present unusual strengths and who would not otherwise be identified in a normal search (see University of Nebraska–Lincoln, Office of Institutional Equity and Compliance); the waiver approach allows these institutions to avoid the issue of strict scrutiny altogether.

ing Inclusion to Attain Excellence), is linked clearly to its diversity plan: "As part of its continuing commitment to provide students with a thriving, intellectually stimulating educational environment, a gifted and diverse faculty is essential" (see "VITAE"). It's also clearly related to the "compelling educational interest" argument of the *Grutter* decision. At UNC as well as at the University of Wisconsin–Madison, diversity is very broadly defined. At North Carolina, the TOP program includes "individuals who grew up in economically disadvantaged circumstances, individuals with substantial professional experience working with minority and economically disadvantaged populations; individuals doing significant research on issues that disproportionately affect minority and disadvantaged populations; and individuals whose teaching or research specialty is in a field that is currently underrepresented in the University faculty" ("VITAE"). At UW-Madison, while not as specific, the program is defined as enabling "departments to hire exceptional faculty members who would greatly enhance the quality and diversity of the department" (UW-Madison TOP initiative). The University of Illinois program is far more explicit. The description of the program that is most directly used by faculty members and department chairs explains that it's meant "to accelerate our recruitment of faculty of color to campus" (Office of the Provost, "Communication #7: Targets of Opportunity Program"). A longer communication, found in a Box folder in the UIUC provost's office site, notes that the program is intended to recruit "leading faculty members among groups that are underrepresented by race, ethnicity, gender, disability, and veterans' status in specific units on campus" ("Communication #7: Targets of Opportunity Program").

The broad language describing the programs is intended to meet the strict scrutiny criteria established in *Grutter* and reaffirmed in *Fisher*. In all cases, these programs are responding to the demands for accountability, both from their governing boards and from their administrations (if not from their state legislatures). All these programs are, at least on paper, required to provide accountability reports to their home offices (mostly provosts), as articulated in their campus diversity plans. At Wisconsin, for example, annual diversity reports are issued to the provost's office by schools and colleges, and as part of these reports, the deans are asked to report on the diversity of their respective departments (that is, in terms of numbers and percentages of individuals who are Black, Hispanic, women, or from other groups that are historically underrepresented in the department's field or fields) and their relative success in recruiting and retaining faculty members from those groups compared with other (that is, majority) groups. But in the TOP programs themselves, no such accountability measures are articulated, leaving uncertain how the success of the programs is understood by those who have implemented and made use of them—not in terms of numbers but in terms of the extent to which the structural and situational vulnerabilities of the individuals who are hired, and the members of the department more broadly, are identified and addressed or ameliorated.

And this problem—how the responsibility of the institution eclipses the rights of the faculty members hired through these programs and their felt location in them—is made more granular in interviews conducted with members of the academic affairs offices (that is, people in the provost's offices who are charged with overseeing the faculty hiring initiative piece of the campus DEI plan) about their TOP or targeted faculty hiring initiatives.[6] Three related issues came up in these interviews, all having to do with the relative absence of acknowledgment of the vulnerabilities inherent in the drive toward faculty diversity, the legal landscape's intransigence, and the nature of the follow-up on the relative "successes" of the initiatives. As I noted earlier, some targeted hiring initiatives establish very broad boundaries for their definitions of diversity, making it difficult to understand how they are addressing the institutional and legislative mandate to redress past instances of discrimination while accounting for the lived lives and situational vulnerabilities of those hired. At one East Coast public university, for example, the target of opportunity program uses a definition—like those at North Carolina and Wisconsin—that includes not only race, ethnicity, and gender but also veterans' status, ability, and social background. This has presented a problem of accounting, if not accountability, at this university: because its institutional research office uses federal categories to determine campus diversity (i.e., Black or African American; American Indian or Alaskan native; Asian, Native Hawaiian or Pacific Islander; and White) while its programs include, for example, Hispanic and other nonracial categories, it is difficult to understand, by the numbers anyway, how successful their program is in diversifying its faculty. At a large midwestern public research university, a similar problem exists. There, women in STEM fields are included because they are historically underrepresented in those fields, but questions have arisen about whether, for example, Hispanic faculty who are not of Mexican descent or Asian American faculty (neither of whom would qualify) should be eligible. The problem, then, at these institutions is that the measures that have been designed to ensure the accountability for the success of the programs haven't accounted

---

6. The information from this section reflects interview data collected between May and December 2021 from discussions with academic affairs officials at nearly a dozen public research universities located in the eastern and midwestern regions of the country. Responses have been anonymized to comply with UW-Madison IRB protocols.

for the breadth of experience (in the form of the "categories" of diversity targeted by the programs) that each of the faculty members hired will bring.

In my interviews I was surprised to learn that there have been few legal challenges to these programs, in particular through the application of strict scrutiny. Part of this, no doubt, comes from the designers' articulation of the aspects of strict scrutiny in their descriptions of the programs available to both internal and external audiences. But as I noted above, because race, for example, is one of a number of identifying characteristics of the faculty members who may be hired, the accountability measures built for these programs suffer from what could only be called—in the neoliberal register—inaccuracy. The experience at a flagship public university in the Midwest is interesting for what it suggests about vulnerability and invulnerability. The creation of a true TOP program had been put into motion there, but the university counsel's office refused to approve the program without providing a "good reason," though it's likely that the counsel's office was less concerned that it wouldn't pass constitutional muster under strict scrutiny and more concerned that it would run afoul of state legislation that prohibited any institution or agency from enacting an affirmative action program. This appears to me to be an instance of what Erin Gilson calls "invulnerability," a "desire to maintain a certain kind of subjectivity privileged in capitalist socioeconomic systems, namely, that of the prototypical, arrogantly self-sufficient, independent, invulnerable master subject" (312). As invulnerable, Gilson goes on, "we cannot be affected by what might unsettle us" (313), which, in this case, is the acknowledgment of people whose experiences—as people, as faculty members, as experts, and as neighbors—may differ radically from their own (which is, by definition, vulnerability). This university doesn't have an initiative that acknowledges race (or ethnicity or any other historically underrepresented identity) as a desired feature of any new hire for its faculty because the institutional invulnerability to even the quite limited criteria established by the *Grutter* and *Fisher* admissions cases as applied to faculty hiring has at this point trumped acknowledgment of the vulnerability of prospective faculty hires.

But perhaps the biggest drawback to these programs is that there is very little follow-up to understand whether the initiatives have had any effect on changing the culture and climate in the units that made the hires or how that culture and climate—improved or not—affected the individuals hired. At a large eastern public university, for example, there's an acknowledged retention problem: because of its closeness to a large city, faculty, and particular faculty of color, find that there are more opportunities to "have an enterprise to run" at institutions that are actually in the city than several miles and a train commute away. At a public research university in the center of the country, retention is also an issue, though there's been little discussion about accountability. According to the person there with whom I spoke, "we hear rumblings" from faculty of color about a lack of mentoring, about problems with establishing community-based research or having it "count" toward tenure, about the misalignment between expectations for research and teaching and the demands on faculty members' time, but these rumblings have apparently not been systematically examined. And at two large public research universities in rural communities far from the nearest large city and that are very predominantly white, retention of faculty from historically underrepresented groups is problematic. At one, which has instituted a program of exit interviews—conducted when a faculty member announces they are leaving the institution—faculty report that finding membership in a community (church, activities-based, social-concerns-based, organizations of people from similar backgrounds) is often the deciding factor in whether a person hired there will decide to stay. But other than exit interviews, there's virtually no systematic attempt to understand the lived lives of faculty members from historically underrepresented groups. At the other midwestern university, the story is very similar, with very little tracking of the success of hires once the funding is provided, though each person hired through its target of opportunity program is assigned two, not one, senior faculty members as mentors. At an urban public research university in the Great Lakes region, more significant efforts have been made to assess the results of its diversity hiring program, both through the use of data based on demographic and comparative information and through exit interviews. The affective dimension of vulnerability, the situational instances of "lack" or deprivation, the moments in which a faculty member's experience is erosive rather than constructive, is there for the asking—those in the offices where faculty diversity hiring initiatives are housed "hear rumblings." But at all the campuses that have such programs, those who are hired leave, or are dismissed at the tenure decision, at higher rates than majority faculty, those who are not by definition targets of opportunity.

To return to the instance with which I began this chapter, what Nikole Hannah-Jones wrote about her experience at the University of North Carolina at Chapel Hill was that she wasn't recognized. UNC failed to recognize the situational—and systemic—vulnerabilities that her presence, as a well-recognized (and to some, controversial) Black scholar, made visible to the campus, to its governing board, to the university's donors, and to the broader community. And this is precisely what scholars from historically underrepresented groups on university campuses say about their own presence: that it brings into stark relief the systemic vulnerabilities that face them nearly every day. As Althea Butler, a faculty member at the University of Pennsylvania, puts it,

"In my own personal experience, we don't have enough people to go around to help with diversity work. You have an issue, you bring it to a nontenured faculty member who is a person of color, or a woman, and they have to do all the heavy lifting because they teach race or some related issue. Everyone's calling them all the time, they can't get enough work done and you've already set that person up for failure" (qtd. in Flaherty, "Scholars Talk").

One of the public research universities whose diversity hiring program I examined created a working group to investigate the reasons for the lagging retention rates of associate professors from historically underrepresented groups, and as part of that group's work, it convened listening sessions with several dozen faculty members to understand the reasons for that lag.[7] What faculty members said during those sessions, in a few cases, was that it was the first time some of them had been asked to describe the lived reality of their experience working at the university. A number of issues stand out in the notes from the working group. First, the toll taken on faculty of color and others from historically underrepresented groups by micro- (and in many cases macro-) aggressions on *students*—let alone on themselves—was significant. Person after person noted that when a Black student is removed from a classroom by police officers for allegedly having spray-painted antiracist graffiti on campus property, or when a trans student is misgendered in class by another student amid snickers from others, this wears on a faculty member's sense that they, too, are being targeted in these incidents. As one faculty member of color said, "The student who was hauled out of the classroom—I had that student in one of my classes, and it could have been my class" that the police invaded. In other cases, the misrecognition of the force of such incidents was directed at the faculty members themselves. One person of Asian descent was told that he shouldn't do so much diversity work since he himself wasn't a person of color so it wasn't his job; another faculty member was asked by her department chair why she was spending so much time working on the health disparities in African American communities, since that kind of work would risk "labelling" the faculty member—who is Black—as far too interested in "race issues" to get promoted.

Faculty members also reported that they all, to some extent, paid a version of what a few in the group called a "Black tax," the invisible work done by faculty from historically underrepresented groups to support students of color and to shoulder the load of diversity work. One recently promoted full

---

7. Notes from the working group, sponsored by the Office of the Provost at this university, were taken and compiled by the vice provost for faculty affairs in the winter and spring of 2019. I have hidden the identity of those quoted in order to protect their privacy and in compliance with the University of Wisconsin–Madison's IRB protocols.

professor cited the case of an assistant professor colleague in a humanities unit who was initially turned down for tenure. The professor noted that despite the colleague's writing an award-winning book, her case was considered weak because she spent her time working with graduate students of color who came to her in order to speak with someone who, unlike their white peers, might understand the challenges they faced. Now, the professor said, more than ever when asked by assistant professors of color whether to take on service obligations, she tells them to say, unapologetically, "no," knowing the toll that such work will take on their chances to make tenure. Another faculty member pointed to the listening session itself as an example of the cultural tax paid by faculty of color. He found it ironic that he was asked to give yet another two hours of his time to address diversity issues when the same was not asked of his white peers. This is consistent with what Robert Head, a longtime and now-retired academic administrator, said of the way higher education does diversity work. "'I find the delegation of antiracism work to Black faculty, in many cases, to be an act of minimization.' The Black faculty members get all the work, with limited influence to change things, while the institution gets to say it's 'doing something'" (qtd. in Flaherty, "Scholars Talk"). A number of faculty in the listening sessions—and not just from arts, humanities, and social science units but also from units in the biological and physical sciences—noted that especially when they were assistant professors they were told to avoid work that could be considered controversial because anything seen as "community-engaged scholarship" might not be considered scholarly enough by tenure and promotion committees and decision-makers beyond the departmental level. In other cases, the lack of support for the mentoring and other diversity work had to do simply with the recognition of time and effort. Some faculty members said they had tallied the hours they had spent, for example, counseling undergraduate and graduate students, creating community in and beyond their units for faculty of color, serving on DEI committees called for in strategic plans, or simply calling out instances of racist or just plain ignorant behavior in the classroom, lab, and formal (committee) and informal conversations. The faculty reported that those hours were valuable, but they were not remunerated for the time and effort—let alone the emotional labor such expenditure requires—either through release time from classroom teaching to make space for such work, a revision of tenure-committee guidelines to recognize the value of community-engaged scholarship, or higher salaries or funding support that would provide at least some recompense for the time.

Richard Reddick, an associate dean for equity in the University of Texas at Austin's College of Education, notes that one of the most significant situational vulnerabilities experienced by faculty from underrepresented groups, and particularly by Black faculty, is that universities can be "'woefully neglectful of what it is like to live' in the surrounding environs" (qtd. in Flaherty, "Scholars Talk"). Reddick asks:

> "What is it like to buy a house in the community? How do local schools affirm Black children? Where can Black scholars find a critical mass to listen to music, appreciate the arts and otherwise build community?" He recalled a professor he once met who realized there were no Black barbers in his rural university town, so he hired one from the nearest city to cut Black students' hair at his own home. It became a community for those students, what . . . bell hooks would call a "homeplace."

Faculty members in the listening sessions noted the same thing. Several Black faculty noted that their department chairs and white colleagues have no idea how difficult it is to raise children in a predominantly white community, not only because, in the case of parents raising Black boys, they have to figure out how to have "the talk" about how to behave if (or more likely when) they are stopped by police officers but also because those children are growing up and being educated in a school system and community climate that has been creating its predominantly white cultural norms for over a century. Parents find that they need to supplement their children's education to provide a cultural counterweight. "Who's going to help me pay for that?" one faculty member asked, while others noted that there's an emotional weight a person carries around when they see themselves "as the only one," the lone Black or queer or disabled person amid others who may or may not be capable of seeing them for who they are. This is a weight, and a felt location, that is difficult for faculty members, let alone their families, to bear.

CONCLUSION: A CASE FOR VULNERABILITY

What was reported in the listening sessions described above, and what has been uncovered again and again in the lived experience of faculty members from historically underrepresented groups, is that despite the acknowledgment by higher education of students' and faculty members' identities and the importance of those identities to the project of public higher education itself over the last fifty years, and despite the responsibility placed on institutions to embrace the regulations imposed on universities by the courts, the pernicious and durable nature of the situational vulnerabilities inherent in one's status as a faculty member in an institution that abides by policy, institutional norms and practices, and history remains. Institutions are, by definition, invulnerable. They tend toward stasis and convention, and they tend to conserve their resources in a way that makes it difficult to turn away from those norms, conventions, and cultures to recognize the ways in which these are not serving its community members particularly well. If we're invulnerable, the experiences cited by the participants in the working group's listening sessions are, to those who convened it (and, I suspect, to nearly anyone who might read the notes), deeply unsettling. It's not surprising, then, that the vulnerabilities expressed by faculty—vulnerabilities created (or, if not directly created, then certainly exacerbated) by the institutions in which they work—are unrecognized. If nothing else, the institution as a set of "routines, procedures, conventions, roles, strategies, organizational forms, and technologies" functions "*as* resistance" or inertia (March and Olsen, *Rediscovering Institutions* 26). The institution's characteristics exacerbate the situational vulnerabilities experienced by faculty of color and others whose experiences have been marginalized. And those situational vulnerabilities act as a constraint on subjects' affective agency. Inasmuch as Vita Pavesich insists that one's constitutive vulnerability is an engine of subjectivity, that it "supplies the *motivation* for becoming autonomous" (8), it's also true, Pavesich continues, that being "corporeally vulnerable [means that we are] biologically incomplete" and that "human beings need a life world that supports, shapes, and informs" that constitutive vulnerability (11).

But what these faculty members report, in describing the conditions that make it harder for the university to retain them even despite the efforts the universities made in some cases to hire them, is that the very institution that has undertaken diversity plans and faculty hiring initiatives and argued for those programs' legality under the courts' compelling interest decisions aren't capable of creating that supportive "life world." And they're not capable of doing so in part because, in Catherine Mills's terms, they haven't recognized the faculty members as full subjects. The norms of the institutions' "world-making capacity necessarily entail[ ] exclusion of that which does not accord with the norm or does not fall within the grid of intelligibility established by it" (140). The institution's recognition of situational vulnerability is trumped by the institutional imperative toward responsibility—accountability, regulation—insofar as the programs devised to hire more faculty from historically underrepresented groups are guided by numbers (the observance of the criterion of "compelling interest" and other aspects of strict scrutiny) rather than by the actual sense of belonging experienced by the faculty members. Even as a "critical mass," these faculty members nonetheless feel marginal because they're *made* marginal. They're made marginal because universities, focused as they are on democracy-as-demographic, on percentages and ratios, overlook the material realities of their lives and the emotional labor required to live them *as* meaningful.

If diversity plans and initiatives to identify and hire faculty members from historically underrepresented groups fail to ameliorate the systemic and situational vulnerabilities of those recruited and hired to join the university community, what is to be done? Sigal Ben-Porath argues that what's needed on campus is what she calls "inclusive freedom," a framework that requires an assessment of the vulnerability inherent in the subject positions of those in the campus community. An inclusive freedom framework is needed because free and open inquiry is only possible when those participating in it "do not find it necessary to hide their identities, because of the harm to their well-being as well as the resultant loss of a valuable opportunity for [them and] their peers [and colleagues] to challenge their own views" and to engage in perspectives informed by experiences other than their own (36). Ben-Porath goes on to examine the notion of vulnerability—in terms of the "harms" cited here—and how situational vulnerabilities such as microaggressions, failures of recognition, and systemic roadblocks to a successful academic career manifest themselves in the quotidian context of university life. In the creation of diversity plans and faculty hiring initiatives with a focus on historically underrepresented groups, institutions would themselves need to be vulnerable. They would not only need to listen to the experiences of individuals who have lived the precarities of predominantly white institutions, actually *hear* them and recognize them, but also to identify the structures and the potential and actual harms that result from those structures and work to interrupt them if not (also) to change them. We need mobility, vulnerability, in-between-ness for faculty, students, and other members of the university to be able to act justly, to uncover and address vulnerabilities, to unsettle and disrupt logics and conventions that need to be reshaped or replaced, and the current model of the university (because of its priority of stasis, loyalty to certain types of stakeholders, and stripping of protections of faculty, such as tenure, from the system) makes the institution invulnerable to these changes, stagnating the university and preventing vulnerability/mobility from doing what we need it to do.

It's that capacity for interruption, I think, that often goes unacknowledged in institutions' assessments of diversity. It remains to be seen whether Nikole Hannah-Jones's decision to reject the tenured offer of the Knight Chair at the University of North Carolina in favor of going to Howard University—where she would be valued and not just tolerated—will have an effect on UNC's actions on diversity and inclusion. Given the entrenched politics in that state, and the simple fact of institutional invulnerability, I'm not placing any bets. But if it does, it'll be because of the durability and mobility inherent in vulnerable bodies. In a discussion of vulnerability organized by Jasbir Puar in 2011, Judith Butler muses on the situation of precarious academic workers, not just in the US but also in Europe and elsewhere, and the desperation of those workers leading them to occasionally take to the streets, forging alliances with students, the unemployed, and the homeless. Butler wonders "what, then, is the political significance of assembling bodies" in these demonstrations, and their answer is that such bodies "are precarious and persistent." They are precarious in that "they are exposed to police force, and sometimes endure physical suffering as a result"; they are persistent in that they are "obdurate and persisting, insisting on their continuing and collective 'thereness' and . . . organizing themselves without hierarchy, and so exemplifying the principles of equal treatment that they are demanding of public institutions" (Puar 168). To be vulnerable is to be susceptible to harm, but to be vulnerable is also to be (dangerously) at the margins, in that those who experience the unequal distribution of political, economic, and ethical resources and power—and who are marginalized as a result—are also marginalized *together*, "shar[ing a] condition of precarity" (170). It's in *this* sense—of the capacity for marginalized bodies to persist and act *together*—that numbers truly matter. Reading Puar with Pavesich and Mills, one can begin to see the conditions of vulnerability described by faculty from historically underrepresented groups at institutions like those examined here as a potential break with the institution, one brought about by the conditions of precarity, leading to a mobility—not a movement to, or toward, or away from any particular point, but an agitation— that contains a kind of power. Of course Nikole Hannah-Jones *moved* from UNC-Chapel Hill to Howard University, but she also created a movement—a mobility—that agitated students, faculty, and community members alike to begin to recognize the conditions of precarity on the campus—and in higher education—that are sometimes rendered invisible in the language of court decisions, diversity plans, and hiring initiatives.

The durability and persistence of the precarious bodies of faculty members who experience racism, discrimination, and misrecognition, let alone legislation and policies based in ignorance and hatefulness—in numbers—are a means of both resistance and solidarity. Butler argues that vulnerability has a relationship to resistance in that despite their marginalization, these faculty members "continu[e] to exist" ("Rethinking" 26) in spaces that appear inhospitable. They form what Stefano Harney and Fred Moten call an "undercommons," a ruptural space amid the institution that gives refuge to those at the institution's margins—not just faculty of color, queer faculty, or those doing work unrecognized by tenure committees because it's not academic enough but also the staff who are sometimes invisible to faculty or the students whose lives are inscrutable to them—who are seen as somehow threatening. These marginalized and sometimes invisible bodies "cause[ ] discomfort (by not fulfilling an expectation of whiteness)" (Ahmed, *On Being Included* 41). Those who work in these marginal spaces are *mobile* and cause trouble, both individually and in concert with others who occupy that same space. It is precisely because of the model of the university (stripping faculty of protections, making individuals marginal, etc.) that faculty are becoming more vulnerable, but it is this vulnerability that gives them the power to disrupt through the undercommons, where precarity and risk (while dangerous to subjects) give the perspective and movement necessary to disrupt the institution. It is only through this being made marginal that we are able to make change.

Nikole Hannah-Jones was right to leave the prospect of employment at the University of North Carolina at Chapel Hill, but not (just) because the institution didn't attend to the diversity on its campus and not because despite that attention it continued to marginalize people from historically underrepresented groups. She was right to leave UNC because, despite its invulnerability—its drive toward responsibility and accountability that ultimately trumped its ability to *see* the members of its community—Hannah-Jones rendered the institution vulnerable. And it also made it possible for Hannah-Jones, an exceptionally talented teacher, journalist, and scholar, to be recognized *as* marginalized, vulnerable, and also on the move. In that moment of marginalization par excellence, she managed to move her corporeal self from Chapel Hill to Washington, DC, but she also moved the capacity of others, those who share the space of the "undercommons," toward being, finally, *seen*. In the meantime, within inhospitable places (as universities are right now), resistance grows through vulnerability, creating an undercommons that both offers refuge to those on the margins and threatens the invulnerable logics of institutions.

CHAPTER 6

Becoming Rhetorical

The 2021–22 academic year was a difficult one for faculty rights and responsibilities in higher education. Daniel Pollack-Pelzner, a tenured Shakespeare scholar at Linfield University, was fired in 2021 without a hearing after publicly complaining about antisemitic remarks made by the university's board president; the university claims that Pollack-Pelzner was engaged in behavior that was harmful to the university. Garrett Felber, a promising and well-regarded tenure-track assistant professor at the University of Mississippi, had his contract terminated after publicly questioning the university's legacy of racism. Felber's department cited his problematic approach to communication with the chair as a reason for his termination. At Collin College, a handful of faculty were terminated for speaking out against their president and other administrators for their response to the COVID-19 pandemic, while others were terminated for their responses to violations of their free speech (in one case, a faculty member was terminated for advocating for the removal of a Confederate memorial in nearby Dallas). In thirty-six states, legislation has been proposed or passed that in one form or another restricts public colleges and universities from teaching about structural racism if doing so would cause students "discomfort, guilt, anguish, or any other form of psychological distress." The irony is that many of these states are proposing bills that would make it possible for students as well as members of the public to bring legal action against faculty members and their universities for teaching material they don't like. And in a much-publicized case, the University of Georgia system has proposed (not unlike proposals discussed earlier in this book at the Universities of Tennessee and Wisconsin) a process of post-tenure review by administrators, not faculty, violating the AAUP's guidelines founded on the latter's expertise and autonomy. (The AAUP has censured the University of Georgia over its violation of faculty rights and responsibilities.)

Each of these cases violates faculty members' rights and responsibilities and interferes with faculty members' responsibilities to create critically engaged citizens with enough expertise to deliberate on matters of public importance and participate actively in the demos. And they trample on faculty members' rights to determine the proper means by which to explore the material and cultural objects and events that are their methodological and disciplinary purviews and to teach the results of their explorations free from fear that they will be fired for doing so. In all these cases, faculty members have defended their positions by arguing that they are doing their jobs consistent with the aims of higher education and its relation to the well-being of the public. And in all these cases, those arguments seem to have had little success. Although Steven Salaita won a monetary judgment against the University of Illinois for breaching his offer of employment, he was nonetheless driven out of academia. Faculty members at universities whose post-tenure review processes were unilaterally changed by state legislatures, or whose models of governance were changed because they granted the faculty too much autonomy, resisted these changes, but in the end, post-tenure review policies, new tenure standards, and legislation eroding free speech and academic freedom were nonetheless put into effect.

The arguments that faculty at public universities use to defend their work—including that they have the expertise necessary to determine the proper standards for evaluating work in their fields, that they have through shared governance a right to determine the policies and standards of due process that will provide the best pedagogical model for educating their students, and that the good of the public is the ultimate aim of the project of higher education—haven't worked. They've failed because the model for faculty work, based on the premises of shared governance, faculty rights and responsibilities, disciplinary autonomy and expertise, and ultimately the honing of a public sensibility that supports the good of the demos, lacks the staying power it once had. Changing attitudes of the public, and about higher education's place in a rapidly shifting and hyper-neoliberal economy, are outstripping the faculty's arguments for their work that are based on the idea of a university and the commonplaces that are used to characterize that idea. So we need to consider whether and how it's possible to recuperate a notion of publicity and of the public action—the *rhetoric*—that would need to be coupled with, if not replace, those more traditional commonplaces in order to reshape their approach to that work.

In this concluding chapter, I want to consider how rhetoric can be put in service of just such a reworking of the faculty's approach to the commonplaces of public higher education in the twenty-first century, one that reflects a rethinking of the idea of publics and publicity. In doing so, I want to make a case that faculty should, in terms used by David Fleming, *become rhetorical* by implementing a rhetorical stance that is closely related to universities' traditional public mission and that also recognizes that the terms of publicity—and of rhetoric—have changed over the last forty years (and with them, the idea of the university's role in that public context and what the implications of such a rhetorical stance look like in the contemporary moment). Becoming rhetorical—recuperating a dynamic notion of rhetoric in public higher education—does two things. It highlights how rhetoric is not only a subject to be taught (a rhetorical education) that is woven through the disciplinary and methodological work of the faculty in public universities. Rhetoric also serves as a means of reconsidering the underpinnings of that very enterprise. It can provide a model for faculty at public universities to make claims for advancing new ways of working and to engage with one another by means of the very precarities and vulnerabilities that I've explored in the preceding chapters. Rhetoric, in other words, can be seen as a way to (re)define our engagements with one another to achieve just outcomes. In the following pages, I revisit the arguments made for the public dimension of faculty work, and in particular, I note the inextricable link between publicity and rhetoric in those arguments. I point out the significant challenges to that work in the changing landscape of public higher education. In doing so, I intend to pull together the theoretical strands of the previous chapters to outline a reconceived rhetorical project—a rhetorical education—that accounts for the mobility, vulnerability, and ethical urgency such precarities demand and that describes in general terms the implications for faculty work in the twenty-first-century public university. I am *not* arguing that faculty members should jettison ideas of democracy, publicity, and public goods; rather, they need to recognize their disadvantages in the current conjuncture and supplement them with other approaches—rhetorical approaches—that more clearly reflect the situation in which they find themselves.

BECOMING RHETORICAL

As I noted in chapters 1 and 3, the public good is understood to be the central aim of higher education and is the foundation of the relative autonomy that faculty, as experts in their fields, wield in the governance of their institutions. The freedom of faculty to wield that power is derived from the protections of citizens to deliberate with one another on matters of public concern and from their perspectives as experts, contributing to what Robert Post has called democratic competence. This argument for higher education, and for the faculty work that promulgates it, is a rhetorical one. Jurgen Habermas and John Dewey, each in their own way, made such an argument about the rhetorical dimension of the project of higher education just as universities were beginning to understand their role as serving the public good. Habermas was addressing the (public) university in Europe and in particular Germany after the Second World War; Dewey was exploring what he called the "problems" in the idea of the public in the years following the First World War. Their common concern is that what we think of as "the public" and "the university"—the *ideas* of the public and the university—are at some distance from the material reality of both entities. Here I explore the implications of that distance in Habermas, Dewey, and other scholars of rhetoric who see a role for an explicitly rhetorical education that likewise is founded on the idea of the university and of the public that fails to take account of the precarious position of both.

Habermas's essay "The Idea of the University: Learning Processes" was written in 1987, twenty years after reformers attempted to recast the German university. It expresses the worry that those reforms were undertaken without fully understanding the relation between the aims of the university and those of the public it serves. The first third of Habermas's essay is diagnostic: since the war, the university is no longer an "organic" instrument of the state or of the public. It has, through bureaucratization and the hyperspecialization occurring predominantly but not only in the natural and physical sciences, become a discrete system of its own, not entirely unconnected to the state but relatively autonomous from both the state and the "idea" of the university that was derived, in the German context, by Humboldt and Schleiermacher (Habermas 6–9). The university's aim was to produce an "autonomous science" that functioned in accord with the scientific system of observation and testing and to produce a means of injecting the discoveries from the sciences into the state through education so that "as ideas are comprehended they simultaneously enter the knower's moral character, thus freeing it from all one-sidedness" (10) by means of the "reconciliatory power of reason" (11). Universities would thus serve as "the birthplace of a future, emancipated society" (11). In this view, concentrated inquiry relatively autonomous from the rough-and-tumble of politics and political interest has a kind of "unifying power" (15) which, located in the university, is sequestered from the state's interests while contributing to the formation of the citizen's moral character. Universities make the state richer not only by creating intellectual capital but also by means of the more active engagement, in the political and cultural sphere, of its citizens through the promulgation of the university's discoveries in the classroom, the laboratory, and the public lecture. What Habermas recognizes—a matter I return to shortly—is that this "idea" of the university works in two ways: it attempts to create an expertise that is developed relatively independently of the political and civic concerns of the state while demanding that the "power of reason"—the "learning processes" of his essay's title—penetrate that independence so that it has a salutary effect on the public. He recognizes that those processes "do not simply stand in an inner connection to the reproductive functions of the life world" (19); rather, they become instrumentalized by the state for whose benefit they supposedly accrue, and the expertise of the faculty is not so much sequestered as it is monetized by those who'd make the most immediate use of their work. For Habermas, the problem with the "idea" of the university is that the integrative power of the sciences—of inquiry—doesn't hold in the contemporary landscape, in part because the sciences have become highly differentiated and in part because the public has become corporatized.

John Dewey comes at things from a different perspective: where Habermas is concerned about the idea of the *university* in a late-stage capitalist economy, Dewey is concerned about the idea of the *public* in such a context, in particular what the role of expertise might be in such a public. Dewey's book *The Public and Its Problems* was published nearly a decade after the end of the First World War, a time in the US when the question of democracy, successfully "defended" in the war, was now open. Essentially the question Dewey addressed was whether democracy and "the public" were more or less the same thing. Dewey's answer—"yes and no"—was controversial at a time when social critics such as Walter Lippman worried that the public's opinion—"commuters reading headlines in the train" (Lippman 63)—would be mistaken for democratic wisdom. In contrast to Lippman's relatively static notion of the public, Dewey proposed a more mobile one, what his editor calls "a permanent space of contingency in the sense that there can be no *a priori* delimitation, except as it emerges from individuals and groups that coalesce in the service of problem solving" that "entails a kind of openness" (35). Lippman believed that, as a bulwark against the public—the commuters on trains—there needed to be an expert class that wasn't just conversant with public opinion but capable of truly understanding it. In order for the public to be both open and engaged in the problem-solving necessary for the public's renewal, Dewey believed that the citizen should at least to some extent also be capable of serving in the role of expert. The citizen knows both what the problems facing the public are—"The man who wears the shoe knows best that it pinches and where it pinches, even if the expert shoemaker is the best judge of how the trouble is to be remedied" (Dewey 224)—and what to do to remedy them. Contrary to Lippman, who'd tell you to go to a cobbler, Dewey would prefer that you'd have enough knowledge to know which cobbler to take the shoe to and how to describe the problem. To understand how to fix the "pinch" that individuals have in common—a public—one must first understand what is common about those pinches. "'We' and 'our' exist only when the consequences of combined action are perceived and become an object of desire and effort" (178), and such perception requires "faculties of effectual observation, reflection and desire," habits "acquired under the influence of the culture and institutions of society, not ready-made inherent powers" (183).

This, for Dewey, is the role of education: to inculcate inquiry—Habermas's science—and distribute its conclusions. Such an education is deliberative: the "omnicompetent" citizen—not the citizen-expert, but the citizen-deliberator—is one who has a modicum of expertise as well as a sense of how to inquire after those issues about which he has less knowledge. What is needed "is the improvement of the methods and conditions of debate, discussion, and persuasion. . . . What is required is that [citizens] have the ability to judge of the bearing of knowledge supplied by others upon common concerns" (Dewey 225). And for Dewey, rhetoric was crucial to this formation. "Communication of the results of social inquiry" is what makes public opinion, not just the communication of the opinion itself. Public opinion, in a true, dynamic, and open public, is "judgment which is formed and entertained by those who constitute the public *and is about their public affairs*" (198–99, emphasis added). It takes account of the objects of knowledge, not just what we think about them. It is deliberative, and it is "scientific," in Habermas's terms, having a relative autonomy from the public itself.

This kind of deliberative education is what the rhetorician David Fleming means by "becoming rhetorical," the creation of civic subjects and the development, in Thomas Miller's terms, of a "critical awareness that established beliefs are mere conventions, and thus open to debate," and in which one masters "the dialectical process of drawing upon received beliefs to speak with public authority" (79–80). For Fleming, such a process of public inquiry is rhetorical in the sense used by Romans such as Quintilian, as a years-long course of study "guided by [the] language [of invention and public discourse] to acquire a practical capacity for such discourse, a faculty of civic life disciplined by deep-seated norms of effectiveness and virtue" (93). Though derived from the scientific disciplines in Habermas's scheme, rhetorical education would create the omnicompetent citizen whose attention to the social *implications* of the knowledge developed in disciplinary inquiry would recognize the complexity of those implications. It would create what Ellen Cushman calls a "metadiscursive dimension" that elaborates on "all disciplinary knowledge by considering how knowledge is made by whom, for whom, and for what ends" (180–81). Ultimately the aim of a rhetorical education is the "rule of justice," one that "allows [Perelman's] universal audience to judge the strength of arguments" (Crosswhite 306). In Perelman's theory of justice, the problem was finding a law that could be applied in all cases and across all strata of human affairs. After working for years to develop such a notion of justice, Perelman gave up, because there will always be the individual case, or a set of cases, for which the law's application would have the violent effect of casting out that which is nonnormative, that which doesn't fit the scheme.

This kind of inquiry—seeking the paradigmatic explanation that would render a phenomenon knowable and excluding instances that could not be handled by the paradigm—works perfectly well for the relatively autonomous sciences, but it worked less well for the creation of a public. Perelman opted instead for a notion of argumentation, of rhetoric, that goes beyond the model of the normative and the excluded, nonnormative case to one that binds the two by means of engagement with the other, consonant with the idea of ethics put forward by Emmanuel Levinas (an idea I return to shortly). James Crosswhite describes the idea of the *intervalle*, an indeterminacy or aporia in argument (see 275) that functions like a threshold, a passage from events to the understanding that the event can't be integrated or isn't integrable but that nonetheless calls for the event to be understood. The intervalle is what *calls for justice*, but it can only be understood by means of deliberation. The public can only *become* a public by means of inquiry, an inquiry that doesn't treat the sciences as autonomous but rather understands the creation of knowledge in the university, or anywhere else, as needing to be reintegrated into civic engagement of citizens so that they recognize how that knowledge pertains to their own situations and, in some cases, makes them susceptible to the others with whom they (seek to) make common cause. This is a rhetorical justice founded on *ethics*, which calls us to engage with others in a way that exceeds science, politics, law, policy, and institutions. It acknowledges that we are potentially vulnerable and that democracy has a tendency to exclude the exception. This is what Thomas Darwin means when he says that rhetoric, and a rhetorical education, is *relational*, evolving from and involving relationships between and among subjects who are thrown together in social relationships. Darwin points to P. Christopher Smith's translation of Aristotle, whose definition of rhetoric is the act of "'taking counsel from others' in dealing with situations that are 'susceptible to being otherwise'" (Darwin 25). Darwin sees in this translation a recognition that "the term *susceptible* reminds us that 'being otherwise' is inherent in any situation where we find rhetoric" (25), which, in Dewey's and Habermas's schemes, is pretty much everywhere, even in those relatively autonomous scientific fields of inquiry.

THE PUBLIC AND ITS PROBLEMS

It's in this relational understanding of the rhetorical force of higher education that one can begin to see a way to supplement the *idea* of the public with an acknowledgment that its *reality* is more complicated—and that public universities are more vulnerable—in its current conjuncture. Dewey recognizes the conditions—"secrecy, prejudice, bias, misrepresentation, and propaganda, as well as sheer ignorance" (226)—that make even the most active rhetorical project of public education tenuous. Habermas wonders whether, in the aporia between the idea of the university and the material realities of the neoliberal economy which—in Christopher Loss's terms—comes *between* the citizen and the state, it is possible to salvage the university as something other than one of Louis Althusser's ideological state apparatuses.

Habermas sees one avenue for this salvage operation in *communication*. If science—inquiry—is no longer enough to make the university an autonomous space for discovery and engagement, rhetoric might be. He writes that the university "contribute[s] to the general socialization processes by introducing students to the mode of scientific thinking, i.e., to the adoption of a hypothetical attitude vis-à-vis facts and norms" by "offering informed interpretations and diagnoses of contemporary events, and by taking concrete political stands" (Habermas 19–20). To bind together the idea of inquiry with the public good, he turns to Schleiermacher, who writes that "the first law of all efforts aimed at knowledge (is): *communication*" (qtd. in Habermas 20). It is "the communicative or discursive forms of scientific argumentation which in the final analysis hold the learning process together in their various functions," forms that involve "the stimulating and productive power of discursive disputes that carry the promissory note of generating surprising arguments" (21–22). But it must be a form of communication—of deliberation—that makes possible the recognition of what is not otherwise capable of being integrated into the public as well as the recognition of what is at the precarious edges of that public. It must also make possible those *surprises* that are not bound by the disciplines in which inquiry takes place and make visible the precarities of social life that are potentially exacerbated by those disciplinary orthodoxies.

The conditions of the university have changed drastically since the Cold War and particularly in the last forty years; the relative independence covetously protected by university faculty and the AAUP has given way to a more elastic relationship between faculty and the private knowledge industry. At the same time, the university's students and faculty have become more aware of how they are interpellated as citizens not just of the university but of their publics, their communities, and their nations, in a global culture that is highly mobile, crisscrossed by movement in the knowledge economy, and vastly more diverse than the relatively autonomous communities of inquiry in Dewey's or Habermas's schemes ever were or could be. "On the one side," writes sociologist of education Gerard Delanty, "it is the latest stage of capitalism in its postindustrial form that is a stage characterized by the predominance of the services, technology, and information. On the other side, the postmodern condition expresses a new kind of politics of plurality whereby political struggles take place on many different levels and cannot be concentrated in any one particular struggle, such as the class struggle" (134).

The tension between these two attitudes is made manifest by a toggling between them, a mobile or plural form of knowledge and knowledge making that stands in opposition to the economy of technocratic managerialism or simple expertise. Like Habermas and Dewey, Delanty sees the function of the university as being "unified" through a kind of communication. Citing Zygmunt Bauman, he notes that the university is no longer a privileged site of knowledge production so much as it is a site of difference and diversity. "According to Bauman, the plurality and multivocality of universities is something liberating and could be the basis of new dialogues" (Delanty 136). The role of the university becomes reflexive, where "cognitive processes," Dewey's inquiry, "not only produce knowledge as content but also give rise to new cognitive structures and identities, a deeper and more far-reaching epistemic shift in horizons" (152). Communication and deliberation, on these terms, are "not merely the transmission of an established body of knowledge" but "the inclusion of as many voices as possible in the construction of knowledge" which is "more creative and experimental," "more responsive to the transformations of cultural models" (154–55). In such a university, the citizens produced are global, technological, and mobile. "In an age characterized by the mobility of capital, labour, communication, food and images, new kinds of rights will emerge which cannot be organized around the centrality of states and national identities" (157) and which can only be mobilized in universities. For Delanty, the idea of the university is to challenge citizens to confront the precarities of the global economy with self-reflexive and deeply critical, and plural, methodologies that form the very ground of the struggles made necessary by the vagaries of the neoliberal economy.

Part of Delanty's argument about the twenty-first-century university is that its publics are constantly shifting and radically mobile. The notion that publics are constantly on the move is consistent with Michael Walzer's claims about the tension in the contemporary public between its associative and dissociative tendencies and about the "profoundly unsettled society" in which we now live (148). And it's consistent, too, with Clark Kerr's and Bill Bowen's assessment that the contemporary university (the "multiversity" in Kerr's terms) has become "fractionalized" and more "pluralistic" even as the value of expertise—often demonized by the public—continues to exert itself (Kerr 32, 27). The capacity for knowledge making, according to Delanty, isn't to stabilize those shifts but to self-reflexively unmoor those stabilities to see what instability yields. The movement causes a shift in the subject, from a member of a relatively stable public sphere to one that is itself constantly on the move. This idea is not unlike that of the Deleuzian *singularity*, the sense that there isn't a single subject whose sense-impressions are synthesized into wholes but a nexus of motion, a radically heterogenous mélange of sense-impressions that, taken together and in its moment, forms a person. Bill Readings's book *The University in Ruins* defines the singularity as "a *minimal node of specificity*" that "offers us a way of discussing the contradictory and multiple ways in which relations of desire (for commodities and other things), power, and knowledge flow among individuals, without having to presume that there is a stable, natural, or logical order of such relations that we have lost and to which we should return" (116).

This idea of communication and deliberative subjects provides an alternative to the ideas of Dewey and Habermas. For them it's through the deliberation of experts that we will at least temporarily stabilize, if not ameliorate, the inequities that rule some out of the court of expertise or, worse, civil society. But what Readings has in mind is "not transparent," and the community is one "in which the possibility of communication is not grounded upon and reinforced by a common cultural identity" but in which that communication takes place in a "network of obligations in which an individual," as singularity, "is not entirely available to the subjective consciousness of that individual, so that we can never pay all our debts" (185–86). This is not to say that disciplinary expertise is jettisoned in favor of those minimal modes of specificity; the creation of new knowledge via expertise is—despite its precarity in a post-truth knowledge economy—a bedrock principle for higher education. It *is* to say that disciplinary expertise must make room for the radically singular, the event that is unconstrained and unmediated by discipline and that requires some other approach to "paying our debts." To be responsible to those others, as singular, is also to be vulnerable to those others; it doesn't involve a contract whose underpinning is freedom of volition or autonomy. In this view, both the university and the public which it purportedly serves are what Giorgio Agamben called "whatever" communities (see *The Coming Community* 1–4), "where the social bond is characterized . . . not as obligation but as *transience*, the solidarity of those who have nothing in common but who are aggregated together by the state of things" (186–87). In this community, what is sought is heteronomy, difference, complexity; we are dependent on one another, not free with or from one another. This is a *rhetorical* community in the sense that it "holds open the question of whether and how thoughts fit together" (191), a community that—like rhetoric—is *transdisciplinary* in the sense that Thomas Darwin suggests, where we are *susceptible* to other ways of thinking, and vulnerable to their effect on us, as singular members of a "whatever" and singular community.

RHETORIC AS MOBILE, VULNERABLE, AND ETHICAL

What would "becoming rhetorical" in this sense mean, and what are its implications for faculty work at public universities? As I've endeavored to show over the previous chapters, I believe that the sense of rhetoric as reasonable, deliberative, tending inexorably if sometimes intermittently toward the good, and in service to a relatively fixed sense of the public or of the demos, is valuable but limiting. We need to recuperate an understanding of rhetoric that is more consistent with the contours of the neoliberal economy and public sphere (if it can be called that), one that is also mobile, that recognizes the vulnerabilities inherent in the human subject and in the communities in which those subjects reside, that understands the ethical urgencies required to address and to ameliorate those precarities when possible, and that accepts the implications of the vulnerabilities inherent in communities and institutions while nonetheless obeying the urgent call to respond to those inequities, injustices, and situational violence that vulnerability sometimes implies.

Rhetoric's relation to movement, particularly the movement of the body in relation to others and to the built environment, has been with us for some time, as Debra Hawhee—in her books *Bodily Arts* and more recently *Moving Bodies*—has made clear. In the latter book, Hawhee examines the writing of Kenneth Burke, whose "sense of mobility and change . . . is crucial for viewing materiality as not holding still even when stasis seems to prevail" (166). For Burke it wasn't just that there was a relation between bodily movement (as in the training rhetors received in, say, delivery) and the capacity of rhetoric to move listeners but also that language consists of "matter/energy in constant motion, taking on shifting forms through shifting relationships" (Condit 332). Mobility characterized by what the body does in relation to other bodies (or what objects do in relation to other objects) in space (motion) and mobility characterized as a capacity inherent in human subjectivity and serving as an engine for the rhetorical enterprise (action) were for Burke held uncomfortably together. They are "irreducibly distinct and yet parallel and complementary, mediated by sensation and attitude—at times undermining, at others duplicating each other, but often, if not always, in effect moving together" (Hawhee, *Moving Bodies* 166). In setting the terms *action* and *motion* together as an irreducible polarity, Burke implicitly called into question whether the outside/inside distinction—matter's motion, humans' action, motion external to us and action internal—holds up. This question has important implications for how we think of rhetoric's role in mobility and in higher education.

I've already noted the usefulness of Alessandra Von Burg's term *stochastic citizenship* because it points to how mobility, understood as a force, calls into question the distinction between exterior and interior, between the material circumstances that cause people to move and what movement is inherent, *in potentia*, and might be made more visible by rhetorical means. Nathan Stormer makes a similar case: mobility is the potential to be otherwise, aligned with what the Greeks called *physis*, "a strange and crucial potential for inconstancy, . . . the expression of vitality, the changes that unfinished, distinct entities are impelled and/or compelled to undergo" (2). Mobility on these terms serves as a "condition of betweenness that isn't physically measurable" (1). As a state of impermanence rather than a characteristic of objects or persons involving a movement of to-and-fro rather than across or toward another or an object, it results in a kind of epistemological homelessness that nonetheless serves as a way to mobilize the precarious location between the public space of the law and the lonelier space outside it.

What's also valuable about the term *stochastic citizenship* is that it stresses that we are all "others"; rather than considering ourselves—in Vico's theory of jurisprudence—members of either the *civis* (citizens, the home-born) or the *hostis* (the stranger, passerby, or noncitizen), we are all to a significant degree also *hostes*, thrown into a world of random movement, and we ourselves are not fixed but also in constant motion, not just from one place to another but also as beings in flux ("inconstancy"). The stochastic also brings some risks. It would be ideal if recognizing ourselves and our fellows as others or *hostes* would consistently encourage us to deal justly with one another and if, to the extent that mobility involves flux and inconstancy, we could nonetheless recognize instances where one could make common cause. But this would ignore the real extent to which mobility, the capacity to be other, is also problematic. As I've noted, in higher education this movement is often linked to the "precariat," those working in academia (lecturers, assistant professors, faculty members from historically underrepresented groups) who live in a state of impermanence and vulnerability rather than a site of potentiality.

What Judith Butler writes about the precarity of social life in "Violence, Mourning, Politics" accurately represents, I think, the circumstances of the mobile subject, buffeted by the material forces at play and the other others with whom the subject comes into contact: we are "undone by each other" (13). As I've argued, mobility involves a constitutive vulnerability in which we are always already in relation to others. That relation has far more to do with the interstices between self and other; as bodies in motion, we are always implicated in lives that aren't our own and that move whether we want them to or not (Butler 17). There's an intimate relation between mobility and being vulnerable: being in relation (and, as a result, being in motion) involves mutuality, a constantly changing interplay of forces—the stasis between polis and oikos, the threshold between action and motion—that leaves us open, as pure potential, and capable of being other; we, and the institutions in which we work, are constantly susceptible to being undone, of (in Butler's terms) losing ourselves, of becoming other.

As Butler has made clear (in *Excitable Speech*), the vulnerability of being addressed and the mobility (or maybe rootlessness) implicated by it carries with it an ethical and political responsibility, the first of which involves recognition: recognition of the other with whom one is implicated and the vulnerable circumstances in which that recognition is made possible. It has the capacity to unsettle us and our disciplinary and institutional conventions, and it also demands the invention of ameliorative measures that reorganize those institutional spaces and norms. But mutual recognition doesn't just happen. One could argue that in the current configuration of higher education, in which tenure and shared governance (which by design attempt to normalize intellectual mobility and mutuality) are threatened, it's easy to understand the tendency for academics to do everything they can to protect tenure and shared governance. It's possible, in other words, that the potential violence of rhetoric, and the constitutive vulnerability that accompanies it, may be misrecognized in the context of a logic that prizes disciplinarity, methodological consistency, and a system of merit, rank, and power. But if we take Petherbridge's point about vulnerability, then rhetorical work—in addition to the work it does to invent paradigms by which expert knowledge is recognizable to its practitioners and its publics—also has a critical dimension that identifies situational vulnerabilities. It has the capacity to (in Nichols's terms) rediscover how those paradigms—and the policies, social contracts, orthodoxies and assumptions—sometimes stand in the way of mutuality and justice through paralysis, academic disenfranchisement, and institutional homelessness. The aim of deliberation, then, is not only to provide institutions ways to recognize these risks but also to reconfigure them by first problematizing the logics in which they are seen not as risks but simply as "the new university" and then reinscribing them as opening new modes of action.

The vulnerability inherent in a rhetoric that's mobile and open carries with it an ethical urgency, one that often enough works against constitutions, policies, and—more generally—politics. As I've noted in earlier chapters, that urgency understands subjects not as givens interrupted by the presence of others but as *constituted by* the interaction with others. It functions like a command that we engage with individuals, from one moment to the next, without regard to the singularity of names, to the limit of the possible. Such encounters make visible the limits of knowledge precisely because "concepts suppose an anticipation, a horizon within which alterity is amortized as soon as it is announced precisely because it has let itself be foreseen" (Derrida, "Violence and Metaphysics" 95). This urgency requires that "there is no circumstance under which we could declare that" human situations of precarity, or of violence, or of injustice, "[are] not our concern" (Campbell 35).

Acting in the context of justice gives "content" to what we do—meanings can be assigned to our actions by our neighbors despite whatever meaning or meaninglessness we ourselves assign. That content must always be acted on in its turn ethically. But ethics and politics occur in the same act toward one individual at a time, knowing—given the presence of the third, the neighbor—that we reside in a community of other individuals whom we can't see at the moment but on whom our action may have a palpable effect. The risk is always that politics—the concern for other others, or for the institution, or for the public—subsumes the engagement with the other in the name of the community, the institution, or the state. The name—the "we" of department or college or university, let alone of race or of intellectual class or discipline—produces the sense of an origin, and what doesn't originate from it is a surplus that must be consumed. But with ethical urgency, *all* action produces a surplus, and the danger to action is a politics that reduces that action to a repetition of the same. Justice is necessary because it continually interrupts the tendency toward unbending orthodoxy or disciplinary intransigence. So the way to engage with others in institutions—to obey the urgency of the ethical in the context of policy, the urgency of other others—is to acknowledge the hiatus between ethics and politics.

As I noted earlier, Giorgio Agamben attempts to work out a notion of human activity that serves as a capacity, an engine for ethical action in a world characterized by flux and potential. He calls this kind of activity "destituent," constituting

> a threshold of indifference between the *oikos* and the *polis*, between blood kinship and citizenship. . . . In transgressing this threshold, the *oikos* is politicized, conversely, the *polis* is "economised," that is, it is reduced to an *oikos*. *This means that in the system of Greek politics civil war functions as a threshold of politicization and depoliticization, through which the house is exceeded in the city and the city is depoliticized in the family.* (Stasis 15, 16)

In Agamben's formulation, stasis marks a zone of indetermination between oikos and polis, between the obligations of the local (to, say, discipline or methodology, or department, or college) and the broader responsibility to the larger community, the public. It is, like the tension between ethics and politics, a threshold between one's responsibilities to those we know and to those we don't. With Aristotle, Agamben asks whether—in the threshold—there is a proper work (ergon) for the human person or whether the human person isn't instead argos, without work, inoperative. Agamben believes the latter: that at the point of hiatus, at the threshold between oikos and polis, the human being is a potentiality that exposes the subject, puts the subject into question, because it "free[s] the living being from every biological or social destiny and from every predetermined task, renders it open for that particular absence of work that we are accustomed to calling 'politics' and 'art'" (17). This mobility is intense, troubling, and potentially deterritorializing.

Thus, the mobility inherent in the capacity that founds deliberation, and that—as stasis—is a kind of internal "civil war" through which the subject becomes other, poses a challenge to institutions because it cannot be contained by the natural law (*physis*), let alone by the polis or the oikos. It exceeds the conventions and constraints we understand to govern our contexts, serving as a mobility—a nondirected and chaotic movement—that has the capacity to hold open the possibility that teacher-scholars toiling in the rhetorical vineyards of higher education might yet transform it because of mobility's unwillingness or inability to abide constraints (of disciplinary convention or of institutional orthodoxies).

THE RHETORICAL IMPLICATIONS FOR FACULTY WORK

There are a number of implications of a rhetorical or deliberative approach to faculty work at public universities that understand work as mobile and inherently vulnerable: for the notion of academic freedom and free speech (and its implications for tenure); for shared governance and the usefulness of policy; for the notion of academic disciplinarity and expertise; and for the precarities inherent in institutional membership or lack thereof. These implications are particularly urgent at a time when the public university faces threats from state legislatures, from its publics, and from its own unwillingness to recognize the vulnerabilities to which faculty members are susceptible as members of an institution that relies on policy, constitution, and the law to the exclusion of the critical examination of the lived lives of those who work and live in their communities. The external threats take the form of legislation that curbs the rights of faculty and staff in shared governance, erodes the protections of tenure designed to protect academic freedom to pursue research wherever it leads, and, most recently, requires universities to recuse themselves from taking positions on "public controversies" while also requiring them to be called to account in readying citizens to enter the marketplace. The internal ones take the form of a faculty gradually ceding its power in governance to deans, presidents, and boards because of a sense that their time in the lab, in the classroom, and in the archive must be preserved. They include a disdain or distrust of the public—Lippman's commuters reading their newspapers on the train, whose own skepticism of disciplinary specialization and expertise has diminished their trust in the value of a liberal arts education—and the maintenance of the disciplinary cleavages that define the internal intellectual structure of the university in the face of the centrifugal forces faced by those disciplines. And they include the hewing to policy—on matters such as faculty rights and responsibilities or the attempts to diversify their faculties and disciplines in order to achieve a more truly ethical institution in which engagement is not understood merely as a "working together" nor deliberation as "thinking together"—in cases where it might be better to engage critically and vigorously with those who are experiencing precarity.

These trends are not sporadic; rather, they represent the culmination of a cultural shift not only in how the general public understands the value of higher education but also—and, for the purposes of this project, most importantly—how those who work in its laboratories, libraries, and classrooms see *themselves*. In their book on university shared governance, William Bowen and Eugene Tobin trace this shift to the late 1960s and 1970s. While the Second World War and the women's and civil rights movements threw open the doors of higher education to a far greater number of students, they also led to an unprecedented boom in funded research. That boom, Bowen and Tobin write, made the disciplinary expertise necessary for such research to be even more sharply distinguished and gave faculty researchers more reason to pay greater attention to their projects and to gravitate away from the responsibilities of shared governance. Coupled with the economic transition in the US away from manufacturing and the aging of the population—forcing states to shift more of their funding from universities and toward other priorities—these trends have led legislatures to see universities as engines of economic growth, rather than as laboratories for young people to learn how to engage civically, and to question what they see as the esoteric (funded) research conducted by university faculty. These trends have worked actively to wrest control of the institution away from the atomized faculty through the erosion of tenure protections and shared governance (see Bowen and Tobin, esp. 99–112). Arguments about the value of a liberal arts education, let alone a rhetorical one—in, say, the mold of Isocrates or in Fleming's terms of becoming rhetorical—as practical, civic training, or as a mode of political thought, or as a critical "equipment for living" don't always work in the face of the economic and social shifts that have led to seeing higher education as a ticket into the service economy. The problem, though, isn't so much that the ground of public higher education is shifting; we've known that for a while now. The problem is that faculty members themselves haven't figured out how to contend with those shifts, how to describe them *among themselves* let alone to others (including legislators, university presidents, or their families). Timothy Barouch and Brett Ommen have diagnosed the problem clearly: in the face of critiques of liberalism offered by rhetorical scholars and their calls for a return to a civic culture that may well no longer exist, we still make use of the same commonplaces—of democracy, shared governance, the autonomy of experts, the public good—to describe what we do but forget that those commonplaces don't stand in for our material circumstances the same way they did forty years ago. They write that we might be better off "not only . . . seeing the shortcomings of liberal public culture, but . . . [finding ways to make] a life within it" (161). They have, with Walzer, diagnosed the problem with the public only hinted at by Habermas and Dewey: that the postmodern and neoliberal public is constituted by singularities, if not atomized individuals, that are constantly moving. Because they are mobile but also constitutively vulnerable, they are also susceptible to situational vulnerabilities that can only be identified by means of critical engagement that goes beyond the bounds of either reason (deliberation) or the methodologies that discipline inquiry. Institutions like the public research university are not static, even inasmuch as writers like Kerr and Bowen and Tobin see the goals of governance and of the administration of university policy as maintaining stability required so that faculty members' work in the classroom and the lab can take place. Institutions have "routines, procedures, conventions, roles, strategies, organizational forms, and technologies" (March and Olsen 22), but they are routines, conventions and strategies that change over time, and they only become recognized *as* institutions by becoming interiorized by those that work in them. We think of institutions as stable only because we are so much in them that the sound of that complexity becomes inaudible against background noise (see Ahmed, *On Being Included* 21).

Becoming rhetorical in the way I've described it above provides a way for faculty to resist the "perpetual structural constraint" of higher education's paradigms, in part by eschewing the liberal characterizations of the university in favor of a rhetorical education that, as Barouch and Ommen might call it, contends directly with "the manner in which its citizens experience life as perpetually *unsettled*" and in which "'being unsettled' [is not] necessarily a bad thing" (172). It's an education that comes with a "'certain level of structural ambiguity' in order to subvert the territorial and bureaucratically resistant characteristics of the university" (173). In order to do so, the faculty member doesn't have to completely abandon the static idea of institution, or discipline, or public, but they will have to augment that idea with the one, from Deleuze and Guattari, that I alluded to in the fourth chapter: nomadism. They describe nomadism as a power, a movement having the capacity for upheaval, for radical change, that isn't ultimately tied or susceptible to the organs of the state. Nomad science doesn't involve theory and practice, hypotheses and conclusion; rather, it is *problematic,* which is to say it is affective, "inseparable from the metamorphoses, generations, and creations within science itself" and develops "eccentrically" (362). Because it deals in singularities rather than universals, "one is obliged to follow when one is in search of [those] singularities of a matter, or rather of a material, and not out to discover a form" (372). Because of its mobility, Deleuze and Guattari characterize this epistemological model as "ambulant." What's important to understand here is that, not unlike the relation, in Kuhn, between normal and abnormal science—in which the latter serves to put the former into question, to describe the inconsistencies and oddities unaccounted for in any paradigm—the ambulant resides *alongside* normal (or royal) science. Expertise and its attendant cultures—disciplinary methodologies, agreed-upon identities, the mechanisms of funding, the policies and practices of scholarship and shared governance—continue apace. But as I've suggested throughout this project, there is a tendency latent in the movements of expertise and faculty work more generally that is stochastic, alloiostrophic, and that moves apart from and against the channeled discussions about policy and problem-solving. In Deleuze and Guattari's model, the ambulant resides *within* and functions coincidentally *with* royal or normal science.

Like Agamben's destituent power (stasis), nomadic mobility is characterized by "a body whose irreducible parts (atoms) occupy or fill a smooth space in the manner of a vortex, with the possibility of springing up at any point.... Nomads have absolute movement, in other words, speed; vertical or swirling movement is [their] essential feature" (381). And like stasis—which in Athens referred to the ambivalence between one's domestic and political affiliations—nomadism doesn't so much refer to the side one comes down on as it does Deleuze and Guattari's "in-between [which] has taken on all the consistency and enjoys both an autonomy and a direction of its own" (380). The faculty member as nomad scientist would also need to understand that the vulnerability afforded by the aporias opened by rhetoric also makes the scholars themselves vulnerable, susceptible to deterritorialization—to undoing—and hence to the possibility that tenure will not protect them from the mobility inherent in their own method. One would need to acknowledge rhetoric's mobility as simultaneously *undoing* its own sense of institutional stability (and of faculty members'—and academic disciplines'—place) at the same time as it provides the material for scholarly work itself. One must also recognize the potential force or power that comes from that vulnerability. This might be difficult for some faculty members to recognize. I would argue, though, that on Petherbridge's account of the critical impulse inherent in vulnerability, it is necessary to recognize the *situational* vulnerability and the real damage being done to higher education in the status quo.

To become rhetorical, faculty would need to deploy the critical dimension of vulnerability described by Petherbridge as an eccentric force on the institutional terrain that they navigate. Rhetoric, then, is a *techne* that just as often suspends direction as it provides the (methodological and policy) material for Kerr's stability. On these terms, the *freedom* (at the root of the terms "freedom of speech" and "academic freedom") is—as I noted earlier in chapter 3—the "alarming possibility of being able," a fear and a vulnerability that results from the recognition that going without destination is breathtaking. To characterize freedom in these terms—as a mobility-without-destination, the eventalization that Nichols describes as acting as a breach or rupture of paradigms beyond the encumbrances of paradigms and ideologies—recasts *academic* freedom as a "potential for inconstancy" that has the capacity to radically call into question fields and methods. Like academic freedom, this kind of mobility ensures a constant engagement with the "more," the eventalization that bogs down modes of thought and notions of identity that so often help us define the academic silos in which we do our work, in both positive and negative ways. (Academic) freedom may provide the stability of the academic (and rhetorical) enterprise that allows departments and disciplines to survive. But it is also an engine that forces them to constantly shift, and it provides the methodology—which isn't really a methodology—that would allow (rhetorical) scholars who work within fields, departments, and institutions to constantly put into question that intellectual and academic ground. And unlike academic freedom, it requires faculty members (as itinerant) to be themselves at times deterritorialized, and it's a deterritorialization that could effectively make institutions such as shared governance and tenure unrecognizable, in turn making a reformulation of them inevitable. As faculty members we are *situationally* vulnerable in institutions whose funding is consistently slashed, where our governance and intellectual rights are threatened, and where our own impoverished notions of diversity bound by law and policy prevent us from critically engaging with the precarities experienced by faculty of color and members of other historically underrepresented communities. It's crucially important to recognize that faculty members, as truly mobile, deploy that mobility as critical engagement—in Dewey's terms, as inquiry—that recognizes the contours of our *constitutive* vulnerability as exacerbated by our participation in an institution that is *designed* to preserve stability. Inquiry, as mobile, helps us see what, in the institution, needs to be unsettled. And that vulnerability also carries with it a force and a power that provides an alternative to fixities residing in those institutions and methodologies.

Becoming rhetorical also calls into question a notion of shared governance that relies on the distribution of power across groups for the purposes of deliberation. Ideally the deliberation that takes place in universities involves the sharing of power and a curb on administrative (or legislative) fiat to ensure the proper direction of the institution. But if Walzer is right, and the contemporary moment is characterized more obviously by solitary and random motion—mobility par excellence—then not only is the deliberation involved in shared governance far less stable and teleologically oriented than we think; it is also a relationality in which those who engage in it are also constitutively vulnerable. To protect shared governance against the predations of a penurious legislature provides no guarantee that the will of the faculty will prevail; for faculty to be *inoperative* means that there are no necessary lanes or spheres of responsibility to which they are delimited, despite the AAUP's guidance. Residing at the threshold of the oikos and the polis—astride disciplines and institutions on the one hand and the public on the other—they are responsible to both, and they are in constant motion. And this is what frustrates deans, provosts, and boards: faculty itinerancy—the capacity for Stormer's "more"—isn't the same as autonomy by dint of expertise but is, instead, a kind of at-large capacity in which faculty members' sphere of influence and authority is both everywhere and constant. This shift will require us to consider alternative forms of governance that preserve constitutive vulnerability's critical dimension.

And it also will require forms of solidarity that aren't only vertical—that aren't based on faculty members' transdisciplinary reorganization of our work, work that may not look like Michael Crow's superimposition of flat multidisciplinary "centers" over the more vertical departmental and school and college units that retain the conventional distinctions that are demanded by the institutional and broader marketplace. It also requires a relationality and an engagement with those whose experience with institutional precarities creates more pronounced, and potentially more violent, dispossessions than those experienced by faculty. These solidarities look more like the ones described by Harney and Moten as an undercommons, institutional zones of "unregulated wildness" created by those vertical organizational structures. These zones aren't departments and colleges or disciplinary conventions and methodologies but rather connections based on experiences of marginalization, exclusion, microaggression, and willed and unwilled ignorance, connections between those who run and do research in the laboratories and pursue independent or collective research and teaching; those who are not on the tenure track; and those who clean the equipment, care for the animals, empty the trash, mow the lawns, and care for students in the dorms and the kitchens. In these zones, there exists "a radical passion . . . such that one becomes unfit for subjection, because one does not possess the kind of agency that can hold the regulatory forces of subjecthood" (Harney and Moten 28). It would be a solidarity reliant not only on collective bargaining agreements, or on forms of shared governance, but also on the assembly of bodies, bodies that are persistent despite policy and constitutions, that in Butler's terms insist on "their continuing and collective 'thereness'" and, in such formations, "organiz[e] themselves without hierarchy." They thus present themselves as forms that are not so much political—that is, as forms that aim toward a public good—as ethical, based on the unequal distribution of vulnerability and that make claims on the institution to ameliorate those situational vulnerabilities by experiencing the presence of those at the margins (see Puar et al. 167–70).

Considering rhetoric's mobility as an *exteriority*, in particular an exteriority to political ideology, institutional fixity, and intellectual paradigms of thought, provides a productive way for faculty members to emerge from the current dilemma in which they—we—find ourselves. The mobility of thought that characterizes a rhetorical project suggests that what goes on at universities like ours can be thought of as a kind of exteriority that can at times challenge "the stable, the eternal, the identical, the constant" that serves as the ideological foundation of a stable public. This is true not only of units in the humanities and qualitative social sciences—represented by units such as the Center on Poverty, Work and Opportunity at the University of North Carolina and the Center for Investigative Journalism at the University of Wisconsin–Madison, both of which were threatened with closure through legislative action in 2015 and 2013, respectively. It's true also of research in the sciences that overturns scientific and political orthodoxies (as with the case of fetal tissue research, which the Wisconsin legislature has attempted to prohibit by introducing bills outlawing the practice) and that follows the implications of the evidence through problematizing ideological and scientific conventions. What's troubling about the mobile dimension of rhetoric described by Burke or Agamben is that it helps us understand reality, and the reality of publicity, as *flux* (Deleuze and Guattari call it "eccentric") and that the mode of thought associated with mobility is the *problem* rather than the *theorem,* the problem which belongs less to the rational order or the public good than to the affective, the metamorphic, the generational and creative. But the other side of the potential to be otherwise is that the faculty member *moves,* is itinerant, and carries with them that movement.

If intellectuals are mobile, then we are not, by definition, wedded to any particular institution or mode of thought and *should be prepared to move.* This is why the protections of tenure are necessary if not sufficient. Tenure is necessary because it protects us to do our work eccentrically. But it's not sufficient if it too closely binds us to methodological orthodoxies or to departmental anchors, to laws of equal opportunity that often stand in the way of making a place in our institutions for those traditionally marginalized; it's not sufficient because it prevents us from understanding that there is no proper work (ergon) for the truly mobile scholar and, as such, no necessary location—department, school, college, or university—from which that work gets done. Those protections must be coupled with Butler's point about vulnerability: if mobility renders the scholar truly stochastic, and if the liberal context in which our work is done is characterized by similarly random, eccentric movement, then our mutual openness to one another renders us susceptible to relations of power regardless of whether they come from the legislature, the president's office, or the dynamics of methodological orthodoxies or the sometimes-cruel institutional politics at the unit level. Tenure isn't a guarantee of fixity, because it simply cannot protect us against the aporias inherent in deliberation, let alone the political economy of higher education. But if we take Petherbridge's understanding of vulnerability as a basis of mutual recognition of others (and of ourselves as becoming-other), tenure is a contract that guards against the situational vulnerability of due-process violations, discrimination, and bias. It doesn't make us invulnerable so much as it prevents *abuses* of vulnerability, knowing full well that intellectual itinerance may be misrecognized as arrogance, disrespect of traditions and norms, or political unorthodoxy. Tenure doesn't eliminate precarity; reconfiguring tenure may go so far as to provide a way to negotiate the conditions of work for academics and others in the institution who, tenured or not, are in a vulnerable position, even when that vulnerability is expressed unevenly.

There's a way to read the action of legislatures, and the opinions about higher education held by the public, with regard to universities as attempts to render them immobile and to arrest their development—to prevent the dissemination of forms of knowledge that don't conform to certain political or intellectual ideologies and to bring institutions under the closer surveillance of the state by, for example, constraining the spheres of influence of the faculty, staff, and students in shared governance by rendering their policymaking actions merely advisory (and, in the language of legislation, "subordinate") to the chancellor and the board of regents or by finding ways around tenure protections. Those actions are attempts to bring mobility to heel by forcing it—in Agamben's terms—to reside only in either the polis, the realm of the state, or the realm of pure interiority. But rhetoric, seen as a capacity to speak founded on a mobility that resonates rather than moves from here to there, is an *opening* of experience. If rhetoric is central to the enterprise of higher education and functions as a kind of threshold between interiority and the polis that is characterized by an intense mobility that oscillates rather than moves, it leads both to vulnerability and to inoperativity. If we faculty members take our roles as rhetoricians seriously, and if we understand rhetoric to be underwritten by the sense of vulnerability and the potential force of mobility laid out here, we may be able to engage with the threats to higher education without resorting to the old-fashioned language of public goods and civic duty and instead by invoking the language of the destituent, the inconstant, and the *more* that owns up to the deterritorializing capacity of the work that faculty members do.

WORKS CITED

Agamben, Giorgio. *The Coming Community.* Translated by Michael Hardt, U of Minnesota P, 1993.

———. "Elements for a Theory of Destituent Power." Translated by Stephanie Wakefield, 2013, https://livingtogetherintheheartofthedesert.files.wordpress.com/2014/02/agamben-elements-for-a-theory-of-destituent-power-1.pdf.

———. *Stasis: Civil War as a Political Paradigm.* Translated by Nicholas Heron, Stanford UP, 2015.

AAUP (American Association of University Professors). "1915 Declaration of Principles on Academic Freedom and Academic Tenure." *AAUP Policy Documents and Reports,* 10th ed., AAUP and Johns Hopkins UP, 2006, pp. 291–301.

———. "1940 Statement of Principles." *AAUP Policy Documents and Reports,* 10th ed., AAUP and Johns Hopkins UP, 2006, pp. 3–11.

———. "On Institutional Problems Resulting from Financial Exigency: Some Operating Guidelines." *AAUP Policy Documents and Reports,* 10th ed., AAUP and Johns Hopkins UP, 2006, pp. 147–48.

———. "Post-Tenure Review: An AAUP Response." *AAUP Policy Documents and Reports,* 10th ed., AAUP and Johns Hopkins UP, 2006, pp. 60–66.

———. "Statement on Government of Colleges and Universities." *AAUP Policy Documents and Reports,* 10th ed., AAUP and Johns Hopkins UP, 2006, pp. 135–40.

———. "Statement on Professional Ethics." *AAUP Policy Documents and Reports,* 10th ed., AAUP and Johns Hopkins UP, 2006, pp. 171–72.

AAUP Committee A. "Statement on Extramural Utterances." *AAUP Policy Documents and Reports,* AAUP and Johns Hopkins UP, 2006, p. 32.

"Affirmative Action Pledged on Berkeley Campus." *New York Times,* 11 Sept. 1983, https://www.nytimes.com/1983/09/11/us/affirmative-action-pledged-on-berkeley-campus.html.

Ahmed, Sara. *On Being Included: Racism and Diversity in Institutional Life.* U of North Carolina P, 2012.

———. *Willful Subjects*. Duke UP, 2014.

Alex-Assenoh, Yvette M. "IDEAL: Our Roadmap for a Fully-Inclusive and Resilient Campus." University of Oregon, 20 Nov. 2020, https://inclusion.uoregon.edu/ideal-our-roadmap-fully-inclusive-and-resilient-campus.

Alger, Jonathan. "When Color-Blind Is Color-Bland: Ensuring Faculty Diversity in Higher Education." *Stanford Law & Policy Review*, vol. 10, no. 2 (Spring 1999), pp. 191–204.

Anderson, Virginia. "Antithetical Ethics: Kenneth Burke and the Constitution." *JAC*, vol. 15, no. 2 (1995), pp. 261–79.

Areen, Judith. "Government as Educator: A New Understanding of First Amendment Protection of Academic Freedom and Governance." *Georgetown Law Journal*, vol. 97 (April 2009), pp. 945–1,000.

Bahls, Steven C. "From Shared Governance to Shared Accountability." *Shared Governance in Higher Education: New Paradigms, Evolving Perspectives*, edited by Sharon F. Cramer, vol. 2, State U of New York P, 2017, pp. 83–120.

Bakke (*University of California Regents v. Bakke*). 1978. https://caselaw.findlaw.com/us-supreme-court/438/265.html.

Barouch, Timothy, and Brett Ommen. "The Constrained Liberty of the Liberal Arts and Rhetorical Education." *Rhetoric Society Quarterly*, vol. 47, no. 2 (2017), pp. 158–79.

Barrett, Minna S., and Duncan Quarless. "Engaging and Keeping Faculty and Students in Governance." *Shared Governance in Higher Education: Demands, Transitions, Transformations*, edited by Sharon F. Cramer, vol. 1, State U of New York P, 2017, pp. 41–68.

Ben-Porath, Sigal R. *Free Speech on Campus*. U of Pennsylvania P, 2017.

Benjamin, Walter. "A Critique of Violence." *Reflections: Essays, Aphorisms, Autobiographical Writings*, edited by Peter Demetz, translated by Edmund Jephcott, Schocken, 1986, pp. 277–300.

Bernard-Donals, Michael. "Divine Cruelty and Rhetorical Violence." *Philosophy and Rhetoric*, vol. 47, no. 4 (2014), pp. 400–418.

Borher, Becky. "Alaska's Governor Makes Unprecedented Cuts in State University Spending." *Los Angeles Times*, 6 July 2019, https://www.latimes.com/nation/la-na-alaska-university-financial-brink-20190706-story.html.

Bourdieu, Pierre. *Outline of a Theory of Practice*. Cambridge UP, 1977.

Bowen, William G., and Eugene M. Tobin. *Locus of Authority: The Evolution of Faculty Roles in the Governance of Higher Education*. Princeton UP, 2015.

Braidotti, Rosi. *Nomadic Subjects: Embodiment and Sexual Difference in Contemporary Feminist Theory*. Columbia UP, 2011.

Brew, Angela. "Disciplinary and Interdisciplinary Affiliations of Experienced Researchers." *Higher Education*, vol. 56 (2008), pp. 423–38.

Bridges, David. "The Disciplines and the Discipline of Educational Research." *Journal of Philosophy of Education*, vol. 40, no. 2 (2006), pp. 259–72.

Brint, Steven. *In an Age of Experts: The Changing Role of Professionals in Politics and Public Life*. Princeton UP, 1994.

Brown, Mark B. *Science in Democracy: Expertise, Institutions, and Representation*. Massachusetts Institute of Technology P, 2009.

Bulman, Drew. "Arranged Marriage: Rastetter Appoints Harreld to UI Presidency, Faculty Say, 'I Object!'" *Little Village Magazine*, 17 Sept. 2015, https://littlevillagemag.com/arranged-marriage-rastetter-appoints-harreld-to-ui-presidency-faculty-say-i-object/.

Burke, Kenneth. *A Grammar of Motives*. U of California P, 1965.

———. *The Philosophy of Literary Form.* U of California P, 1973.

Butler, Judith. "Academic Norms, Contemporary Challenges: A Reply to Robert Post on Academic Freedom." *Academic Freedom after September 11*, edited by Beshara Doumari, Zone, 2006, pp. 107–42.

———. *Excitable Speech: A Politics of the Performative.* Routledge, 1997.

———. "Rethinking Vulnerability and Resistance." *Vulnerability in Resistance*, edited by Judith Butler et al., Duke UP, 2016, pp. 12–27.

———. "Violence, Mourning, Politics." *Studies in Gender and Sexuality*, vol. 4, no. 1 (2003), pp. 9–37.

CAFT (Committee on Academic Freedom and Tenure). "Report on the Investigation into the Matter of Steven Salaita." University of Illinois Urbana-Champaign Faculty Senate, 23 Dec. 2014, https://www.senate.illinois.edu/af1501.pdf.

Campbell, David. "Deterritorialization or Responsibility: Levinas, Derrida, and Ethics after the End of Philosophy." *Alternatives: Social Transformation and Humane Governance*, vol. 19, no. 4 (1994), pp. 455–84.

Chancellor's Task Force on Diversity. "Report." University of North Carolina at Chapel Hill, 26 Apr. 2005, https://acrobat.adobe.com/link/review?uri=urn:aaid:scds:US:9ef13da5-5858-3603-8d20-fd11134be079.

Charis-Carlson, Jeff, and William Petroski. "Iowa Lawmaker Looking to End Tenure at Public Universities." *Des Moines Register*, 12 Jan. 2021, https://www.desmoinesregister.com/story/news/education/2017/01/12/iowa-lawmaker-looking-end-tenure-public-univerisities/96460626/.

Clary-Lemon, Jennifer. *Nestwork: New Material Rhetorics for Precarious Species.* Pennsylvania State UP [forthcoming].

Clayton, Taffye Benson, et al. "2014–15 Diversity Plan Report." University of North Carolina at Chapel Hill, 2015, https://acrobat.adobe.com/link/review?uri=urn:aaid:scds:US:179989db-95b8-31ff-92c2-704b901389f6.

Condit, Celeste. "The Materiality of Coding: Rhetoric, Genetics, and the Matter of Life." *Rhetorical Bodies*, edited by Jack Selzer and Sharon Crowley, U of Wisconsin P, 1999, pp. 326–55.

Critchley, Simon. *The Ethics of Deconstruction: Derrida and Levinas.* Blackwell, 1992.

Crosswhite, James. *Deep Rhetoric: Philosophy, Reason, Violence, Justice, Wisdom.* U of Chicago P, 2013.

Crow, Michael M., and William Dabars. "Toward Interdisciplinarity by Design." *University Experiments in Inter-disciplinarity: Obstacles and Opportunities*, edited by Peter Weigart and Britta Padberg, Transcript Verlag, 2014, pp. 13–36.

Cushman, Ellen. "Beyond Specialization: The Public Intellectual, Outreach, and Rhetoric Education." *The Realms of Rhetoric: The Prospects of Rhetorical Education*, edited by Joseph Petraglia and Deepika Bahri, State U of New York P, 2003, pp. 171–87.

Daniel, James Rushing. "Freshman Composition as Precariat Enterprise." *College English*, vol. 80, no. 1 (Sept. 2017), pp. 63–85.

Darwin, Thomas J. "Pathos, Pedagogy, and the Familiar: Cultivating Rhetorical Intelligence." *The Realms of Rhetoric: The Prospects of Rhetorical Education*, edited by Joseph Petraglia and Deepika Bahri, State U of New York P, 2003, pp. 23–38.

Davis, Diane. *Inessential Solidarity: Rhetoric and Foreigner Relations.* U of Pittsburgh P, 2010.

DeCesare, Michael. "Back to the Past: Imagining the Future of Shared Governance." *Shared Governance in Higher Education: Vitality and Continuity in Times of Change*, edited by Sharon F. Cramer and Peter L. K. Kneupfer, vol. 3, State U of New York P, 2020, pp. 147–61.

Deemer, Rob, et al. "Improving Shared Governance through Bylaws, Technology, and Collaboration." *Shared Governance in Higher Education: Demands, Transitions, Transformations*, edited by Sharon F. Cramer, vol. 1, State U of New York P, 2017, pp. 3–39.

DeFour, Matthew. "UW-Madison Dean Acknowledges School's Failure to Address Sexual Harassment." *Wisconsin State Journal*, 22 Nov. 2017, https://madison.com/wsj/news/local/education/university/uw-madison-dean-acknowledges-schools-failure-to-address-sexual-harassment/article_12d43b02-9f73-504f-9bc2-d60621a9611e.html.

Delanty, Gerard. *Challenging Knowledge: The University in the Knowledge Society*. Society for Research into Higher Education & Open UP, 2001.

Deleuze, Gilles, and Felix Guattari. "1227: Treatise on Nomadology:—The War Machine." *A Thousand Plateaus*, translated by Brian Massumi, U of Minnesota P, 1987, pp. 351–423.

Derrida, Jacques. *Adieu, to Emmanuel Levinas*. Translated by Pascale-Ann Brault and Michael Naas, Stanford UP, 1999.

———. "Violence and Metaphysics." *Writing and Difference*. Translated by Alan Bass, U of Chicago P, 1978, pp. 79–153.

Dewey, John. *The Public and Its Problems: An Essay in Political Inquiry*. Swallow Press, 1927/2016.

DiPietro, Joseph. "The Truth About Post-Tenure Review Policy." University of Tennessee, 24 Feb. 2018, https://mailchi.mp/tennessee.edu/the-truth-about-post-tenure-review-policy.

Diprose, Rosalyn. "Corporeal Interdependence: From Vulnerability to Dwelling in Ethical Community." *SubStance*, vol. 42, no. 3 (2013), pp. 185–204.

Douglass, John Aubrey. "Shared Governance at the University of California: An Historical Review." https://escholarship.org/uc/item/07q345d0.

Duderstadt, James J. *A University for the Twenty-First Century*. U of Michigan P, 2000.

Eckes, Suzanne E. "Diversity in Higher Education: The Consideration of Race in Hiring University Faculty." *Brigham Young University Education and Law Journal*, vol. 2005, no. 1 (2005), pp. 33–52.

Faculty Legislation II-303. "Protected and Unprotected Expression in a Work-Related Setting." Faculty Policies and Procedures and Faculty Legislation. University of Wisconsin–Madison, 2017, https://policy.wisc.edu/library/UW-882.

"Faculty Policies and Procedures." Chapter 7. "Faculty Appointments." University of Wisconsin–Madison, 2019, https://policy.wisc.edu/library/UW-807.

"Faculty Policies and Procedures." Chapter 8. "Faculty Rights and Responsibilities." University of Wisconsin–Madison, 1986, https://policy.wisc.edu/library/UW-808.

"Faculty Policies and Procedures." Chapter 8.01. "Faculty Rights and Responsibilities." University of Wisconsin–Madison, 2020, https://policy.wisc.edu/library/UW-808.

"Faculty Policies and Procedures." Chapter 9. "Discipline and Dismissal of Faculty for Cause." University of Wisconsin–Madison, 1986, https://policy.wisc.edu/library/UW-809.

"Faculty Policies and Procedures and Faculty Legislation." University of Wisconsin–Madison, 2019, https://secfac.wisc.edu/governance/faculty-legislation/.

"Faculty Rights and Responsibilities." Michigan State University, 1984, https://hr.msu.edu/policies-procedures/faculty-academic-staff/faculty-handbook/faculty_rights.html.

Fields, Cheryl M. "Report on Affirmative Action." *New York Times*, 15 Jan. 1975, https://www.nytimes.com/1975/01/15/archives/report-on-affirmative-action.html.

Finkin, Matthew W., and Robert Post. *For the Common Good: Principles of American Academic Freedom*. Yale UP, 2004.

Fisher v. Texas (Fisher v. University of Texas at Austin et al.). 2016. https://www.law.cornell.edu/supremecourt/text/14-981.

Flaherty, Colleen. "Debate at University of Tennessee over Posttenure Review Plan." *Inside Higher Education,* 27 Feb. 2018, https://www.insidehighered.com/news/2018/02/27/debate-university-tennessee-over-posttenure-review-plan.

———. "Hiring Booms." *Inside Higher Education,* 24 Mar. 2021, https://www.insidehighered.com/news/2021/03/24/defying-trends-ohio-state-and-syracuse-will-hire-many-new-tenure-track-faculty.

———. "Scholars Talk about Being Black on Campus in 2020." *Inside Higher Education,* 21 Oct. 2020, https://www.insidehighered.com/news/2020/10/21/scholars-talk-about-being-black-campus-2020.

Fleming, David. "Becoming Rhetorical: An Education in the Topics." *The Realms of Rhetoric: The Prospects of Rhetorical Education,* edited by Joseph Petraglia and Deepika Bahri, State U of New York P, 2003, pp. 93–116.

Foley, Megan. "Of Violence and Rhetoric: An Ethical Aporia." *Quarterly Journal of Speech,* vol. 99, no. 2 (May 2013), pp. 191–99.

Foucault, Michel. *Essential Works of Foucault,* vol. 1. *Ethics, Subjectivity, and Truth.* Edited by Paul Rabinow, New Press, 1997.

———. *Essential Works of Foucault,* vol. 3. *Power.* Edited by James D. Faubion, New Press, 2000.

———. *Power/Knowledge: Selected Interviews and Other Writings 1972–1977.* Edited by Colin Gordon, Random House, 1980.

Fuller, Steve. "Disciplinary Boundaries and the Rhetoric of the Social Sciences." *Knowledges: Historical and Critical Studies in Disciplinarity,* edited by Ellen Messer-Davidow et al., UP of Virginia, 1993, pp. 125–49.

Geiger, Roger L. *Research and Relevant Knowledge: American Research Universities Since World War II.* Transaction, 2008.

"General University Policy Regarding Academic Appointees." University of California at Berkeley, 2017, https://www.ucop.edu/academic-personnel-programs/_files/apm/apm-015.pdf.

Gerber, Larry G. "'Inextricably Linked': Shared Governance and Academic Freedom." *Academe,* vol. 87, no. 3, pp. 22–23.

———. "Professionalization as the Basis for Academic Freedom and Faculty Governance." *Journal of Academic Freedom,* vol. 1 (2010), https://www.aaup.org/JAF1/professionalization-basis-academic-freedom-and-faculty-governance#.X_2lqi2ZPxs.

———. *The Rise and Decline of Faculty Governance: Professionalization and the Modern American University.* Johns Hopkins UP, 2014.

Gilson, Erin. "Vulnerability, Ignorance, and Oppression." *Hypatia,* vol. 26, no. 2 (2011), pp. 308–32.

Glenn, Cordelia A. "Affirmative Action After *Bakke.*" *Cleveland State Law Review,* vol. 32, no. 4 (1983), pp. 681–712.

Goodlad, Sinclair. "What Is an Academic Discipline?" *Cooperation and Choice in Higher Education,* edited by Roy Cox, University of London Teaching Methods Unit, 1979, pp. 4–18.

Grutter v. Bollinger. 2003. https://caselaw.findlaw.com/us-supreme-court/539/306.html.

Gutmann, Amy, and Dennis Thompson. *Democracy and Disagreement.* Harvard UP, 1996.

Habermas, Jurgen. "The Idea of the University: Learning Processes." *New German Critique,* vol. 41 (1987), pp. 3–22.

Hamer, Emily. "Records Show Walker Wanted to Change Wisconsin Idea." *Badger Herald,* 27 May 2016, https://badgerherald.com/news/2016/05/27/records-show-walker-wanted-to-change-wisconsin-idea/.

Hannah-Jones, Nikole. "Statement on Decision to Decline Tenure Offer at University of North Carolina–Chapel Hill and to Accept Knight Chair Appointment at Howard University." NAACP Legal Defense Fund, 6 July 2021, https://www.naacpldf.org/press-release/nikole-hannah-jones-issues-statement-on-decision-to-decline-tenure-offer-at-university-of-north-carolina-chapel-hill-and-to-accept-knight-chair-appointment-at-howard-university/.

Harney, Stefano, and Fred Moten. *The Undercommons: Fugitive Planning & Black Study*. Minor Compositions, 2013.

Haskins, Ekaterina. *Logos and Power in Isocrates and Aristotle*. U of South Carolina P, 2004.

Hawhee, Debra. *Bodily Arts: Rhetoric and Athletics in Ancient Greece*. U of Texas P, 2004.

———. *Moving Bodies: Kenneth Burke at the Edges of Language*. U of South Carolina P, 2009.

Holley, Karri. "Defining Governance for Public Higher Education in the Twenty-First Century." *Governance and the Public Good*, edited by William G. Tierney, State U of New York P, 2006, pp. 199–206.

Irwin, Megan. "ASU Inc." *Phoenix New Times*, 26 Apr. 2007, https://www.phoenixnewtimes.com/news/asu-inc-6445696.

Isocrates. *Areopagiticus*. Translated by George Norlin, Loeb Classical Library, Isocrates, vol. 2, Harvard UP, 1929.

———. "Hymn to Logos." *Nicoles*, translated by George Norlin, Loeb Classical Library, Isocrates, vol. 1, Harvard UP, 1928, pp. 26–43.

Jencks, Christopher, and David Riesman. *The Academic Revolution*. U of Chicago P, 1968/1977.

Kelderman, Eric. "In Iowa, Public Colleges Scramble to Ward Off Claims of Bias and Threat to Tenure." *Chronicle of Higher Education*, 3 Feb. 2021, https://www.chronicle.com/article/in-iowa-public-colleges-scramble-to-ward-off-claims-of-bias-and-threat-to-tenure.

Kerr, Clark. *The Uses of the University*, 5th ed. Harvard UP, 2001.

Kezar, Adrianna J., and Daniel Maxey. *Envisioning the Faculty for the Twenty-First Century: Moving to a Mission-Oriented and Learner-Centered Model*. Rutgers UP, 2016.

Kidd, Charles V. *American Universities and Federal Research*. Harvard UP, 1959.

Klein, Julie Thompson. "The Dialectic and Rhetoric of Disciplinary and Interdisciplinary." *Interdisciplinary Analysis and Research* (January 1983), pp. 35–74.

Labaree, David F. *A Perfect Mess: The Unlikely Ascendancy of American Higher Education*. U of Chicago P, 2017.

Lavin, Chad. *The Politics of Responsibility*. U of Illinois P, 2008.

Lenoir, Timothy. "The Discipline of Nature and the Nature of Disciplines." *Knowledges: Historical and Critical Studies in Disciplinarity*, edited by Ellen Messer-Davidow et al., UP of Virginia, 1993, pp. 70–102.

Lippmann, Walter. *The Phantom Public*. Harcourt Brace, 1925.

Loss, Christopher P. *Between Citizens and the State: The Politics of American Higher Education in the 20th Century*. Princeton UP, 2012.

Lyons, Beauvais. "Message from Faculty Senate President." University of Tennessee-Knoxville Faculty Senate, 16 Mar. 2018, https://senate.utk.edu/wp-content/uploads/sites/16/2018/03/president-eppr-message.pdf.

———. "Report on the Proposed BOT Policy on the Expanded Application of the EPPR Process." University of Tennessee-Knoxville Faculty Senate, 18 Feb. 2018, http://senate.utk.edu/wp-content/uploads/sites/16/2018/02/2-18-2018-Proposed-BOT-Policy-on-Expanded-Application-of-the-EPPR.pdf.

Maeroff, Gene I. "'Quotas' Assailed in Faculty Hiring." *New York Times,* 8 Dec. 1974, https://www.nytimes.com/1974/12/08/archives/quotas-assailed-in-faculty-hiring-hook-among-signersn-goals-not.html.

March, James G., and Johan P. Olsen. *Rediscovering Institutions: The Organizational Basis of Politics.* The Free Press, 1989.

Massumi, Brian. *A User's Guide to 'Capitalism and Schizophrenia': Deviations from Deleuze and Guattari.* Massachusetts Institute of Technology P, 1992.

McCaughey, Robert M. "The Transformation of American Academic Life: Harvard University, 1821–1892." *Perspectives in American History,* vol. 8 (1974), pp. 239–334.

McMurtrie, Beth. "The Promise and Peril of Cluster Hiring." *Chronicle of Higher Education,* 13 Mar. 2016, https://www.chronicle.com/article/the-promise-and-peril-of-cluster-hiring/.

Messer-Davidow, Ellen, et al. "Introduction: Disciplinary Ways of Knowing." *Knowledges: Historical and Critical Studies in Disciplinarity,* edited by Ellen Messer-Davidow et al., UP of Virginia, 1993, pp. 1–21.

Michigan Constitution of 1850. https://www.legislature.mi.gov/documents/historical/miconstitution1850.htm.

Michigan Constitution of 1963. Article VIII, Education. https://www.legislature.mi.gov/(S(hd5hypuruaj00x3mya14vd55))/documents/mcl/pdf/mcl-Constitution-VIII.pdf.

Miller, Thomas P. "Changing the Subject." *The Realms of Rhetoric: The Prospects of Rhetorical Education,* edited by Joseph Petraglia and Deepika Bahri, State U of New York P, 2003, pp. 73–89.

Mills, Catherine. "Normative Violence, Vulnerability, and Responsibility." *Differences,* vol. 18, no. 2 (2007), pp. 133–56.

Nichols, Robert. *The World of Freedom: Heidegger, Foucault, and the Politics of Historical Ontology.* Stanford UP. 2014.

Nowotny, Helga. "Dilemma of Expertise: Democratising Expertise and Socially Robust Knowledge." *Science and Public Policy,* vol. 30, no. 3 (June 2003), pp. 151–56.

Ohio State University, The. Author interview with vice provost for faculty affairs. 26 Aug. 2021.

Oleson, Alexandra, and John Voss. *The Organization of Knowledge in Modern America, 1860–1880.* Johns Hopkins UP, 1960.

Olivas, Michael A. "The Supreme Court Made the Right Decision on Fisher." *Inside Higher Education,* 24 June 2016, https://www.insidehighered.com/views/2016/06/24/supreme-court-made-right-decision-fisher-essay.

Owens, Patricia. *Between War and Politics: International Relations and the Thought of Hannah Arendt.* Oxford UP, 2015.

Parker, Kim. "The Growing Partisan Divide in Views of Higher Education." Pew Research Center, 2019, https://www.pewresearch.org/social-trends/2019/08/19/the-growing-partisan-divide-in-views-of-higher-education-2/.

Pavesich, Vida. "Vulnerability, Power, and Gender: An Anthropological Meditation Between Critical Theory and Poststructuralism." *Essays in the Philosophy of Humanism,* vol. 22, no. 1 (2014), pp. 3–34.

Petherbridge, Danielle. "What's Critical About Vulnerability? Rethinking Independence, Recognition, and Power." *Hypatia,* vol. 31, no. 3 (Summer 2016), pp. 589–604.

Pettit, Emma. "'Ousted' from Academe, Steven Salaita Says He's Driving a School Bus to Make Ends Meet." *Chronicle of Higher Education,* 19 Feb. 2019, https://www.chronicle.com/article/ousted-from-academe-steven-salaita-says-hes-driving-a-school-bus-to-make-ends-meet/.

Pickering, Andrew. "Anti-Discipline or Narratives of Illusion." *Knowledges: Historical and Critical Studies in Disciplinarity,* edited by Ellen Messer-Davidow et al., U of Virginia P, 1993, pp. 103–22.

Pinch, Trevor. "The Culture of Scientists and Disciplinary Rhetoric." *European Journal of Education,* vol. 25, no. 3 (1990), pp. 295–304.

Plato. *Protagoras: A Socratic Commentary.* Translated by B. A. F. Hubbard and E. S. Karnofsky, U of Chicago P, 1983.

Post, Robert C. *Democracy, Expertise, and Academic Freedom: A First Amendment Jurisprudence for the Modern State.* Yale UP, 2012.

———. "The Structure of Academic Freedom." *Academic Freedom after September 11,* edited by Beshara Doumari, Zone, 2006, pp. 61–106.

Puar, Jasbir, editor. "Precarity Talk: A Virtual Roundtable with Lauren Berlant, Judith Butler, Bojana Cvejic, Isabell Lorey, Jasbir Puar, and Ana Vujanovic." *TDR: The Drama Review,* vol. 56, no. 4 (2012), pp. 163–77.

Pusser, Brian. "Reconsidering Higher Education and the Public Good: The Role of Public Spheres." *Governance and the Public Good,* edited by William G. Tierney, State U of New York P, 2006, pp. 11–28.

Quarless, Duncan, and Minna S. Barrett. "Governance Structures: Perspectives on Administrative Task Forces in Shared Governance." *Shared Governance in Higher Education: Demands, Transitions, Transformations,* edited by Sharon F. Cramer, vol. 1, State U of New York P, 2017, pp. 117–51.

Readings, Bill. *The University in Ruins.* Harvard UP, 1996.

Reichman, Henry. *The Future of Academic Freedom.* Johns Hopkins UP, 2019.

Reisig, Michael D., et al. "Assessing the Perceived Prevalence of Fraud among Faculty at Research-Oriented Universities in the USA." *Accountability in Research: Policies and Quality Assurance,* vol. 27, no. 7 (2020), pp. 457–75.

Rescher, Nicholas. *Cognitive Systematization: A Systems-Theoretic Approach to a Coherentist Theory of Knowledge.* Basil Blackwell, 1979.

Rosenberg, Charles E. "Towards an Ecology of Knowledge: On Discipline, Context, and History." *The Organization of Knowledge in Modern America, 1860–1920,* edited by Alexandra Olson and John Voss, Johns Hopkins UP, 1979, pp. 221–32.

Rutgers University. Author interview with vice president for academic affairs. 27 Aug. 2021.

Sabsay, Leticia. "Permeable Bodies: Vulnerability, Affective Powers, Hegemony." *Vulnerability in Resistance,* edited by Judith Butler et al., Duke UP, 2016, pp. 278–302.

Schlissel, Mark S., et al. "Many Voices, Our Michigan: Diversity, Equity & Inclusion Strategic Plan (2016–2021)." University of Michigan, Oct. 2016, https://diversity.umich.edu/wp-content/uploads/2016/10/strategic-plan.pdf.

Schneider, Pat. "Regent John Behling: UW Needs Post-Tenure Review Policy to Satisfy Accountability Concerns." *Capital Times,* 18 Sept. 2015, https://madison.com/ct/news/local/education/university/regent-john-behling-uw-needs-post-tenure-review-policy-to/article_c1a30400-0f99-5580-9cdc-e6312a0c7ca5.html.

———. "UW Board of Regents Give Administrators Final Word in Faculty Reviews." *Capital Times,* 8 Dec. 2016, https://madison.com/ct/news/local/education/university/uw-board-of-regents-give-administrators-final-word-in-faculty-reviews/article_a34a1817-eb78-5be0-8c60-8e983c748d39.html.

———. "UW-Madison Researchers React to Robin Vos's 'Ancient Mating Habits of Whatever' Remark." *Capital Times,* 8 Nov. 2014, https://captimes.com/news/local/writers/pat_

schneider/uw-madison-researchers-react-to-robin-vos-ancient-mating-habits-of-whatever-remark/article_3c87294e-6176-5b8f-94d0-5e1e401e633f.html.

Schuster, Jack H., and Martin J. Finkelstein. *The American Faculty: The Restructuring of Academic Work and Careers.* Johns Hopkins UP, 2006.

Scott, Joan Wallach. "The Critical State of Shared Governance." *Academe,* vol. 88, no. 4 (July–Aug. 2002), pp. 41–48.

Senate Council, University of Tennessee-Knoxville. "Minutes, 19 February 2018." https://senate.utk.edu/wp-content/uploads/sites/16/2018/02/Exec.-Minutes-February-2018.pdf.

South Dakota Legislature. "House Bill 1012." South Dakota Legislative Council. 2022, https://sdlegislature.gov/Session/Bill/23006/226040.

State Higher Education Executive Officers Association. "SHEF: State Higher Education Finance" report for FY 2019. 2020, https://shef.sheeo.org/wp-content/uploads/2020/04/SHEEO_SHEF_FY19_Report.pdf.

Stormer, Nathan. "Everything Moves, Even When It Doesn't." University of South Carolina Rhetorical Theory Conference, Columbia, SC, 2–3 Oct. 2015.

Strauss, Valerie. "How Gov. Walker Tried to Quietly Change the Mission of the University of Wisconsin." *Washington Post,* 5 Feb. 2015, https://www.washingtonpost.com/news/answer-sheet/wp/2015/02/05/how-gov-walker-tried-to-quietly-change-the-mission-of-the-university-of-wisconsin/.

Stripling, Jack. "As the Crow Flies." *Inside Higher Education,* 16 July 2010, https://www.insidehighered.com/news/2010/07/16/crow-flies.

Sutton, Jane S., and Mari Lee Mifsud. "Towards an *Alloiostrophic* Rhetoric." *Advances in the History of Rhetoric,* vol. 15, no. 2 (2012), pp. 222–33.

Taylor, Angus E. *The Academic Senate of the University of California: Its Role in the Shared Governance and Operation of the University of California.* Institute for Governmental Studies Press, 1998.

"Tenure at UW-Madison." Office of the Secretary of the Faculty, 2019, https://secfac.wisc.edu/tenure/.

Tiede, Hans-Joerg. *University Reform: The Founding of the American Association of University Professors.* Johns Hopkins UP, 2015.

Tierney, William G. "The Examined University: Process and Change in Higher Education." *Governance and the Public Good,* by Tierney, State U of New York P, 2006, pp. 1–10.

Turner, Bryan S. "Discipline." *Theory, Culture, and Society,* vol. 23, nos. 2–3 (2016), pp. 183–86.

United States Department of Labor. "Title VI, Civil Rights Act of 1964." https://www.dol.gov/agencies/oasam/regulatory/statutes/title-vi-civil-rights-act-of-1964.

University of Alaska. "Constitution of the University of Alaska Fairbanks Faculty Senate." https://docs.google.com/document/d/115wSK_MfZfNmirHyVIacNUYtTtYS1t1M14E8GTrTewI/edit.

———. "Strategic Pathways." https://www.boarddocs.com/ak/alaska/Board.nsf/files/ADXU4T7A47C4/$file/Strategic%20Pathways%20BOR%2016%20September%202016.pdf.

"University of Alaska Anchorage Resolution Recommending Suspension of President James Johnsen." https://drive.google.com/file/d/1Dp42QxODRBn6pW_OcdOT14ENZgVMhXwI/view.

University of Alaska Board of Regents, "Policy on Financial Exigency." https://www.alaska.edu/bor/policy-regulations/files/04.09-financial-exigency.pdf.

University of Alaska System. "UA President Jim Johnsen Withdraws from University of Wisconsin Search." Press Release, 12 June 2020, https://www.alaska.edu/opa/enews/2020/612/.

University of California Regents. "Regents Policy 4400, University of California Diversity Statement." 2010, https://policy.ucop.edu/doc/4000375/Diversity.

University of California, Riverside. "Provost Announcement: Cluster Hiring." Dec. 2014, https://acrobat.adobe.com/link/review?uri=urn:aaid:scds:US:4db85b4e-a768-3c5e-ac1c-699f475e9577.

———. "UC Riverside Cluster Hiring Initiative." Dec. 2018, https://accreditation.ucr.edu/sites/g/files/rcwecm2321/files/2018-12/overview_of_ucr_cluster_hiring_initiative.pdf.

University of California, Riverside, Faculty Senate. "Faculty Senate Cluster Survey." 12 Jan. 2016, https://app.box.com/s/6vyla0ivjka3uji5ipcm6i9n8q5k8drn.

University of California, Riverside, Office of the Chancellor. "UCR 2020: The Path to Preeminence." July 2010, https://strategicplan.ucr.edu/sites/g/files/rcwecm2701/files/2019-03/ucr_2020_-_final.pdf.

University of California, Riverside, Office of the Vice Chancellor for Research and Economic Development. "Cluster Status Update Memo." 6 Nov. 2017, https://app.box.com/s/c9ar98zjd0cra0c7ufwekolskq43cb6k.

University of Illinois. Author interview with vice provost for faculty affairs. 9 Sept. 2021.

———. Emails released in response to public records request. N.d., https://www.uillinois.edu/common/pages/DisplayFile.aspx?itemId=294204.

University of Illinois System. "Statutes of the University of Illinois." 12 Nov. 2020, https://www.bot.uillinois.edu/governance/statutes.

University of Illinois Urbana-Champaign, Office of the Provost. "Communication #7: Targets of Opportunity Program (TOP)," Aug. 2022, https://uofi.app.box.com/s/w22wjx02wg48sfvebywjnjop15y8h6ty/file/429057326074 [PDF].

———. "Communication #7: Targets of Opportunity Program (TOP)." N.d., https://provost.illinois.edu/policies/provosts-communications/communication-7-targets-of-opportunity-program-top/.

University of Michigan. "Professional Standards for Faculty." Standard Practice Guide Policies (RPG 201.96), 2018, https://facultyhandbook.provost.umich.edu/1-d-professional-standards-for-faculty/.

University of Michigan Board of Regents. "By-Laws." May 2020, https://regents.umich.edu/governance/bylaws/.

University of Michigan Senate Assembly. "Senate Assembly Statement on Academic Freedom." *University of Michigan Faculty Handbook,* 2010, https://www.provost.umich.edu/faculty/handbook/1/1.C.html.

University of Minnesota, Twin Cities campus. Author interview with vice provost for faculty and staff Affairs. 17 Sept. 2021.

University of Nebraska–Lincoln. Author interview with vice provost for faculty affairs. 23 Aug. 2021.

University of Nebraska–Lincoln, Office of Institutional Equity and Compliance. Search Waiver Request. N.d., https://www.unl.edu/equity/search-waiver-requests.

University of North Carolina at Chapel Hill. "VITAE (Valuing Inclusion to Attain Excellence) Hiring Guidelines." N.d., https://academicpersonnel.unc.edu/policies-and-procedures/faculty-recruitment/vitae-hiring-guidelines/.

University of North Carolina at Chapel Hill Trustees. "Trustee Policies and Regulations Governing Academic Tenure in the University of North Carolina at Chapel Hill." 2018, https://facultyhandbook.unc.edu/wp-content/uploads/sites/15431/2018/11/2018-11-15-Trustee-Policies-and-Regulations-Governing-Academic-Tenure.pdf.

University of North Carolina Board of Trustees. "UNC Policy Manual." 2020, https://www.northcarolina.edu/apps/policy/index.php?tab=policy_manual.

University of Tennessee Board of Trustees. "Policies Governing Academic Freedom, Responsibility, and Tenure." 23 Mar. 2019, http://senate.utk.edu/wp-content/uploads/sites/16/2018/03/BT006_3-23-2018.pdf.

University of Tennessee Board of Trustees, Committee on Academic Affairs and Student Success. "Proposed Revisions to Board Policies on Academic Freedom, Responsibility, and Tenure." 23 Mar. 2018, https://trustees.tennessee.edu/wp-content/uploads/sites/3/2018/11/March-23-2018-Full-Board-Signed.pdf.

University of Tennessee–Knoxville Senate. "Letter of Concern Regarding Post-Tenure Review." 16 Mar. 2018, http://senate.utk.edu/wp-content/uploads/sites/16/2018/03/Letter-to-BOT-2018-Post-Tenure.pdf.

University of Texas at Austin, UDIAP. *University Diversity and Inclusion Action Implementation and Resource Guide.* 30 Mar. 2017, https://diversity.utexas.edu/diversity-and-inclusion-action-plan/implementation-and-resource-guide/.

University of Wisconsin. "Selection Process for System President, Chancellors, Vice Chancellors and UW System Senior Leadership Positions." Regent Policy Document 20-27, 2022, https://www.wisconsin.edu/regents/policies/selection-process-for-system-president-chancellors-vice-chancellors-and-uw-system-senior-leadership-positions/.

University of Wisconsin–Madison. "Hostile and Intimidating Behavior." University of Wisconsin–Madison, 2014, https://policy.wisc.edu/library/UW-872.

———. "Post-Tenure Review Policy." UW-Madison Faculty Senate, Faculty Policies and Procedures 7.17. 7 May 2018, https://policy.wisc.edu/library/UW-807#Pol807_7_17.

———. "Report of the Cluster/Interdisciplinary Advisory Committee to Evaluate the Cluster Hiring Initiative." July 2008, https://facstaff.provost.wisc.edu/wp-content/uploads/sites/208/2017/07/ClusterReport_2008.pdf.

University of Wisconsin–Madison, Office of the Provost. "(TOP) Faculty Diversity Initiative." N.d., https://facstaff.provost.wisc.edu/faculty-diversity-initiative/.

University of Wisconsin System, Board of Regents. "Budget in Brief: University of Wisconsin-Madison." 2021, https://budget.wisc.edu/content/uploads/Budget-in-Brief_2020-21_Web.pdf.

———. "Commitment to Academic Freedom and Freedom of Expression." Regent Policy Document 4-21, 2017, https://www.wisconsin.edu/regents/policies/commitment-to-academic-freedom-and-freedom-of-expression/.

———. "Periodic Post-Tenure Review in Support of Tenured Faculty Development." Policy Document 20-9, 8 Dec. 2016, https://www.wisconsin.edu/regents/policies/periodic-post-tenure-review-in-support-of-tenured-faculty-development/.

Urban Universities for Health. "Faculty Cluster Hiring for Diversity and Institutional Climate." Urban Universities for Health / National Institutes for Health, Apr. 2015, https://www.aplu.org/wp-content/uploads/faculty-cluster-hiring-for-diversity-and-institutional-climate.pdf.

Urbinati, Nadia. *Representative Democracy: Principles and Genealogy.* U of Chicago P, 2006.

Veysey, Laurence R. *The Emergence of the American University.* U of Chicago P, 1963.

Von Burg, Alessandra Beasley. "Mobility: The New Blue." *Quarterly Journal of Speech*, vol. 100, no. 2 (May 2014), pp. 241–57.

———. "Stochastic Citizenship: Toward a Rhetoric of Mobility." *Philosophy and Rhetoric*, vol. 55, no. 4 (2012), pp. 351–75.

Walzer, Michael. *Politics and Passion: Toward a More Egalitarian Liberalism.* Yale UP. 2004.

Warren, Mark E. "Deliberative Democracy and Authority." *American Political Science Review*, vol. 90, no. 1 (1996), pp. 46–60.

Wasserman, Ed. "Harreld Selection: A Tale of Two Searches." *Iowa City Press-Citizen*, 30 Sept. 2015, https://www.press-citizen.com/story/opinion/contributors/guest-editorials/2015/09/30/harreld-selection-tale-two-searches/73024712/.

Weeden, Darnell. "Back to the Future: Should *Grutter*'s Rationale Apply to Faculty Hiring? Is Title VII Implicated?" *Berkeley Journal of Employment and Labor Law*, vol. 26, no. 2 (2005), pp. 511–44.

Wess, Robert. "Burke's Dialectic of Constitutions." *Pre/Text*, vol. 12, nos. 1–2 (1991), pp. 10–30.

Whittington, Keith E. *Speak Freely: Why Universities Must Defend Free Speech*. Princeton UP, 2017.

Wilson, John K. Email with author, 8 Aug. 2020.

———. "What's Wrong (and Right) about the CAFT Report on Salaita." *Academe Blog, AAUP Magazine*, 31 Dec. 2014, https://academeblog.org/2014/12/31/whats-wrong-and-right-about-the-caft-report-on-salaita/.

Wisconsin Assembly. "2021 Assembly Bill 735." Madison, WI. 2021, https://docs.legis.wisconsin.gov/2021/related/proposals/ab735.

Wisconsin State Legislature. "Chapter 36, University of Wisconsin System." https://docs.legis.wisconsin.gov/statutes/statutes/36.

———. "Chapter 36.01, University of Wisconsin System, Statement of Purpose and Mission of the University of Wisconsin." 1973, https://docs.legis.wisconsin.gov/statutes/statutes/36.

Wise, Phyllis. "Email to faculty." CAFT report 62. 22 Aug. 2014, https://will.illinois.edu/nfs/08-22-2014_Wise_Email_On_Salaita.pdf.

WISELI (Women in Science and Engineering Leadership Institute). "Results from the 2019 Study of Faculty Worklife at UW-Madison." University of Wisconsin–Madison, 2020, https://wiseli.wisc.edu/wp-content/uploads/sites/662/2020/01/SFW2019_TT_FINAL.pdf.

Working Group on the Retention of Mid-Career Faculty from Historically Underrepresented Groups. Notes. University of Wisconsin–Madison, January–February 2019.

Zamudio-Suarez, Fernanda. "Missouri Lawmaker Who Wants to Eliminate Tenure Says It's 'Un-American.'" *Chronicle of Higher Education*, 12 Jan. 2017, https://www.chronicle.com/article/missouri-lawmaker-who-wants-to-eliminate-tenure-says-its-un-american/.

Zerai, Assata. "Diversity and Inclusion: Goals and Actions Proposed for the 2018–23 Campus Strategic Plan." Office of the Associate Chancellor for Diversity, University of Illinois Urbana-Champaign, 2018, https://blogs.illinois.edu/files/7831/601837/127668.pdf.

INDEX

academic freedom: alternative model of, 89–92; democratic competence and, 74, 77–81, 86, 91–92; democratic ideal and, 11; democratization, separate spheres, and, 73–75; development of, 72–73; governance and, 25; mobility and, 70–71, 75–76, 89; post-tenure review, 78–82, 91; as potential for inconstancy, 167–68; public opinion and, 81–82; Salaita case, speech rights, and oppressiveness of the demos, 82–88; state efforts to eliminate tenure, 68–69; university statements on, 77–78

accountability: diversity initiatives and, 126, 135n4, 138–40; governance and, 37–38; interdisciplinarity and, 111–12; post-tenure review and, 80–81

Agamben, Giorgio: on destituency, 19, 21, 40, 163, 167; on *oikos* and polis, 48, 54, 64, 65, 91, 163, 171; on radical engagement, 91–92; on stasis, 40, 75, 163; on "whatever" communities, 159

Ahmed, Sara, 6, 90

Alger, Jonathan, 131n1

alloiostrophos, 103–5, 120

Althusser, Louis, 156

ambulant, the, 166–67

American Association of University Professors (AAUP): on academic freedom, 72–73, 77, 87; on exigency process, 30; on extramural utterances, 86–87; on faculty as appointees, not employees, 35–36, 40, 44, 47, 69; on "proper work," 41; on responsibility, 9–10, 44, 53; on rights/responsibilities, 47; on shared governance, 25–26; "Statement of Principles" (1940), 10; University of Georgia censured by, 150

Anderson, Virginia, 65–66

anticonservative bias, presumption of, 69

appointees vs. employees, faculty as, 35–36, 40, 44, 47, 69

Arendt, Hannah, 48, 64

Aristotle, 8, 11, 19, 75, 156, 163

Arizona State University, 115–16

Association of Governing Boards of Universities and Colleges (AGB), 25, 27

autonomy: disciplinarity, interdisciplinarity, and, 94–98, 104–6, 113–14, 116, 118; expertise and, 19; faculty misconduct and, 64; governance and, 30, 36–37; order vs., 27–28

axiomatists, 102

Bahls, Steven C., 26, 27, 28
Bakke case, 129
Barouch, Timothy, 70, 165, 166
Barrett, Minna S., 33
Bauman, Zygmunt, 157
Behling, John, 37
Benjamin, Walter, 31, 37
Ben-Porath, Sigal, 126–27, 146
Black Lives Matter movement, 110
Black studies, 110n3
"Black tax," 142–43
Bowen, William G., 38–40, 158, 164–66
Braidotti, Rosi, 90
Brennan, William, 38
Brew, Angela, 102
Brint, Steven, 97–98
Brown, Mark, 100, 117–18
bullying case, 59–63
Burbules, Nick, 84
Burke, Kenneth, 7, 14, 45, 65–66, 70, 75, 159–60, 170
Butler, Althea, 141–42
Butler, Judith, 6, 76, 123, 133, 147, 161, 169

Cattell, James, 10
Center for Media and Democracy (CMD), 34
circulation, 101–2
Citizens United, 74n1
Civil Rights Act (1964), 127–28
Clark, Geoffrey, 116
Clary-Lemon, Jennifer, 103
cluster hiring programs, 94, 106–15
coherentists, 102
collectivities, 6–8
Collin College, 149
commonplaces, 7–12, 17–19. *See also* academic freedom; autonomy; consensus; deliberation; democratic commonplaces; mobility; publics and publicity; stability
consensus: governance and, 22–24, 29–33; interdisciplinarity and, 113; mobility and, 26, 36, 39–43
constitutions, 50–51, 65–66, 78. *See also* policy

constitutive vulnerability: as commonplace, 17–18; defined, 6–7; as engine of subjectivity, 145; positive implications for, 21
Crosswhite, James, 30–33, 42, 155
Crow, Michael, 115, 169
Cushman, Ellen, 155

Daniel, James Rushing, 71
D'Anieri, Paul, 108, 111
Darwin, Thomas, 155–56, 159
Davis, Diane, 18, 52–53, 61, 66
DeCesare, Michael, 27
Deemer, Rob, 26
Delanty, Gerard, 12, 26, 117, 119, 157–58
Deleuze, Gilles, 18–19, 118–19, 158, 166–67, 170
deliberation: beyond law, 39–40; democratic competence and, 11; Dewey and deliberative education, 154; governance and, 26–40; the public, communication, and, 156–59; rhetoric and, 30–31; risks and, 162; self-deliberation, 25, 26, 32; situational vulnerability and, 43; sympathy vs. relationality, 42–43; University of Alaska and failure of, 29–33; violence and, 31–32
democratic commonplaces: about, 10–12; academic freedom and, 73–75, 82, 88; responsibilities to public and, 46–47. *See also* publics and publicity
democratic competence: academic freedom and, 74, 77–81, 86, 91–92; deliberation and, 11; interdisciplinarity and, 105
departments, academic. *See* disciplinarity and interdisciplinarity
Derrida, Jacques, 52
destituency, 19, 40–41, 75–76, 88, 163
Dewey, John, 152, 153–54, 156–58, 165, 168
DiPietro, Joseph, 79–80
Diprose, Rosalyn, 132
disciplinarity and interdisciplinarity: academic disciplines and overspecialization, 95–97; alloiostrophic model (relational, coherentist, and socially robust), 102–5, 120; Arizona State University overhaul case, 115–16; attraction of interdisciplinarity, 101; autonomy and, 94–98, 104–6, 113–14, 116, 118; circulational model, 101–2; cluster hiring programs, 94, 106–15; discipline and policing function, 97;

expertise and, 93–94, 99–105; the interdisciplinary revolution, 93–94; Readings on "ruin" and institutional pragmatism, 116–17; rhetorical work of disciplines, 98–100; transdisciplinarity and nomadism, 117–20

diversity, institutional: backlash against, 123, 125–26; "Black tax," emotional labor, and, 142–43; conditions of precarity, undercommons, and, 132, 147–48; in constitutional law, 129–30; DEI statements and plans, 134–37; Hannah-Jones case, 121–22, 146–48; hiring initiatives, 133–44; inclusive freedom framework, 146–48; lived experience, situational vulnerability, and, 123–24, 126–27, 131–33, 140–48; micro-aggressions, 142; microhistory of, 124–27; retention issues, 140–41, 142; rights/responsibilities tension and, 134–35; synchronic approach vs. numerical and diachronic, 127–30, 135n4; Target of Opportunity initiatives, 137–40

Dixon v. Alabama Board of Education, 125

donor pressure, 74n1

Dreschel, Robert, 34

due process, 45, 55–59

Dunleavy, Mike, 22, 29–30, 32

Eckes, Suzanne, 130–31n1

emotional labor, 142–43

ergon, proper, 19, 41, 76, 170

exigency, financial, 30

exit interviews, 141

expertise: autonomy and, 19; democracy and, 46; democratic egalitarianism vs., 74; disciplinarity, interdisciplinarity and, 93–94, 99–105; transgressive potential of, 102–3

faculty work. *See* academic freedom; autonomy; disciplinarity and interdisciplinarity; *ergon*, proper; expertise; rights-and-responsibilities model; vulnerability

Felber, Garrett, 149

felt location, 123, 127, 128–29, 133, 139, 144

Finkelstein, Mark, 95

Finkin, Matthew, 47, 48, 86

Fisher v. Texas II, 130, 138, 140

Fleming, David, 151, 154–55, 165

Foucault, Michel, 51–53, 62, 65, 88–89, 91–92, 99, 115

freedom: inclusive, 127; mobility and, 70–71; as mobility-without-destination, 167; policy and, 51–52; rights/responsibilities and, 45, 64. *See also* academic freedom; speech, freedom of

Fuller, Steve, 100

funding cuts, state, 1–2

Geiger, Roger, 93, 96, 126, 128

Gerber, Larry, 38, 39, 46

GI Bill, 8, 95, 124, 125

Gilson, Erinn, 6, 140

Glenn, Cordelia, 131n1

good, public. *See* public good

governance: beyond law, 39–40; consensus and, 32–33; definition and principles of, 22–24; destituent power and, 40–41; development of, 24–25; disciplinarity and, 100, 105; interdisciplinarity and, 107–8, 110–11, 114, 120; mobility, deliberation, and, 25–33, 40–42; public goods and, 23, 35–38; rhetoric and, 168–69; University of Alaska case, 22–23, 29–33; University of Wisconsin case, 33–38; vulnerability and, 41–43

governmentality, 51, 53–54

Grutter v. Bollinger, 129–30, 138, 140

Guattari, Felix, 18–19, 118–19, 166–67, 170

Habermas, Jurgen, 152–53, 155–58, 165

Hannah-Jones, Nikole, 121–22, 141, 146–48

Harney, Stefano, 20, 147–48, 169

Haskins, Ekaterina, 32–33, 39

Hawhee, Debra, 70, 159–60

Head, Robert, 143

Higher Education Act (HEA), 124–25

hiring initiatives: cluster programs, 94, 106–15; DEI statements and plans, 134–37; Target of Opportunity (TOP), 137–40

Hofstadter, Richard, 46

Hook, Sidney, 128

Howard University, 121–22

"Idea of the University, The" (Habermas), 152–53
identities: autonomy and, 75; constitutions and, 50; Delanty on, 157–58; disciplinary, 98–99, 102; diversity initiatives and, 17, 124–26, 131–35, 144–46; "the more" and, 167–68; the precariat and insecurity of, 71; rights/responsibilities and, 9; shift toward, in higher education, 125; shifting, 15, 18, 39, 116
information technology, 39
interdisciplinarity. *See* disciplinarity and interdisciplinarity
intervalle, 155
Isocrates, 11, 28, 32, 165

Jencks, Christopher, 96
Johnsen, Jim, 22–23, 29–30
Johnson, Kristina, 94
justice: the *intervalle*, deliberation, and, 155; the law vs., 31, 36, 55; Perelman's theory of, 155; rhetoric, ethical urgency, and, 162–63; rhetorical, 155–56; rights/responsibilities and, 45, 51–55, 61–63, 66–67; sexual harassment case, procedure, and, 55–59
justice vs. the law, 31, 36

Kerr, Clark, 23, 36, 39, 158, 166, 167
Kidd, Charles, 96
Kirby, Audrey, 33
Klein, Julie Thompson, 102–3
knowledge: consensus vs. dissensus on, 10; fragmentation of, 12; shifting publics and, 158; socially robust, 103; transdisciplinarity and construction of, 119–20
Kuhn, Thomas, 166

Latour, Bruno, 117–18
Lavin, Chad, 8, 45, 47, 49–50, 65
law: deliberation beyond, 39–40; ethical vs. political responsibility and, 66–67; justice vs., 31, 36, 55; violence and, 31
Lenoir, Timothy, 99–100, 104
Lernfreiheit and *Lehrfreiheit*, 72
Levinas, Emmanuel, 15, 52, 61–62, 155
Linfield University, 149

Lippman, Walter, 153–54, 164
listening sessions, 142–44
Locke, John, 8
Loss, Christopher, 8–9, 15–16, 122, 128, 156
Lyons, Timothy, 111–12, 114

majority, tyranny of, 74–75
Mifsud, Mari Lee, 103
Miller, Thomas, 154
Mills, Catherine, 132–33, 145, 147
mission, institutional, 33–34
mobility: academic freedom and, 70–71, 75–76, 89; autonomy and, 36; bodies, movement of, 159–60; commonplace of, 18–19; communities and, 64–65; eventalization and, 167–68; as exteriority, 169–70; governance and, 25–33, 40–42; hyperglobalized economy and, 41–42; nomadism, 18–19, 118–19, 166–67; "passion" and, 63; policy and, 54; rhetoric and, 159–63, 169–71; stochastic citizenship and, 160–61
Morrill, Richard, 27
Morrill Acts (1862 and 1890), 2, 8, 9, 39
Moten, Fred, 20, 147–48, 169

Nancy, Jean-Luc, 19
neoliberal paradigm: Delanty on, 12; free speech and, 88; governance and, 42; identities, shifting, 12, 18; interdisciplinarity and, 16; mobility, freedom, and, 70; rhetoric and, 159; singularities and, 165; workforce needs and student preparation, 3–4, 6, 27, 34–36. *See also* accountability
Nichols, Robert, 51–54, 65, 88, 89, 162, 167
nomadism, 18–19, 118–19, 166–67
Northern Illinois University, 128
Nowotny, Helga, 102–3

O'Connor, Sandra Day, 129–30
oikos and polis: academic freedom and, 75–77, 91; free speech and, 88; impermeable boundaries and, 59; mobility, vulnerability, and, 161; responsibilities in communities of, 19; rights/responsibilities and, 48, 53–54, 62, 65; threshold of indifference between, 163. *See also* polis

INDEX • 189

Oleson, Alexandra, 95
Olivas, Michael, 131n1
Ommen, Brett, 70, 165, 166
openness to others, radical. See constitutive vulnerability
Owens, Patricia, 48

Pavesich, Vita, 145, 147
Penn State University, 137n5
perceptions of higher education, 2–3
Perelman, Chaïm, 155
Petherbridge, Danielle, 6–7, 18, 42, 161–62, 167, 171
Pickering, Andrew, 101–2
Pinch, Trevor, 98–99
Plater, William, 41
Plato, 31–32
policy: application of, vs. justice, 54–55; ethics, politics, justice and, 14–15, 31; governance and, 22, 32–33, 37–38; procedure vs., 58; rights/responsibilities and, 50–53, 65–66; state policy, higher education as tool of, 8–9
polis: deliberation and, 32, 39; democracy commonplace and, 11; disciplinary expertise and, 100; law vs. laws and, 62, 63; mobility and, 171; post-tenure review and, 80–81. See also democratic commonplaces; oikos and polis
Pollack-Pelzner, Daniel, 149
Post, Robert: on AAUP statements, 47, 72; on academic freedom, 73–74, 76, 77, 80–82, 86, 89–90; on democratic competence, 11, 15, 100, 105, 152; on norms vs. public opinion, 48
post-tenure review, 37, 78–82, 91, 150
power: destituent, 19, 40–41, 75–76, 88; donor pressure and, 74n1; nomadism as, 166
pragmatism, institutional, 116–17
precariat, 71, 161
procedure, strict adherence to, 55–59
Progressive movement, 9, 46, 73, 96
proportionality, 62–63
Puar, Jasbir, 147
public good: academic freedom and, 69–73, 82; autonomy and, 98, 152; commonplace of, 23; consensus and, 26; consolidated responsibilities and, 8; democracy and, 10–11; diversity and, 134; governance and, 33–38, 41; higher education viewed as, 2; knowledge creation and, 122; private goods vs., 2, 35. See also rights-and-responsibilities model
public opinion, 81–82, 153
publics and publicity: academic freedom and, 82; Dewey and Lippman on, 153–54; governance and, 30; majority, tyranny of, 74–75; mobility and, 26, 36; multiple constituencies, 54; perceptions of, 3; shifting, 5, 10, 158. See also democratic commonplaces; responsibility

Quarless, Duncan, 33

Readings, Bill, 116–17, 158
Reddick, Richard, 143–44
Reichman, Henry, 73, 77, 89
Rescher, Nicholas, 102–3
responsibility: capacity for response, 18; commonplaces of, 8–10; governance and, 26; individual vs. collective, 8. See also accountability; rights-and-responsibilities model
retention, 140–41, 142
rhetoric: about, 149–51; alloiostrophos, 103–5; becoming rhetorical, 151, 152–56, 167; Crosswhite on, 30–31; deliberative education and, 154–55; democracy and, 11; disciplines, rhetorical work of, 98–100; education, rhetorical, 20–21, 151, 152, 155–56, 166; governance and, 28; implications for faculty work, 164–71; as mobile, vulnerable, and ethical, 159–63; the public, communication, and deliberation, 156–59; recognition and, 42; vulnerability and critical perspective of, 20
Riesman, David, 96
rights-and-responsibilities model: AAUP and, 9–10; about, 44–48; associational and mobile communities and, 64–65; bullying case and proportionality, 59–63; campus speech and, 3–4; conflicting responsibilities, 46–48, 60; constitutions, policies, freedom, and justice, 49–53; diversity initiatives and, 122–23, 131–35, 137; ethical vs. political responsibility and justice, 66–67; neoliberal era and,

12; *oikos*, polis, and, 48, 49; policies as exigent, 65–66; policy documents and hiatus, 53–55; the rights-responsibility pairing, 44–45; sexual-harassment case, procedure, and due process, 55–59; theories of education, responsibilities-based vs. rights-based, 9. *See also* responsibility

Rosenberg, Charles, 99

"ruined" university, 116–17

Sabsay, Leticia, 133

Salaita, Steven, 77, 82–88, 91–92, 150

Schleiermacher, Friedrich, 152, 156

Schuster, Jack, 95

sexual harassment case, 55–59

singularities, 158–59, 165–66

situational vulnerability: about, 5–6, 21; constitutive vulnerability and, 6–7, 145; deliberation and, 43; diversity initiatives, lived experience, and, 123–24, 126–27, 131–33, 140–48; interdisciplinarity and, 120; rhetoric and, 162

Smith, P. Christopher, 156

solidarity, 19–20, 42, 43, 169

speech, freedom of: AAUP on extramural utterances, 86–87; democratic competence and, 74; First Amendment, 84–85, 88, 91; legislation on, 3–4; Salaita case, 83–88, 91–92

spheres, proper, 23, 31, 35–41

stability: autonomy vs. order, 27–28; governance and, 23, 31, 36; mobility and, 26; rhetoric and undoing of, 167

stochastic citizenship, 18, 70–71, 119, 160–61

Stormer, Nathan, 18, 70, 88, 160, 169

Sutton, Jane, 103

sympathy, 33, 38, 42–43

Target of Opportunity (TOP) initiatives, 137–40

tenure: AAUP statements on, 72–73; cluster hiring programs and, 114n4; democratic competence and, 77–78; democratization and, 73–75; mobility and, 71; as necessary but not sufficient, 170–71; post-tenure review, 37, 78–82, 91, 150; as protection of academic freedom, 69–70, 72–73, 90–91; state efforts to eliminate, 68–69

Tiede, Hans-Joerg, 46, 48, 73

Tierney, William, 10–11

Tobin, Eugene M., 38–40, 164–66

transdisciplinarity, 117–20

Turner, Bryan, 97

undercommons, 20, 132, 147–48, 169

University of Alaska, 22–23, 29–33

University of California, 129, 135n4

University of California, Berkeley, 65, 128

University of California, Riverside, 94, 108–13

University of Georgia, 150

University of Illinois at Chicago, 94

University of Illinois at Urbana-Champaign, 82–88, 91–92, 136, 136n4, 138, 150

University of Michigan, 129, 135n4

University of Mississippi, 149

University of Nebraska–Lincoln, 137n5

University of North Carolina, 135n4, 136, 170

University of North Carolina at Chapel Hill, 121–22, 137–38, 141, 146–48

University of Oregon, 135n4, 136

University of Pennsylvania, 141–42

University of Tennessee, 79–81

University of Texas at Austin, 130, 137n5, 143–44

University of Wisconsin, 33–38, 125

University of Wisconsin–Madison, 2n2, 34, 37, 54n2, 78, 94, 107n2, 114n4, 136, 138–39, 170

Veysey, Laurence, 24, 72, 95, 96

Vico, Giambattista, 75, 160

violence: deliberation and, 31–32; governance, the law, and, 31, 32–33; language as, 37; mobility and, 76; solidarities and, 43

Von Burg, Alessandra, 18, 70, 75, 90, 160–61

Vos, Robin, 89

Voss, John, 95

vulnerability: about, 4–7; affective dimension of, 141; constitutive, 6–7, 17–18, 21, 145; as eccentric force, 167; governance and, 41–43; hyperglobalized economy and, 41–42; inclusive freedom and, 127; invulnerability, 140, 145, 148; mobility, intimate relation with, 161; precarious bodies and, 147–48; publics and, 4–5; resistance, relationship to, 147–48; solidarity and, 19–20; synchronic, 130; transdisciplinarity and, 118. *See also* situational vulnerability

Walker, Scott, 34, 35, 68
Walzer, Michael: bullying case and, 60; on collectivities, 6; on communities, 49–50, 65–66; on the contemporary moment, 43; on mobility, 18, 63, 70; on policy impasse, 54; on the public, 5, 158; on shifting neoliberal identities, 12; on solitary and random motion, 168

Weeden, L. Darnell, 130n1
Whittington, Keith, 74, 77, 89
Wilcox, Kim, 108
Wilson, John K., 87, 89
Wise, Phyllis, 83–88

Yiannopoulos, Milo, 3

Zaun, Brad, 68

www.ingramcontent.com/pod-product-compliance
Lightning Source LLC
Chambersburg PA
CBHW020947230426
43666CB00005B/212